From the Other Side
of the Desk

From the Other Side of the Desk

Students Speak Out About Writing

Linda Miller Cleary
University of Minnesota at Duluth

Boynton/Cook Publishers
HEINEMANN
Portsmouth, NH

Boynton/Cook Publishers Inc.
A subsidiary of Reed Elsevier Inc.
361 Hanover Street, Portsmouth, NH 03801-3912
Offices and agents throughout the world

Every effort has been made to contact copyright holders and students for permission
to reprint borrowed material. We regret any oversights that may have occurred and
would be happy to rectify them in future printings of this work.

Library of Congress Cataloging-in-Publication Data
Cleary, Linda Miller.
    From the other side of the desk: students speak out about writing/
    Linda Miller Cleary.
        p.   cm.
    Includes bibliographical references and index.
    ISBN 0−86709−282−3
    1. English language—Composition and exercises—Study and teaching
    (Secondary)—United States—Case studies.   I. Title.
    LB1631.C54   1991
    808'.042'0712−dc20   91−23918
                                                                        CIP

Printed in the United States of America.

99 98   EB   4 5 6 7

To my mother and father
and to Jed and Sarah.
For their infinite patience at different stages in my life.

Contents

Acknowledgments

With thanks to all those whose effort and cooperation enabled me to write this book:

First and foremost, to the forty eleventh-grade writers who gave up hours in their busy lives to let me hear of their experiences with writing. I regret that they must remain anonymous. Special thanks to Elana, who read a good portion of the first draft from a student's point of view.

To some of their teachers whom I also wish I could identify: Mr. L., Mrs. M., Mr. R., Ms. N., Ms. Goodstream, and Mr. O'Neill. They orchestrated their curricula to tap their students' energy and strong interests.

To students of mine who helped with the research a year at a time: Andrea St. George Jones, Constance Nylund, Susan Richardson, Eva Spranger, and Louise Covert. And to the other University of Minnesota, Duluth, students who took the stories of these forty developing writers to heart as I rehearsed for this book.

To teachers and colleagues who read various drafts or parts of drafts and who encouraged me in revision: Cal Benson, Mara Casey, Pam Erickson, Leo Hertzel, Sally Hudson-Ross, Michael Linn, Nancy Lund, Constance Mathew, Robert Kosuth, Josephine Ryan, Pat Shannon, Georgia Swing, and Neil Wittiko.

To mentors who have read and responded early in the process of this research: Judith Solsken, Earl Seidman, Charles Moran, Michael Linn, Donald Murray, and Sonia Nieto.

To the women in writing groups who responded to the ideas and the writing along the way: Chris Bresnahan, Kate Finnegan, Harriet Gott, Lou Lipkin, Mary Bray Schatzkamer, Alice Schleiderer, and Joan Snowden.

To my editor, Bob Boynton, who, like the best writing teachers, let this work be my own.

This book was supported, in part, by a Grant-in-Aid from the University of Minnesota.

Introduction

I confess. In 1966, when I announced my first writing assignment as a student teacher, my eleventh-grade students groaned. Of course, my students groaned less as I became better at teaching, but even in my thirteenth year I knew there were more groans than there needed to be. As a teacher, I pondered their origin and worked to reduce them, but I didn't have time to make those groans a focus for serious study until I began graduate work and research pursuits in 1980. Now, as I train teachers in northern Minnesota who are about to go out and meet local groans, I feel compelled to write about what I have learned. There have been enough groans.

This book is about what has gone wrong for forty eleventh-grade writers from urban, suburban, and suburban/rural schools, from the East Coast, the Midwest, and the West Coast. It explores the writing experience of successful writers, unsuccessful writers, and ESL writers; it includes students whose teachers have had writing-project training and students whose teachers haven't. The book examines forty writers' responses to their teachers and peers, as well as the institutions, curricula, and social factors that have affected their relationship with writing.

The forty eleventh-graders who generated the material for this book wouldn't all have been my favorite students. Nevertheless, I grew to respect each of them by hearing of their writing experiences in long and multiple interviews, by observing them in writing classes, and by listening to them say everything out loud that came into their minds while writing. Of course, these forty writers can't talk for all the developing writers in the nation, but they tell us enough so that we can begin to ask some very important questions, and they can send us in the direction of answers to the central question of this book: What goes wrong for developing writers?

Writing isn't easy. As I write the introduction for this book that has been six years in the making, I'm in just the place to say that. At worst, writing is so onerous a task that it is only the consequences of not doing it that keep me going. I'd rather be dancing, canoeing, or even cleaning the house. I struggle when my writing feels futile, impossible, vulnerable to criticism, or boring—like writing yet another long-range plan for an administrator who has neither interest in nor funds for the English Department.

At best, writing is engaging, compelling, and challenging—and hard work. This book is about writing at its best and its worst, and writing it has been the best and the hardest work I have ever done. There hasn't been a moment when I haven't wanted to finish the book, but there have been moments when I have roamed the wild parks of Duluth trying to order the muddled plans swirling in my head, when I've ranted to my dog about uncooperative chapters, and when I've lost a day of work with the mistrike of a key. Nevertheless, from my first interview to my last, I've felt compelled to write this book. These forty eleventh-grade students have filled me so full of tales, perspectives, and insights that I might have exploded without a pen in hand or computer keys under my fingertips. Ironically, my best-yet writing experience is mostly about what has gone wrong for forty eleventh-grade writers; in finding my voice, I'm writing about the obstacles students meet in maintaining theirs.

Overview of the Book

In the chapters ahead we'll look at the kinds of things that went wrong for forty developing writers, at what made them struggle for voice and then lose their desire to write. As a reader interested in students and writing, you'll come to this reading with your own set of questions, and because of the breadth and depth of what these students have to say, you may even find answers to questions I haven't yet posed. I want this to be a book in which the reader makes some of the meaning. In most books, authors say what they think is true and then prove it using examples. In this book, students give you their views of their writing experiences, but I don't offer interpretations until you've probably come to some of your own. Their accounts will immerse you in the complexity of students' perceptions of classroom reality and will compel you to examine that reality so you can develop new ways of thinking not only about students but also about curriculum that capitalizes on student individuality.

Students' voices are the backbone of the book. A profile of a student introduces each chapter, using the student's own words woven from recorded interview material. The student talks of writing experiences that shed light on the chapter topic and give a graphic understanding of what students bring to the writing classroom. In each chapter except the first, in addition to a main student voice, I include what other students had to say about the chapter topic and offer some observations and conclusions of my own. Thus, though one student is the soloist in each chapter and the other students are the chorus, we all take part in the composing.

In chapter 1, I describe the research process I went through with Tracy; further, her experience raises questions that provide a frame for the rest of the book. In chapter 2, we hear about what went wrong for Carlos and other unsuccessful writers. In chapter 3, we listen to Elana and other successful writers as they talk about what made writing troubling and unsatisfying even for them. Chapter 4 focuses further on Elana and how her life outside of school complicated the writing she was doing in school. In chapter 5, Lisa and other students talk about how peers make writing both distressing and engaging. Chapter 6 focuses on Jenny and other ESL students who were mainstreamed into English classes; this chapter discusses issues of language and of dialect that also beleaguer the unsuccessful student introduced in chapter 2. In chapter 7, we listen to Doug and Joseph and look more focally at the secondary writing curriculum with the question, "Why does the struggle for voice begin for most students in the secondary school years?" Although ideas for teaching are embedded in each chapter, the final chapter is dedicated to that purpose. Thus, in chapter 8, we look at the positive side of what's happening in secondary schools and use Kathy's, Danny's, Brittany's, and Anne's experiences to explore writing curricula that can make writing satisfying and fulfilling.

Chapter One

Tracy
The Research, The Questions

To really understand the things that Tracy and the others have to say, it is important for you to know how I chose these forty students, and also to know how I found out what they had to say, how I recorded the perspectives that they had to offer on writing. I will describe how I went about my research with Tracy, so you can get a close view of the research process that I used with all forty students. This chapter is not entirely about the research, however, because Tracy's experience introduces questions about the writing experience that will be explored in the rest of the book.

Finding the Students

The most challenging part of this research was getting to the students. I had to clear my method with two universities' human subjects review boards, and I had to get my project approved by four superintendents, nine principals, and nine English Department chairs. All these steps are important in that they safeguard students from irresponsible research, but the process became simpler when I got to the teachers. And when I finally sat down with students like Tracy, the research became compelling.

I chose eleventh-graders for the study because I wanted the students to be able to reflect on their experience; I chose not to go through the research process with twelfth-graders because I knew too well what it was like to work with students who have one foot out the high school door. I sought out many different kinds of students so that I might try to understand a broad range of writing experience. I wanted a diversity of region, gender, ethnicity, and social class, so I sought students from three different regions of the United States, from different ethnicities, from basic, standard, and advanced tracks, and from different sorts of schools. For instance, I wanted to have a female minority student from an advanced writing class in an inner-city school whose parents were of the working class. Tracy was the closest I could find. Her father was a factory foreman and her mother was a florist in the local supermarket. In other categories, there were many students in each pool, and I was able to take the names of those willing and then select my participants' names out of a hat. Figure 1–1 will tell you about each participant in the study and how they fit in with the categories that I set up. You will probably want to refer to this figure as you read on in the book.

The forty students who finally went through this research process offered diverse views, but by no means did they represent perfectly the whole population of sixteen- and seventeen-year-olds nationwide. First, students had to be willing, and there were a few who weren't for reasons that I will never know. Further, the study missed students who had dropped out of school before I had the chance to find them in eleventh-grade classes. Finally, because I was seeking diversity, there was a higher percentage of minority students in the study than there was in the schools.

Listening to Tracy: The Interviewing and Profiles

When I finally walked into Tracy's fifth-period class, it wasn't hard to find her. She was the only black female student in the advanced writing class of her inner-city school. She was stamped as a successful student by her elementary school, had been placed in its "gifted classes," and had remained in advanced classes thereafter. She was an ironic counterbalance to the only white young woman in the basic writing class of the same district. I observed Tracy writing in class and then met her during the study hall she had after that class. I told her: "I want to write for teachers. I'd like them to know what it's like for students to learn to write." Like most of the students, Tracy was eager to be included in the research. Tracy asked a few questions, gave prompt assent, and selected a pseudonym so she could talk about teachers and peers without feeling vulnerable. Student selection of pseudonyms was interesting in itself: those with common names wanted more exotic ones, those with exotic names went for more common ones, and ESL students most often

Figure 1–1
Participants

Pseudonym	Race/Ethnicity	School Setting	Gender	Level Tracked	Occupation	
					Mother	Father
Alice	White	Rural/Sub	Female	Standard	High Schl. Math Teacher	Retired Const. Wkr.
Carlos	P. Rican	Rural/Sub	Male	Basic	Unemployed	Truck Driver
Chris	White	Rural/Sub	Male	Advanced	Teacher	Civil Servant
David	White	Suburban	Male	Basic	Owner Beauty Par.	Const.
Doug	White	Suburban	Male	Advanced	Housewife	Exec. V.P. Mfr. Corp.
Elana	Jewish	Rural/Sub	Female	Advanced	Administrator	Professor
Elizabeth	White	Rural/Sub	Female	Advanced	Lawyer	Professor
Frank	White	Rural	Male	Standard	Housewife	Unemployed Fact. Supervisor
Fred	White	Urban	Male	Standard	Laid off Factory Worker	Unemployed Fact. Worker
George	White	Suburban	Male	Basic	Library Aide	Mechanic
Heidi	White	Suburban	Female	Standard	Prison Guard	Welder
Iris	P. Rican	Inner City	Female	Basic	Homemaker	Unemployed Fact. Worker
Jenny	Korean Immigrant	Suburban	Female	Standard	Homemaker	Truck Driver
Joel	Jewish	Rural/Sub	Male	Mainstr. ESL	Adoptive/Anesthetist	Homemaker
John	White	Urban	Male	Standard	Teacher	Health Adm.
Joseph	M-Phillipino F-White Am.	Suburban	Male	Advanced	ESL Tchr/Secretary	Ins. Salesman
Kathy	White	Suburban	Female	Advanced	Editor	Engineer
Kevin	White	Suburban	Male	Advanced	Student/Housewife	Minister
Lilly	Vietnamese Immigrant	Suburban	Female	Standard	Blk. Mrkt.	Bus Driver
Lisa	White	Rural/Sub	Female	Mainstr. ESL	Adoptive: Clerk	Businessman
Matt	Indian Immigrant	Rural/Sub	Male	Standard	Housewife	Unemployed Acct.

Name	Ethnicity	Setting	Gender	Level	Mother	Father
Meg	White	Suburban	Female	Basic	Housewife	Deliv. Man/Real Est.
Mona	Maltese Am: 1st Generation	Suburban	Female	Basic	Housewife	Deliv. Man/Real Est.
Orion	White	Rural/Sub	Male	Basic	School Cook	Electrician
Patti	Chinese/From Vietn.	Urban	Female	Standard / Mainstr. ESL	Piece Work	Fact. Worker
Paul	Black	Suburban	Male	Basic	Secretary	Comm. College Counselor
Peco	Korean Am. 1st Generation	Suburban	Male	Advanced	Owns Small Business	Owns Small Business
Portia	White	Suburban	Female	Standard	School Libr.	Deceased Teacher
Rikka	White	Suburban	Female	Advanced	Elem. Teacher	Soc. Wrkr. (Absent)
Sandy	White	Urban	Female	Advanced	Secretary	Warehouseman
Shannon	White	Suburban	Female	Basic	Bartender	Const. Wrk.
Sherry	White	Suburban	Female	Basic	Bartender	Electrician
Sonia	Black	Inner City	Female	Basic	Secretary	Fact. Supervisor
Tim	Am. Indian	Reservation	Male	Basic	Unempl.	
Tom	Jap. Am. 1st Generation	Suburban	Male	Standard	Owner—Auto Shop	Deceased Owner—Auto Shop
Tony	Vietnamese Immigrant	Suburban	Male	Standard / Mainstr. ESL	Deceased	Fisherman/Merchant
Tracy	Black	Inner City	Female	Advanced	Store Clerk	Fact. Supervisor
Vance	White	Suburban	Male	Standard	Secretary	Student/Laborer
Vicky	White	Suburban	Female	Standard	Secretary	Insurance Agent
Zac	Black	Inner City	Male	Basic	Fact. Supervisor	Mach. Operator

Summary:

Ethnicity	Setting	Gender	Level
22 White	8 Rural/Sub	20 Male	12 Advanced
4 Black	4 Inner City	20 Female	13 Basic
2 Puerto Rican	1 Reservation Sch		15 Standard
2 Jewish	22 Suburban		
3 First Gen. Am.	4 Urban		
1 Am. Indian	1 Rural		
5 Immigrant			
1 Phillip. Am.			

wanted very American names. Sometimes students took weeks to come up with the names they wanted, and Orion Quest actually researched possibilities. Tracy, however, knew immediately what she wanted to be called, and upon stating her new name, she pulled out her calendar so that we could set up times for three interviews. As much as possible, I scheduled interviews at least a week apart so that students had time between interviews to reflect on their writing experience.

Figure 1–2 details the material covered in the three hour-long

Figure 1–2
Interviews

Interview I — *What has writing been like for you from the time you first remember until the present?*

What do you remember of writing before you began school? How did you learn to write?

What was writing like for you in elementary school? junior high school? high school?

Did your parent(s) help you with writing? How was that? Who else helped you with writing (neighbors, grandparents, siblings, peers)? When was the help useful? Was any of it upsetting?

What kind of writing did you see your parents/siblings doing?

Tell me about a time when writing was really (good/bad) for you.

Tell me about where you lived and what your schools were like.

Can you recreate _____ for me? You haven't said much about _____?

I'm trying to get a sense of _____. (. . . and other open-ended questions)

Interview II — *What is writing like for you right now?*

Tell me as many stories as you can about what writing is like for you now.

What are all the kinds of writing you do inside and outside of school? Tell me about a typical day and how writing fits in that day.

How do you go about writing a paper for school from the time you get the assignment until you hand in the finished paper? Give as many details as possible. What is the process like for you? When is it exciting, or hard?

How do other people help or hinder that process?

Some people say that writing is uncomfortable, even distressing to them. Is that ever true for you? How?

I'm trying to imagine you at home writing. If I had a picture, what would it look like? Where do you write, when, how, with what?

What makes writing easy for you? What gives you a problem with writing? What do you worry about? Do you try to figure out what teachers want when you write?

Interview III — *What sense do you make of your experience with writing?*

Thinking about your past experience with writing and with school and your present experience with writing, what sense do you make of the whole thing? How do you understand that experience? (Asking the question in several different ways helped.)

What things are important to you in your life? How does writing connect with what is important?

Are you realizing anything through these interviews about schooling and its effect on you? How has the experience of writing been good/ bad/exciting/distressing/frustrating? How did you understand that?

What is there that seems important to you that we haven't covered? (Follow up from prior interviews)

---

interviews, but let me say a little more about the interviewing process. Each interview began with a broad question. In the first interview, I asked Tracy, "Tell me about your experience with writing from the first time you remember doing it until the present." The second interview began: "What is writing like for you in the present?" and the third interview: "What meaning/sense do you make of your experience with writing?" I didn't need to use many of the back-up questions listed on the chart with Tracy because she offered the answers on her own when answering the broader question. She talked the proverbial blue streak, but other students needed the further prompting that the additional questions offered. Nevertheless, toward the end of Tracy's first interview, I noticed that she hadn't said much about her parents' connection with her writing, so after she had run out of things to say, I asked her whether adults had helped her in her writing. As we will see in the following profile, Tracy's family was tremendously supportive of her in her schooling, but when it came to specific help on specific assignments, they simply hadn't had the education to offer help. This was very different from what happened in the families of other advanced students. So as students started talking, my own questions about students' experience were forming and reforming.

The interviewing that I did with Tracy and the others is called "in-depth phenomenological interviewing" (see Seidman, et al., 1983; Seidman, 1991; Schutz, 1967; Schuman, 1982). This approach to research assumes that the meaning students make of their experience with writing affects the way they go about it. Indeed, as we soon shall see, the sense that Tracy makes of her experience with writing in past years affects the way she goes about writing in the present. I have constructed the following profile of Tracy from excerpts of interview material. To make these profiles readable, I deleted large portions of material, rearranged and combined sections of interview material when a subject arose in more than one interview, changed verb tenses to make the rearranged material hang together, deleted hundreds of *you know*'s and *like*'s, and altered names of friends, teachers, and places to protect Tracy's anonymity. As you read what she has to say about her experience with writing, I hope you'll be forming questions as I was about what went wrong for Tracy, either in the margins of the book or in the margins of your mind.

A Profile of Tracy

My mother made so much about my writing before I even went to school. I loved to just scribble and scribble and show it to my mother, and she say, "Oh! That's wonderful," and pin it up on the walls. She had bunches of paper, a big box of pencils, and I remember her buying me a whole bunch of crayons. In school there were big green cardboard things around the walls with letters on them, and my teacher used to have a big stack of letters laid out on the floor, and she would say: "Which one is *C*," and we would run to it. We used to have thick-lined yellow paper, and we would have like an *F* and number three to practice on. They'd put a big star on it if we did it right, and we'd have grape juice and graham crackers. We'd go to the library every day after lunch, and we'd take home stars for our writing. You better believe that everyone who came to my house had to see that star. If we finished all our work early, we could go up to the library by ourselves and take out a book, other times we would have to walk in lines with the teacher. That was a lot of fun, picking out your own book.

My mother was really good friends with the library teacher, so she always used to pick me to be in things, 'cause she lived next door. In third grade I was the spokesman . . . spokesperson for a real T.V. show just for our elementary school, and we interview someone every week, and I wrote the scripts. I had to do quite a bit of writing. It wasn't a bad feeling when writing turned into a job. I remember in sixth grade my English teacher wanted me and two other girls to write a play to help the younger kids in first and second grade to learn the library resources, so I wrote out my script as if I was a girl asking how you're supposed to use the library. So that was fun, and we had to act it out for the kids, and that was another writing experience. In junior high we had working cycles, you could work in the office, or the school bank, or with gym teachers, so I worked in the office, and I was introduced to typing. That year I was picked for a gifted class, and we would meet every week and go off to a different place. We went to a marina, a zoo, an author's house, and we had to describe where we went.

We moved north in eighth grade. My father moved first; he's a foreman. Then two years later, my mother and sister and me and grandparents in the same house. The first marking period in the new school I wasn't really into school. Mr. Howes gave us a lot of work. Vocabulary wasn't a problem, just look up the words, but we did philosophy stuff. We had to think of what Aristotle was saying, Plato was saying, or read all those myths. They didn't talk the language we talked. It just seemed so far away; I just couldn't get it. The second marking period was really hard. I had to get my brain thinking again. I had to struggle so hard. Sometimes it was just so hard 'cause you had to do so much all at once, to remember so much about getting it right and then write about stuff that was so confusing.

I just hated going to that class. Go, just sit there, and I didn't participate. We had to interpret the philosophy and stuff; that was hard for me in eighth grade. We had to do a report; I was the first person he picked to read out loud. He picked on me a lot. Mr. Howes, he picked on me for everything. If I missed a word, he would have a fit. Another missed, he wouldn't say anything. I said no need of trying harder because he was just going to find something wrong with it. We had a yellow bus that came through the neighborhood, so we'd stand around waiting, and I said, "I have Mr. Howes first period. I hate that man." And they'd say, "Why you hate him?" You see, my friends that took my bus weren't in that hard English class. So around homeroom time, that subject came up, and I say, "I hate that English class because I try my best, but he always picks on me and stuff." And they [others in her English class] used to say, "Yeah, he does pick on you." I thought he hated me, and I hated that class. I stopped doing assignments.

At the beginning of the last marking period, Mr. Howes called me up to his desk, and he said, "Tracy, I think you're a very good student. I'm not trying to pick on you, I just think you have good abilities, and I think you can do much better than what you are doing. So don't get uptight when I call you up about a sentence. Just read over your work. Don't be in such a hurry to get it over

with." It was just a relief to know that he wasn't picking on me for
bad reasons, that he was picking on me because be thought I had
good abilities. I thought he hated me, and I hated him for that
reason. I just didn't care about the work, just did it to get it done.
After that he became a nice teacher. I didn't regret going to the
class, and I started to put effort into the work, getting the writing
done. My mother never had to tell me to do good in school, I just
did it. I never had a punishment, or spanking, but when she means
it, she means it. She told me I have to study, that I'm not dumb or
anything. She know I can do the work, and I'm just not doing it. So
I did it.

There weren't many black people in my city who had made it,
so later in junior high when my teacher broke us up to interview
the elderly people of the city, it added a lot when my friend Jay and
I interviewed the first black man to work in the school systems of
this city. I learned so much. I began to understand how it might be
for me as a black person—easier than it was for him, but still not all
that easy. We interviewed him every week at the town library about
his life story and how he got interested in writing and becoming
a teacher and how it was for him to be the first black with
predominantly white teachers and everything. All the interview
stories were combined into a small book and it's in the junior high
library now. I think writing then was—getting out into the
community and getting information from people who knew
something about a particular thing that I wanted to know. That's
how it was in ninth grade. But in tenth grade it was mostly books,
books, books, and writing compositions about books, constantly
writing.

My mother always said that she never went to college and
wished she would have went to college. My father always hanged
up all my report cards and papers when I'd bring them home. He
always tells me that he wants me to do better than he did, because
he couldn't go to college. [Even though] my father drives me to
school every morning and could tell me, he writes to me about two
letters every year and tells me how proud he is of me, really
personal letters and mails it to me. Tells me how much he loves me
and how much he wants me to do good and everything. They
always said that it's my choice if I want to do good at school. They
would never pressure me into doing anything I didn't want to, [but]
they act concerned with my education. They always go to open
house at school together. My sister went for two years and then
dropped out, and now she says she wished she would a finished, so
I said I might as well go to college, so I went to the college
preparatory high school in the city. I would be the first in our

family to go through college completely. I haven't asked my parents for any help since I was in elementary school because they think I can work it out pretty well by myself, but I asked my sister for awhile.

Tenth grade didn't do anything spectacular in writing; we read about six or seven books and we had to write a theme on every book we read; that's about it and book reports with lots and lots of examples. In eleventh grade it was better, we went to a crematorium, museum, planetarium, wrote journals, and wrote about our trips, learned to use microfilm. She thought I should not stick to easy words but to elaborate using bigger words. She wanted me to write more like a newsperson, going by the fact.

Now it's [writing's] pretty easy. I get hard assignments, but there is not strain on my mind to do the writing. When a teacher gives an assignment, I usually think it over, try to take notes, jot down my thoughts before I just go round and write it. It is one of my best subjects; I can express myself pretty good. It is not something I just love doing. If I have to do it, I do it. But if I don't have to write, then I don't write. I can't really think about anything I really like about it. I try to improve it when I can. I have these opportunities to improve it. I took a writing workshop class cause I thought that would help me improve because I know when I get to college I will have to do a lot of writing. What else can I say. I don't get excited about it. Sometimes I like it if I know I have to write an experience. I don't usually get excited about writing about anything else. Inside of school I mostly read a book and do a short essay. That's practically all the type of writing I do.

I don't do much writing outside of school anymore. One time I got mad at my great grandmother, and I went upstairs and instead of yelling back at her, I just went upstairs and wrote at my little desk. When I was little, my grandfather gave me this little desk, and I still use it. [Also,] I write a lot of notes in school. When I have SAT class, I usually hurry up and do it real quick, and then just write notes to my girlfriend. I forgot to mention that, and my father's mother, she usually writes me occasionally, and I write her back, about three times a year. That's it.

When I do an essay on the book, I read over whatever page she wants us to do, and then just jot down notes from the reading, then I do a rough draft, try to get all my notes together, then I just do the final draft, just write it over in case it's sloppy. I do it at that same little writing desk; my books are in my lap. It's so comfortable, and I'm so used to it.

When I take my time, I usually get things right. I can remember a few corrections about the wrong tense, about singular when it should be plural, but it wasn't really a major problem for me, as I see in lots of kids. My mother constantly corrects me when I talk improper. My great-grandmother talks not really bad, but sometimes I can't understand her that well. I think it came from the slaves. But my mother and father they don't really, and I think I pick up most of my language from them and from doing good in school. Good English just came easy to me. I'm in a predominantly white school now. I can't remember feeling badly about the English that I used, but when I first moved up here, I really couldn't communicate well with some of the kids in my neighborhood because some of the words I just didn't even know. I thought maybe I wasn't hip or whatever; they would break it down for me. When I'm in a class I make sure that I don't make mistakes; I'm weighing in the back of my mind, "Correct that; it's not right." But at home, usually I just talk any way that I want to. And with my friends, I'll switch my vocabulary to slang. Sometimes, if it's late at night and I'm doing a rough draft, and write it over really quick, I'll use the wrong tense or something. But when I take my time, I usually get it right. I can remember corrections about the wrong tense, about singular when it should be plural. And it isn't really a major problem for me, as I see in lots of kids that is a major problem. I don't know where it originated. Well, I think it originated from slaves when they were brought over here from Africa.

When I write, I worry about a word that's repeated throughout the paper, and it makes the paper boring. So I try to use a variety of words that mean the same. I use a Thesaurus. And I also worry about length. Usually a teacher doesn't specify a length. I try to make it over a page. I worry about length because I don't want to make it too short or too long. I try to make it about one and a half pages. I can never remember Mr. Abruzzi ever giving us a limit. So I used to write it, and sometimes I would get carried away, and at the end he would always comment, "a little too lengthy," or if I didn't he would say, "You could use more; add another paper onto this." He tried to make us figure out for ourselves what was the right amount. I think that's why I worry about it now. I can remember Ms. Dell telling me that a paper on *Huckleberry Finn* was too long, that I used too many examples. Dr. Heller had always told me to use lots of examples. So I didn't figure that one out. So now I have to switch over to her way. Now, when I write something for her, I use about half the examples to shorten it. It's not hard; as long as they explain I can get the hang of it.

I just finished my term paper; that was a little hard at the little desk, had to use the bed. Finding a topic was hard; he told us we couldn't do it on any disease, on any sports, or any people 'cause we were limited. At first I had abortion, but he said it was like a disease. I was really interested in it medically, ethically. Then I had alcoholism, and he said that was disease too. Then I said suicide, but that was wrong too. And then finally I came up with divorce and how it affects children, and then I finally got it approved. That was the worst time for me, getting stuck on that topic. I couldn't put any of my own experience in it because divorce didn't affect me much at all. I remember glancing through magazines trying to find something that wasn't wrong.

I found an article about divorce and how it affects children, so then I wrote that down as a thesis statement and got it approved. It was frustrating 'cause I didn't want to scrounge around to get up eight typed papers. We had to get five resources; I had eight. Then we had notecards from all eight of the books. Then I sorted them, and then I wrote the whole thing, using some of my words, then theirs, then mine, then theirs. He corrected the rough draft, and then I typed it correcting each error and then typing until another [error]. I just didn't feel like writing the whole thing over again. I started retyping it on Saturday afternoon, due Monday, but I only came up with six and a half pages. I was glad I hadn't turned my book in yet, 'cause I had to come up with a bunch of little extras. I just added it all on to the end at the last minute. It came up to eight pages. I got 86, the highest in the class, but he said he'd rather I turned in not enough pages than spoil it and add on other stuff that I didn't really need. I was so mad. I was going to turn it in at only six and a half pages, but sometimes he can be so strict, so I added on.

When I do a paper for a specific teacher, I always try to figure out what they want. That seemed like the most trouble throughout school, living up to what they expect out of your writing and stuff. When I was with Mr. Abruzzi, I did it his way; Dr. Keller, I did it his way; Ms. Dell, I did it her way. And I think that's what made writing feel more like work than pleasure. Each year the work would get harder and harder. When I get a hard assignment, I read the question over and over and over, trying to pick out what my teacher wants me to say, what they're trying to get at. I try to use a variety of words, a longer word, stuff like that. And now in eleventh grade, it's more and more, and you have to learn how certain teachers want it done. I don't get excited about it. I do it because I know it has to be done. I think I know what my teachers want from me now. I hope another teacher doesn't come along and change things again.

After college I guess I'll be somewhere in the medical field, doing something so I can be my own boss, probably not as much writing, maybe little things on patients' charts or something or writing down prescriptions for medicine. I don't think that writing will be as extensive after I get out of college. Dr. Heller, my tenth-grade teacher, was really enthused with my writing. When my parents came for open house, he told them he thought I should be a writer for a living! He gave me a big encouragement in writing, but I don't think writing is for me. I don't see it in my future. If I didn't have to do it I just wouldn't do it. When I was little, I thought it was wonderful. But now, it's work, something that you have to do. When I was little, I used to show my parents all my work. Now I just stuff it in my notebook or throw it away.

In Tracy's experience we see writing at its best and at its worst. As a young child, like other children, she learned to speak because she wanted to. Children learn language because they are by nature inquisitive, responsive to feedback, imitative, observant, and expressive. In elementary school, Tracy brought these same human attributes to writing. Tracy's early writing career seemed ideal; writing was exciting and engaging work. Further, she was successful, and she had support from parents, grandparents, and teachers. She liked the feelings of self-determination and competence that language gave her in her world. Tracy is a success story in almost every respect, but even praise did not keep her wanting to write. Although all the questions that Tracy's experience raises about writing (questions about criticism, confidence, motivation, dialect, and support from teachers, parents, and peers, among others) are questions addressed in this book, I think it's important to focus on one major question here because it permeates so much of what these forty students had to say and because it forms an overall frame for this book: *Why do Tracy and so many other secondary students lose their inner inclination to write? What goes wrong for developing writers?*

We are told by researchers and theorists that writing is a way to come to know one's own thoughts and feelings and that it is a way of letting others know those thoughts and feelings. Writing is one way of engaging in the self-expression that makes us human. It's also a way of acting upon our world, a way of getting things to happen for us, not to us. Of course adolescents develop competing interests of many kinds, but is it inevitable that they must lose interest in a mode of expression that has such potential for satisfaction?

The interview material gathered in this study is an important way to begin to study these questions because it permits us access to students' perspectives on what has gone wrong, but it is not the only method that I used.

Observing Tracy

I observed Tracy and the other students while they wrote in class on at least three separate occasions, once before their first interview and at least twice thereafter. On my second observation, Tracy started to work on the in-class essay on *Huckleberry Finn* before most of the other students even sat down at their desks. As she wrote, she sat so still that it seemed from my vantage point that only her pen and her gold earrings moved. She seemed to concentrate on her own work despite hostile questions that her confused class-mates had for the teacher about the assignment; she wrote steadily for forty minutes, breaking her contact between pen and paper only when she searched in her book for appropriate quotes. She finished her "copy-over draft" a full five minutes before anybody else in class finished theirs. She seemed more focused on writing that day than any other student I observed at any time in the study. This particular observation validated the view that I had of Tracy in the interviews. She was an earnest young woman who was intent on being "the good student." The observations of Tracy and the others allowed me a glimpse of these developing writers in their school settings, and these observations often enabled me to ask questions that further clarified their experience.

Immediately following the second and third observations, I made a point of chatting with Tracy and the others about the writing, although I couldn't always record those conversations verbatim since they often occurred in crowded corridors on the way to the students' next class. "I have trouble getting all the examples the teachers want," Tracy said that day, "so I have to work really hard to make sure I get it done." She didn't know yet that her new teacher would be wanting fewer examples. Her frustration with finding what the teacher wanted wasn't new, but she was about to have another go-round with it.

Composing Aloud; What Goes On in the Conscious Attention

I also observed as Tracy composed aloud. After a few practice tasks designed to get her used to composing aloud, I asked her to do two teacher-assigned tasks, saying aloud everything that came into her mind while she was writing. The composing-aloud sessions gave me a glimpse of what was going on in the conscious attention of these writers. Psychologist Herbert Simon (1982) says that the conscious attention is a place where thoughts and feelings are intertwined and where the mind works on a task. The human body might carry on numerous tasks simultaneously if it weren't for what he terms "the bottleneck" of conscious attention.

Writing is hard work because there's just so much you can concentrate on at once while you're writing, and anything that's upsetting seems to take priority, interrupting concentration needed for that writing. I constructed Figure 1-3 to help myself see patterns in the occurrences of things that interrupted students' concentration while they were composing. I will refer back to this figure in talking about individual writers in later chapters.

Writing was not easy for Tracy, even though she was generally successful at the end of a task. On the task recorded on Figure 1-3, she concentrated on ideas, word choice, planning, and revision, as did most of the other advanced writers. But Tracy also was interrupted in her composing process by the attention that she needed to give to syntax ("Do I need -ed on that verb?"); this was most likely a result of her impetus to be correct, to remove the vestiges of the black English that she talked about in her interviews. On three occasions during the recorded composing-aloud session, Tracy interrupted her work with concern over whether she was doing what the teacher expected. On two of these occasions she expressed her desire to quit or to be doing something else. Tracy had talked in her interviews about some of the reasons that writing was hard enough to make her feel like quitting in eighth grade. "I had to struggle so hard. Sometimes it was just so hard 'cause you had to do so much all at once, to remember so much about getting it right and then write about stuff that was so confusing." Tracy echoed what other students in the study had to say about why writing was harder than other school endeavors. Elana said:

> When you do math, you have one formula, and you do multiple problems with this same formula. You don't have to think about it. But when you write something . . . , your mind has to be constantly flowing, coming up with new ideas, new structures, to form these ideas, not just to write them, but to do it in an attractive creative manner. And you have to be thinking about all those things at once while you're writing. And it's hard work. And when I have some of these other things [grandfather's death and teacher's criticism] on my mind, I absolutely cannot write. I cannot do it. I get so preoccupied with trying so hard to not be preoccupied with these other things that it gets to sort of spaghetti, and it gets awfully messy.

Composing-Aloud Data (A): Things That Interrupted Basic Writers

	CARLOS	DAVID	GEORGE	IRIS	JOHN	MONA	ORION	PAUL	SHANNON	SHERRY	SONIA	TIM	ZAC
(sentences)	11	8	9	6	6	13	27	5	20	17	6	8	7
(minutes)	35	19	23	12	14	20	35	8	10	24	10	7	15
Spelling	16	3	2	1	1					2			6
Aesthetics	1												
Syntax	9							1		1	1		2
Punctuation	3										1		1
Convention	1					2							
Idea Generation	12	10	8	1	4	3	2	14	1	6	3	1	3
Word Choice	1		1		3		1			1	1		
Planning	1	2				3			2				
Recursion	10	1	1	2	1		2	2		5	2	1	8
Outside Life		4	1		2								
Audience													
Revision													
word/sentence	3		4			4	2	2		3	3	1	
paragraph											2		
Blocks—impetus to quit					4								
Amusing Oneself	1		3										
Passive Voice													
Colloquialism													
Inner Critic													
Writing Environs		3										1	
Self-Evaluation													
Self-Approval			2			1				4			
Style													

Figure 1–3

Composing-Aloud Data (B): Things That Interrupted Standard Writers

	ALICE	FRANK	FRED	HEIDI	JENNY	JOEL	LISA	MATT	PORTIA	TOM	VANCE	VICKY
(sentences)	9	17	13	7	13	16	20	15	14	5	10	10
(minutes)	25	42	12	18	19	25	40	12	48	21	32	28
Spelling							7	1		1	7	
Aesthetics			3				1				2	
Syntax							5	4			1	
Punctuation		1	2				3				1	
Convention						1	2					1
Idea Generation	8	6	6	7	7	10	55	13	29	5	8	10
Word Choice	6	4	1	1			13	3	2		2	
Planning	3		1	2	3	8	9	3	6		5	2
Recursion	2	15	2	4	1	2	16	7	7	7	19	7
Outside Life							3				1	1
Audience	1					1	1				2	2
Revision word/sentence	2	7		1	3			6	4	8	10	6
paragraph	2	1								1	3	
Blocks—impetus to quit	3	2	1				4	1	3			
Amusing Oneself							1					
Passive Voice												
Colloquialism	1											
Inner Critic						1	2					
Writing Environs							1		2		1	
Self-Evaluation		2									2	
Self-Approval												
Style		1					1		3			1

	CHRIS	DOUG	ELANA	ELIZABETH	KATHY	KEVIN	JOSEPH	MEG	PECO	PORTIA	RIKKA	SANDY	TRACY
(sentences)	12	3	8	19	6	13	10	8	13		21	13	15
(minutes)	40	29	40	15	37	45	45	60	37	48	40	22	20
Spelling	1									1			
Aesthetics	1						1				6	1	
Syntax	1												5
Punctuation													
Convention			1		1		1				2		
Idea Generation	22	5	28	15	8	17	26	7	19	29	13	7	15
Word Choice	8	4	13	2	4	5	1	7	2	2	15	3	4
Planning	30	2	18	6	14	17	7	11	19	7	12	3	20
Recursion	3	2	2	3	7	1	6	5	4	7	9	7	3
Outside Life			4	2	2	1			1				
Audience	7		1			1			1			1	1
Revision													
word/sentence	14		11	6					2	4		3	6
paragraph												2	2
Blocks—impetus to quit	5	2	2	1		2	2		1	2			2
Amusing Oneself	4			1			2	1		1		2	
Passive Voice	2		1	2									
Colloquialism	3												
Inner Critic	4	2	5	2		1				2	1		1
Writing Environs	2	2						1					
Self-Evaluation				1				3			5	1	
Self-Approval	1			4	1			1		3			
Style	3												

Before looking at the complexities of what goes wrong for these students, it's important to understand that composing is a complex task by its very nature. Analysis of composing-aloud sessions helps us to see the complexity that writing holds for students, and connecting that information with interview and observation data further clarifies how that complexity fits in with students' response to writing.

Even those of us who live to some extent by the pen and who are the survivors of our educational systems can understand what Tracy and Elana meant when they said that writing is hard. Many of us probably also know about writing when it becomes a struggle, when emotions connected with our lives or with the context for writing complicate the writing process. As we explore what students like Tracy have to say about writing, we will see that it was not hard work but other factors that kept them from being able to concentrate on the hard work of writing — that made them struggle for voice.

Though the rest of this chapter will look to Tracy for examples, the focus will return to the qualitative research I used. I make some strong statements about curriculum and pedagogy at the end of this book, and I want you to know how I moved *from* observing and listening to individual students *to* coming to conclusions about the curricula of the schools that they attended and *to* advocating change.

Truth, Inner Voice, and Tracking

When I first started this research, I thought I was going to have to search for the truth within what the students had to say. I had my share of "the dog ate the paper" excuses as a teacher, but in taking Tracy and the others seriously, in hearing them trying to make sense of their experiences, I began to know that these students were working hard to relate their perceptions of what happened to them with their writing, to make me understand. It was *their perceptions* of what had happened with their writing that informed their attitudes, opinions, and feelings about writing.

Truth — who is to say what truth is all about? I'm sure some of these students' teachers, even the exonerated Mr. Howes, would give different renditions of the interactions that they had with the students. I haven't given teachers equal time here because my purpose is to understand what was going on for the students: what their perceptions of reality were and how those perceptions affected their behavior. Part of what the book attempts to do is to enable teachers to see the learning experience from students' perspectives, to become sensitive to the kind of things they react to. Mr. Howes became sensitive somehow to Tracy's perception of what was going on and acted to change it. We can see how both his sensitivity and his high expectations were important to Tracy and her future in school.

What's recorded in this book are some honest perceptions from students who seemed to realize that I really wanted to collect and understand their experience. Before they trusted me, when they were trying to figure out what I wanted from them or when they were trying to entertain me, they often started with "an outer voice." But when they sensed that I was just interested in understanding their experience with writing, I would get "an inner voice," the voice that was both relating and trying to understand that experience.

The inner voice was a thinking voice: thinking to remember, thinking to get what happened into words, thinking to understand it and fit it together with present experience. I could even hear the difference on the tapes. The inner voice would come on as the students became interested in rendering the past; it moved in when they trusted me and out when they suddenly wondered what I was thinking of what they were saying. As I became better at interviewing, I was able to move them back to the inner voice, usually with a question that indicated acceptance and reflected back to them what I sensed they had said: "So your year with Mr. Howes was a difficult one?" After that question, Tracy began to tell me about the difference between the beginning and the end of the year. This book is filled with the inner voices of students.

This research attempts to gain entry into the conceptual world of the participants, to capture the meaning that they conferred on what they did and on the way other people reacted to what they did. Students, like the rest of us, mediate experience by interpretation. We can't give them a stimulus and expect a standard response, because each is a unique individual. The initial meaning that Tracy made of Mr. Howes' critical stance toward her writing was what, she said, made her "want to quit." These are the kinds of things that we as teachers sometimes can't see from the other side of the big desk. In order to understand, it helps to see how students define and understand their experience. Further, sometimes students need help in sorting out meaning. Tracy needed help in understanding why she didn't hold her usual "best" student status in Mr. Howes' class. Mr. Howes helped her sort that out.

One of the things that kept me walking and thinking in one of Duluth's parks for hours one day was how to group students and issues in chapters so that I could talk about them honestly and productively. In my original research plan, I selected students from basic, standard, and advanced classrooms. I wanted to look at students as they fell into the "ability" groups established by their schools. Each school was tracked, and the criteria for tracking varied across schools. Students were placed in tracks on the basis of testing, self-tracking, and/or performance in previous classes. Twelve students came from their school's advanced writing or English classes, fifteen from the standard, and thirteen from the basic. Original selection was fairly simple, but finding a way to deal with differences in "ability" levels in this book was very difficult, for I truly believe that almost every student has innate ability to be successful in school and that lack of success is a complex interaction of dynamics connected with race, class, schooling, and circumstance.

But in my trek up Hartley Hill in Duluth that day, I began to see a better way of talking about writers. I divided them as they saw themselves: successful or unsuccessful. Their decisions about whether they were successful or unsuccessful were based in part on what was reflected to them from their teachers' responses to their writing and in part on the level of their track. The unsuccessful students had been placed in the basic or remedial track; they were generally students who didn't feel good about themselves as writers, and most were students who had given up hope of or interest in becoming good writers. Successful students, who were in standard or advanced classes, didn't necessarily feel themselves to be excellent writers, but they were perceived by their schools as being generally successful, and they had come to believe it. And, of course, every grouping becomes a generalization that doesn't work for every writer. For instance, Tracy would have considered herself unsuccessful in the first part of seventh grade and successful by the end of the year; Lisa swung between feeling successful or unsuccessful depending on how peers or teachers responded to her writing on a particular day; Matt took on symptoms of both groups simultaneously for logical reasons that I will relate later.

If You're Interested in Data Analysis

One of the problems in this research was in getting *from* thousands of pages of interview transcripts, transcriptions of composing-aloud sessions, and observation notes *to* conclusions about what went wrong for these forty developing writers. There was both a tremendous variety and a strong continuity in the experiences of these students.

As previously described when talking about Tracy and Figure 1–3, analysis of the composing-aloud data was developed to indicate instances of interruptions in the students' focused attention during composing. Interruptions occurred when attention was drawn to a variety of composing or personal concerns. In describing the writing processes of successful and unsuccessful writers, this analysis was important because it linked with what students said about their writing in interviews.

I looked for connections among things different participants said and did by working out a complicated system by which I filed and cross-filed excerpts of interview transcripts and field notes according to category codes. The heavy cross-filing that occurred was indicative of the complexity of the research topic. The file folders that represented category codes did not remain constant throughout the research. At one time there were 123 files, but I added, deleted, and subsumed category codes as I went along. In early analysis, I began to see differences in how unsuccessful and successful students responded to their writing curricula and to their teachers and peers, and how this affected their concentration and motivation.

To deal with issues in their complexity, I had to look at each category code as described by the whole range of students, then as described by different groups of students (successful, unsuccessful, those whose teachers did or didn't teach writing as a process, ESL students, workshop students). I also had to look carefully at highly cross-referenced categories; for instance, in writing chapter 4, "Elana Continued: When Life Gets Tough," I had to pull files from each region that connected in any way to this topic (category code files used: distressing life situation, family and writing, peer involvement in writing, cathartic writing, struggle, emotional disruption, worries, conscious attention, out-of-school writing, and junior high trauma). Finally, in writing about the profiled writers, I had to be fair to the data generated from interviews, classroom observations, and the composing-aloud sessions of the particular writer.

This analysis of the interview, composing-aloud, and observation data connected the experiences of the different participants so that the complex dynamics of the interaction among thought, emotion, and the writing process could be studied. Pat theories and conclusions did not emerge full-blown. In this analytic induction, theories arose and were discarded, to be replaced with new and more complex theories and explanations as discrepant data appeared. Thus, insights gleaned from all phases of the research process led to an emerging theory about what was going wrong for these developing writers: about how emotion interacted with thinking to limit concentration during writing and how writing motivation interacted with this dynamic.

Conclusion

Sometimes researchers feel strongly while they're researching; some people think that doesn't make for objective research. I can't promise that I have conducted this research without emotion, but I can promise that I have presented these students fairly. The quotes that I have selected to illustrate the conclusions I have drawn in this book are representative of the very large majority of the students or of groups of students. Significant deviations from what the majority had to say are discussed as such.

Actually, I have had strong feelings in this research process. I have felt compelled, even politicized, by hearing the experiences of the forty students. It didn't start right away. The first writer didn't make me want to write a book. I started out with just twelve writers, and I learned a lot from them, and then as the group expanded, their stories and experiences continued to be compelling. They had so much to say but no forum in which to speak. I wanted to make sure their voices — sometimes despondent, sometimes angry, sometimes confused, sometimes enthusiastic — were heard.

Chapter Two

Carlos
Dismantling the Cage of the Unsuccessful Writer

The students in this study who had been relegated to the "basic" or "remedial" or "vocational" classes had long since lost interest in things academic. They were unsuccessful as writers and as students, and they were caught in circumstances they could neither see nor fully understand. Their language was nonstandard, they weren't fluent in getting thoughts into written words, nor were they adept in reading. They had received prolonged criticism, they had become defensive, and they felt bad about themselves as students and writers. This chapter will explore these students' problems as well as the complex social constructs that brought them about.

Carlos was among these students, but he was one of the lucky ones. In his early elementary years and in his recent school years, teachers had become important to him; they had made a difference. As a result, when I worked with Carlos, he was beginning to see the bars of the cage that held him, and he was able to accept his teachers' active measures to assist him in dismantling that cage. His perceptions of his writing experience provide us with a way to view the complex circumstances that beleaguer the basic writer.

Carlos began his life in a large city, where his Puerto Rican mother spoke Spanish and where his eleven brothers and sisters taught him what he called "street talk," a dialect of English that showed Spanish and black English interference. In third grade Carlos went to a reform school where teachers attempted to bring his language closer to standard English through almost four years of remedial exercises. Later, he moved to a New England town where he attended junior and senior high school.

I first saw Carlos when he entered the English office of his high school. His height and rugged good looks were at odds with the boyish grin that spread across his face as his teachers greeted him and joked with him. His drama coach, Mr. O'Neill, brought him over to meet me, saying, "Here's an eleventh-grader you can learn from." He was right; I learned a lot from Carlos.

A Profile of Carlos

When I was a little kid in kindergarten, I was trying to write my name and couldn't. Or at least the teacher didn't like it. I scribbled this way, up and down first, and then sideways. And then I took the pencil and went, "Argh"! I hated writing. Now I do a lot of writing at this high school, and I don't write very well.

When I got to first grade, the teacher made me do a lot, but the only thing I liked was watching T.V. I got left back in first grade. I stayed back and I liked it. I'd watch still more T.V. I didn't know I'd stayed back. Next year I went downstairs to ESL. She [the teacher] was Spanish, and she would translate and say it was my language too. I spoke English out on the street, but at home I spoke Spanish. [Now] my English is terrible. My English, to me I understand what I am saying; to other people, they don't understand. I just don't wanna speak—I don't know what words to use. My English crashes into Spanish. It mixed together. If I ever try to speak Spanish, Spanish people would say, "Are you Spanish?" I say, "Yes." They say, "You don't talk like you're Spanish; you don't know how to speak well." My mother is always telling me I should be ashamed. I don't feel like I'm Spanish; I don't feel like anything. I just feel . . . like a plant.

When I got to second grade, I had Miss Banducci. I loved to read in her class. She let me read a lot in the group. I would always sit right across from her, and I just go, "Ah, Miss, can I read?" In third grade I had Miss Hirsch; she was my favorite. I did a lot of math, spelling, learning big words, learning how to do script, learning how to write and all that. They didn't mind run-on sentences, but they got to that later.

I used to run away, sometimes afraid to get punished, sometimes [with my brother] Juan. He didn't go to school much. He got put into a reform . . . training school. That same year I got into trouble. One time my friends broke into a shopping mall. I didn't know where we were going; I was too scared to say anything. It was dark out. We had to crawl to get out. I got caught then by the police.

My mother knew a little English when she went to the courtroom with me. I whispered that I wanted to go. My brother Juan was already there at the training school. He was my best brother. She said it out loud to the judge.

It [training school] was nice; I have a picture at home. We'd go swimming, we'd go skating, and every Sunday we'd go to church if we wanted to. Miss Hirsch—my third-grade teacher—she came to see me at that school, to take me to the movies, on my birthday and on Christmas Day, and she wrote me letters, a lot of letters. I liked that, but missing my mom—that's the only thing I hated because then she never visit me in three years. Only once my uncle came.

And I didn't like the school [part]. I didn't like writing; I didn't know how to make a sentence. Every day I had to write. First goes my name, the date, then the weather, what's it like. If I get it wrong, I got to rewrite it—all over again. I didn't know how. The teacher said I was bad at making up stories, too short. When I was a kid, I was dumb, too dumb. And I still am 'cause I'm way behind. I didn't know how to write the story. I knew I'd be getting it wrong. Then I'd have to rewrite it again, and again, and again. No wonder I refused to write, but they made me do other exercises. But it was always wrong, too. Everyone talked like I did there 'cause we all came from the city and city talk. We understood what we say—blacks, whites, and Spanish. But when we go to school, we had to correct that.

There was this one lady came there. She told me how to start writing again. She'd say, "Write down what you can and what you know." I liked the way she helped me on things. She also taught me how to do plants—apple trees. I got a plant that big, and then it died. She said, "Write down on paper why it died." I passed it in, and she gave me a hundred. I felt good 'cause I'd see what's happening, and I'd just write it down. But she left the program. I stopped writing again.

I wondered why I stopped. Now I realize why. I guess it's the way someone's looking at it. Analyzed it. [In third grade] I like[d] to write and I see what I wrote 'cause nobody's gonna grade it. I['d] just write and write, but I don't know I'm wrong so I write. And I try to write about dogs in the city, how they are mean. [But] when I got to that school, things that I did I know are wrong. So I just sorta stopped. Why should I write when everything's always wrong?

After two and a half years I came north [to where my mom had moved] on the train, and I went to junior high up here. I loved it. But I hated [the resource room]. It made me feel dumb. I didn't understand the classes and had to go in for extra help. Mr.

Kendrick taught me a lot, how to express words like: "I woke up this morning. I watched the sun rise while I lied in the bed. And I got up, touched the cold floor, and I walked on the cold floor and opened the curtain, look out of the curtain, see a glare of light coming from the sun, hitting the ice, glaring up at my face. And I could feel the warmth from the glass, from the sun hitting the ice and the glass." And like, he taught me that. It was fun, but I want to forget what my grade was. I had to write journals every day. My journals were really short. I didn't write very well.

I learned fragments in ninth grade — fragments. You put them together. I always put past tense into present tense. I still do that. It just comes to me as I'm writing to put it into the present tense. My writing was always a mess. I can't even read my own writing. I would write something down fast like, "My name is Carlos." I'd forget the "is." I hate to read my own writing, [but] I got used to it now. There's a lot of writing at high school. I had to do a lot of writing for every course. My writing got better. And I know more, and I know I write longer, instead of short. And it takes me forever to put my thoughts down on a piece of paper; I gotta do a five-page paper and get it long enough. So I have to proofread it and see what's wrong with it and all that. I look over the essay, make my sentence clear, make it sensible, and make it clearly 'cause it doesn't look right.

I have to have tutors in school 'cause I can't get the work done by myself, 'cause I don't know how to put it into words. Some words I don't know what it means. Mary Sue, [my tutor], helped me on another paper. That's when I get a lotta corrections. I got a B+ on it. She tells me how to make it clearly and neat. In this film class I looked at a movie, so I know what to say. It's memory. I know examples from the movie. I never read. The reading, it's terrible. I never even read the [assignment] papers and things. I mean I don't like to read. I think about it before I write — what I'm going to say, how I'm going to start it. I get all the examples and then write it. I read it silently. I make sure it's right. I read it slowly and make sure I understand it. I go over it to see if I left any words out, and make capitalizations. To me I don't know what sounds right.

It's hard for my mom, 'cause she has eleven kids. I don't tell any of my friends that I'm poor, but I think my friends know. I can't get in so much trouble [now] 'cause my mom's going through so much. My mother never helped [in school work]. My mom doesn't know how to do it. I would take home books, and I never do it 'cause of what's going on in the house. I try to do my writing but I can't. I don't have a table in my room. When I write in the kitchen, my brothers and sisters and then my mom comes in the kitchen and cook and I have to leave. And so much noise, and the cat gets on the table. "Get off cat; get away from my writing." And then the T.V. comes on, and then my mom is cooking. But if I try to write, I smell the food, and I go taste it. I go back to my table, and I have grease all over my hands and get a messy paper. And the telephone rings. I don't write at home.

Mary Sue, my tutor, is helping me. At Mary Sue's I sit at a small table in the kitchen. I write my term paper. I have books over here, paper here, extra, and the book I'm working with. When I write sometimes I forget the radio's on. When my favorite music comes on, I hear that. I stop and start singing with the music. There's something there that keeps me company. After I finish singing, I go, "Oh no! I got to go back to writing."

In writing you have to do a lot of thinking. It hurts my head. I don't know what to say. I worry about when it's due, about how long is it gonna take, and how long they want it. I look over the questions again and again and again until I get the idea what they want. And I worry what's the paper gonna look like, am I gonna typewrite it or not? If I type it, it's too short. I worry how neat it's gonna be. Is the sentence right? My tense is right? Did I use the right word, I mean, past tense all the time? I always forget that.

In school I am dumb. Not to adults, but with students I am. When I talk to people, I have to use examples to make them understand me. And it takes a long time. I can't write nothing right. I get mad 'cause I don't believe how dumb I am. The ideas are not dumb; it's my writing. I cannot put it into words. And knowing what to write. I read the directions over and over and over. And sometimes I don't read them — just ask friends. When I was a kid, I was dumb, too dumb. And I still am because I'm way behind. Because I was supposed to be a senior this year, and I should have been higher, on my level, 'cause I'm in a lotta basic classes. I hate being in basic level. But I am gonna have to do it. They [tried to] put me in ESL again, and I didn't want to be in ESL 'cause I know I was way above that. I know I got the capability to learn, nothing is helping to bring it out. And I notice that — that my family's always in basic and low; I don't know why. My uncle wants me to graduate. I would be the first one in my family to graduate.

I never wrote that much until this year. I'm in Upward Bound. It started last summer, that's why I have a tutor. I know that I'm getting smarter. But not in the speed I wanted to. And I wonder, how the people look at me. Why am I going to graduate? And when I don't know so much. I wish that I went back, to be born again, to do better. I want to dance on stage, act, help people. And the other thing is making people happy! Makes me feel better. Especially in the English office. Everybody smiles when I come in. I want to go to acting school. Somebody told me Yale is excellent. After I'm successful, I'll help my mom. Plus I listen to my horoscope. It says, "You have to push to where you want to be and think that you can do it."

Carlos's View of Himself as a Writer

As I worked with students who had been placed in classes at the lower end of the tracking system, I began to see that most of them secretly believed their problem with writing was a problem with their intellect. This was one of the things that Carlos taught me. As our work unfolded I realized that his view of himself as a student and a writer profoundly affected his work. After his second year of first grade, he had begun to feel good about himself in school. "I like to write and see what I write 'cause nobody's gonna grade it," he said, describing his second- and third-grade experience. Miss Hirsch was, perhaps, the reason he trusted teachers more than the other basic writers. But when Carlos was in what he called "training school," he lost his positive perception of himself as a student and writer. "When I got to [that] school, things that I did I know are wrong. . . . Why should I write when everything's always wrong?" He found a logical way to keep himself from the feelings that writing engendered; except for a brief respite during his work with the apple-plant teacher, he resisted writing. And while he avoided writing, students in other elementary schools were becoming fluent in putting their ideas into writing.

After he moved north to a junior high school, Carlos had a few teachers who gave him the opportunity to write and others who kept him focused on exercises and word-level correctness. Carlos attended a high school where the faculty was sensitive to the difficulties of students whose first language was not standard English. Nevertheless, he had a wound that was not easily healed. Although he was frequently reassured by his teachers, Carlos went back and forth about how he felt about himself. His nagging feelings of inadequacy, his "hidden injuries of class" (Sennet and Cobb, 1973) surfaced on every possible occasion. While observing Carlos in his film class (his first class that wasn't designated as basic), I began to understand how painfully sensitive he was to peer opinion. "I knew as soon as I see the assignments paper coming that I wouldn't understand," he told me one day after class. "But I'm embarrassed to ask questions in front of the class, but I could ask Mr. Marsh. And the boy next to me was in basic, too, so he wouldn't think I'm stupid. But I could only ask the advanced girl spelling, 'cause I hear advanced kids asking spelling." Carlos's self-consciousness limited his access to useful help from peers. His perseverance was a tribute to his teachers' approach; by caring, they provided the impetus he needed to keep writing.

Unlike many basic writers Carlos was in the process of accruing self-regard from his Upward Bound tutor, Mary Sue, from his drama coach, Mr. O'Neill, and from other teachers and friends. When he and his ideas were taken seriously, he felt better about himself as a human being, and a writer, and he found reason to try.

Carlos and his low-prestige, dialect-speaking peers spent their early years learning that they were not good students. Much of this chapter will focus on how to help them to separate the real reasons for their difficulties in school from their misassumptions about their abilities — misassumptions based on the negative response they have received to their work along the way. As Carlos began to feel better about his abilities, his willingness to work increased. He was lucky to have teachers who trusted in his ability to improve.

Fluency Problems and Overload

Carlos's story tells poignantly of his struggle with writing, but only when I observed him composing aloud and writing in the classroom did I fully understand the agony of the battle he was waging. He sat at his desk with books and papers spread on the desk's surface and on his lap. While he was intimidated by books, he trusted their ideas more than he trusted his own. He groaned and swore under his breath, and in moments of greater frustration, pounded his forehead with his palm, as if to force the clogged words and ideas onto the page. When Carlos had to concentrate on too many aspects of writing at once, he couldn't do it. He wasn't automatic enough at the simplest aspects of writing to be able to get his thoughts into words easily. If he tried to concentrate on the more complex aspects of his assignments, he hit a sort of overload. Hayes and Flower, (1984, p. 124) term it "cognitive overload," but the overload was not entirely cognitive. The frustration that accompanied the overload was a further emotional burden, and it prolonged his struggle with the process.

When Carlos said aloud what he was thinking while he was writing, the cause of his overload and subsequent frustration was evident. He said things in standard English and then wrote them in his dialect, and he wrote things in standard English that he had rehearsed in dialect. He spelled the same words correctly and incorrectly in the same sentence. He often practiced a sentence before actually writing it but then was interrupted by one of his many concerns and forgot the meaning he was trying to make. He made mistakes when he reread the text to "get back on track," and these mistakes were cause for further confusion in his process. This made for a stop-and-go process that was further interrupted by worries about content, length, deadline, neatness, tense, and word choice.

Most of Carlos's worries promoted a consciousness that should have improved his written expression. But when the worries ganged up on him, he had little room in his conscious attention for the actual writing. Though his process was like that of a third-grader dealing with spelling, capitalization, and paragraphing, he was trying to accomplish eleventh-grade writing. And indeed there were signs of the eleventh-grade writer in his process that were not common to the other basic students I studied.

Teachers were pushing Carlos along in his academic career and had urged him into an untracked class called "Film." In the planning he did for a research paper on Bette Davis, he showed skill and creativity in organization, but he was unable to implement them in his writing. "I want to go back and tell about her movies and the roles she's played," he said before putting pen to page, "and then gradually go back to how she started . . . the way she learned." But when he began to write, he struggled with syntax, spelling, and synthesis of material from several books, and he couldn't carry out his plan. He pounded his head with his fist, said, "Oh, damn. . . . Oh well," and changed to a chronological presentation of her life. He couldn't cope with a nonchronological format when there was so much else to concentrate on. In this and in three other observed instances, Carlos began with rather sophisticated writing plans, but in reaching a state of overload, he reverted to the chronological organization that was more automatic for him. The groans, sighs, and forehead-drumming were outward symptoms of his inner struggle with writing.

Carlos needed time with pen and paper to work beyond the word-by-word struggle. He needed to write daily and to limit what he must attend to while he did this writing. Mary Sue, his tutor, was learning that students do better when they can divide the writing process. She began to encourage Carlos to use his strong oral skills to generate ideas as she took notes. She asked him to freewrite, to list, to cluster, and finally to reap the best from these ideas and to incorporate them into a plan. Then she directed him to write the draft without worrying about spelling or dictate a draft to a tape recorder and then transcribe it. Only as a last step did she help him to "correct" his draft. Nevertheless, time was running out for Carlos. Mary Sue was only a temporary assistant to him, and if he is on his own again with writing before he becomes fluent, the frustration of writing and its accompanying self-deprecation may end his endeavor. Problems with language as well as with overload and self-confidence complicate his writing process.

Language

I found a rich mélange of students in the "basic" or "remedial" or "vocational" classes. They included black, Hispanic, immigrants, and working-class white students with one thing in common: none spoke standard English. In nine schools — urban, suburban, and rural — the story was the same, and although I know that tracking is a complex social phenomenon (Apple, 1982; Connell et al., 1982; Rist, 1970), it seemed to me that "ability" tracking was based in a profound way on language.

Carlos said: "My English is terrible. . . . My English crashes into Spanish. . . . I don't feel like I'm Spanish; I don't feel like anything. I just feel . . . like a plant." And in Carlos's composing-aloud sessions, it became clear that his English had crashed into his Spanish, a sort of syntactic derailment. He often used English words with Spanish syntax; he followed the wrong rules or rules that were incomplete. Subject/verb agreement and formation of plurals were constant problems for him, and yet his·errors had a Spanish logic. In an essay on the film version of *The Grapes of Wrath*, Carlos wrote, "The Joad were able to sell some of their furnitures." His mistake, "The Joad," is understandable because the Spanish equivalent, *Los Joad* is plural but has no plural marker on the noun. Carlos should have used *furniture* as a collective noun, yet he used *furnitures* in accord with the plurality accorded to *los muebles*. In his sentence, "There were enough job," he confused *job* and *work*, which use the same word in Spanish (*trabajo/work*; *trabajos/jobs*).

The interaction of black English, Spanish, and working-class English that Carlos learned in the streets may explain the verb tenses that he identified as present tense: reduction of consonant clusters in black English leads to omission of past-tense markers (passed = pass; laughed = laugh). Carlos said, "To me I understand what I'm saying." (More Spanish syntax, but the meaning is clear.) He can't write acceptably without assistance, and his tutor has to help him "make it clearly." (The Spanish verb "*hacer*," to do or to make, takes an adverb; whereas the English verb, to make, requires an adjective.)

Though Carlos had spent hours of classroom time doing exercises, he didn't apply those exercises when he wrote. The exercises, in fact, kept him from getting down to writing. Ironically his strategy in editing was to make corrections on the basis of whether it sounded right to his confused ear.

It's tempting to say that because of Carlos's Spanish background, language is a bigger problem for him than for most basic writers, but in my investigations, that wasn't the case. Working-class English and black English posed as much difficulty for the other basic students as Carlos's complex dialect caused for him.

Each basic writer in my study suffered from the subtlety of dialect difference. Many of their teachers interpreted their problems as poor grammar and ignorance rather than use of different dialects. Smitherman reports, "Research on language attitudes consistently indicates that teachers believe black English-speaking youngsters are non-verbal and possess limited vocabulary. They are slow learners or ineducable. Their language is unsystematic and needs constant corrections and improvement" (Smitherman, 1985, p. 50). There is inequity in America's school system that values only one subculture's language and doesn't provide adequate help to those who have to learn it. Disparity between a student's home language and standard English created a gulf into which the basic writers fell. In this gulf they felt ashamed and stupid; they blamed themselves instead of differences in dialects; and they rarely received the individualized instruction they needed to bridge the gap, to get out of the pit of self-contempt. If we choose one dialect of English to call standard and reward those who master it with status and economic privilege, then we owe it to students who don't speak that standard dialect to help them master it, no matter what the cost. By the time bilingual/bidialectal students graduate from high school, they should be conversant in both dialects and able to write effectively in the standard one.

Paulo Freire urges that teachers of poor children be trained to see that all children speak beautifully, to respect them in the way that they speak and think, but then to teach them what he calls the "cultivated pattern of language" so that they have a better chance in the world (Freire, 1990). Carlos's ESL teacher did this for Carlos in his second year of first grade, but after that one year, the school absolved its responsibility for his language difference until he became involved in the Upward Bound program. Then Mary Sue became an adjunct to Carlos's endeavors.

Mary Sue was training Carlos to be self-sufficient in the first two stages of his writing, but she would be long needed in the essential last stages, for it is in revision and editing that serious attention to language can best take place. She began to help Carlos see the specific differences between his oral language and standard English. Carlos had been thinking in terms of right and wrong rather than in terms of different dialects for different purposes or situations. Some teachers have students keep logs of these dialect differences. Figures 2–1 and 2–2 show how Carlos might have logged some of his differences. After each draft Carlos and Mary Sue looked for the nonstandard constructions together. They started by logging the most frequent mistakes and then went on from there, "one problem at a time" (Collins, 1979). This process helps students to take ownership of errors and to make sense of teacher feedback. Conscious understanding of how personal language is different from formal written language enables nonstandard dialect students to become conscious that their problem is one of language and not of intellect.

Reading Problems

In Carlos we can begin to see the complexity of the problems of the basic writer. His difficulties with the way he views himself as a writer, his overburdened process, his difficulties with language, and our next subject, his carefully hidden difficulty with reading, all work together to make writing a struggle.

At first, Carlos had difficulty talking to me about his problems

Figure 2–1
Usage, Grammar, and Punctuation Log

Personal Grammar	Written Grammar	Reasons for Differences
my brothers house	my brother's house	I need to put in an apostrophe to show ownership.
We took the following items, a camera, a backpack, and a canteen.	We took the following items: a camera, a backpack, and a canteen.	I should use a colon (:) when I introduce a series.
people were throw out of the house	people were thrown out	irregular for the past part. — like shown or grown

Derived from Van de Weghe (1983).

Figure 2–2
Spelling Log

Correct Spelling	My Misspelling	Why the Word Confused Me	Helps for Remembering
The Joads	The Joad	because I use the Spanish plural form of names	Add an "s" to last names to make plural
California	Californio	probably Spanish	Ends in "ia" like Lithuania
furniture	furnitures	because it's one of those collective nouns	Collective nouns like children don't need the "s"
whole	hole	because they sound the same	The hole I want to climb in doesn't have "w"
kept	kepted	the past tense "ed" rule, but this one's irregular	Like other "eep" verbs — weep/wept, sweep/swept

Derived from Van de Weghe (1983).

with reading. Though teachers had let him know that he was not "dumb," but just "behind," he said to me in the final interview: "Teachers say I'm not dumb because I know how to read. So does everybody else. Well, some people in the streets don't know how to read. But I think I am dumb in the school, I mean with the students, not to adults." Perhaps he and other basic students go to great lengths to hide their difficulties with reading because reading problems are so linked in their minds with "stupidity." Toward the end of my time with Carlos, Mary Sue said to me, "I think Carlos may have some trouble with reading." He had shielded the truth so cleverly that it took Mary Sue nearly eight months of tutoring him in writing to realize it.

At first Carlos's stance with his tutor frustrated her. He made what seemed to be only half-hearted attempts to read the complex assignment sheets and handouts on film criticism and then simply refused. It was better to appear lazy or obstinate rather than illiterate. His subterfuge protected him, but again there was a toll. If he and other basic writers avoid evaluation and help in reading, they'll get none.

Carlos's difficulty with reading made getting material together for a paper difficult at best. It also meant he had less experience with the written code he was trying to emulate. Carlos couldn't remember reading a complete book on his own. By avoiding reading, he had missed exposure to standard language and conventions of written code. To some extent, ability to use written code, ability to use standard constructions and to gain sentence sense, paragraph sense, story sense, and correct spelling comes through reading by a sort of osmosis (Clay, 1972; Heath, 1983; Pearson and Johnson, 1978; Wells, 1986).

Finally, inept reading interfered in his writing process. His difficulty with reading further interrupted his already stop-and-go writing process. In his *Grapes of Wrath* composing-aloud session, he read *said* instead of *sold* as he reread his text. This mistake in rereading caused him to lose his train of thought, caused yet another interruption in his crowded process. Carlos said to me, "Sometimes I can't read my own writing. I leave out words. I have to read it over and over again." Struggling with reading during the actual composing process was a common occurrence for him.

Carlos needed to begin to read at a level he could understand and about subjects that interested him. He had neither the prior knowledge nor the reading skills to read academic articles about film criticism. But his interest in his heritage, jazz dance, theater, and psychology was a strength that he might have brought to reading.

Carlos and Consciousness

Though Carlos was caught somewhere between feeling good about himself and bad about himself as a student and a writer, in his eleventh-grade year he was becoming more conscious of his real problems in writing. His new ability to see himself as "behind" instead of "dumb" decreased both the defenses he used and the inadequacy he felt in writing and in other learning. With most of the basic students, defenses remained as barriers to the consciousness of what their real problems were and of the effects of those problems. Because Carlos had support and advocacy from his teachers through the years, the defensive barrier that he had set up for himself was thinner. And as he identified the reasons he had difficulty in school, he began to blame his problems less on his intellect and more on his circumstances. The oft-repeated "Now I realize why" was one such indication that this had happened. When I asked him whether he received help on his work from home, he realized for the first time that most students had received help from their parents or older siblings. Suddenly he felt less reprehensible because he had to have a tutor. Before he said, "I have to have tutors in school, 'cause I can't do the work." Now he said, "I didn't know other kids got help."

Other statements that Carlos made indicated a growing consciousness of factors that influenced his writing. "My ideas are not dumb. It's my writing; I cannot put it into words." When I showed him how Spanish syntax interacted with his writing, he said, "I didn't know I had a Spanish grammar" and more worries about his intellect slipped away. For most basic writers, defenses blunt the sting of "that buried sense of inadequacy that one resents oneself for feeling" (Sennet and Cobb, 1973, p. 58). Carlos's emerging consciousness of the reasons for his problems became a strength that he brought to his work. While Carlos's struggle paralleled that of most of the thirteen basic writers I interviewed, it was different in some respects. Due to the good work and advocacy of some teachers, he had not given up the fight when I met him. He was still trying.

Additional Bars to the Unsuccessful Writer's Invisible Cage

Basic writers confront a complex construct of problems. So far we have considered several of Carlos's concrete problems with overload, language, and reading and have referred to social problems of confidence, of teacher's attitudes and expectations, of the family's ability to help, and of the pedagogical problems that the well-entrenched, exercise-based, remedial writing programs pose. There are additional problems, however, that are more subtle. They are harder to detect and hence more debilitating. To adapt a metaphor used by Marilyn Frye to describe women's circumstances, these young developing writers found themselves in an invisible cage.

> Cages. Consider a bird cage. If you look very closely at just one wire in the cage, you cannot see the other wires. If your conception of what is before you is determined by this myopic focus, you could look at that one wire, up and down the length of it, and be unable to see why a bird would not just fly around the wire any time it wanted to go somewhere. ... It is only when you step back, stop looking at the wires one by one, microscopically, and take a macroscopic view of the whole cage, that you can see why the bird does not go anywhere; then you will see it in a moment. It will require no great subtlety of mental powers. It is perfectly obvious that the bird is surrounded by a network of systematically related barriers, no one of which would be the least hindrance to its flight, but which, by their relations to each other, are confining as the solid walls of a dungeon. (Frye, 1983, pp. 4–5)

Occasionally I ran into some things that the eleventh-graders in my study said and did that didn't make sense. It would have been simple to ignore what didn't make sense, but I have found that it is often the discrepant data that hide the gold mine, the new understandings. Some things that didn't originally make sense had to do with the invisible cage.

Defenses

The first discrepancy was one that I had been working to understand since my first days of teaching. It had not taken me long as a teacher to realize that though basic students had not performed well in the eyes of their schools, they were not lacking in intelligence. These students recounted their past experiences in vivid detail, yet their memory of writing was very different from that of the more successful students. Basic writer Orion recalled only glimpses of his writing experience, but he remembered other parts of his school years down to the locker number. Zac couldn't remember any writing in seventh or eighth grade, but he could recite the name of every boy that was in his seventh- and eighth-grade English class. Wasn't writing assigned to Zac and Orion, or did they just forget it?

The modes of writing reported by these students were grammar and usage exercises, answering textbook questions, short-answer tests, and vocabulary and spelling sentences (not so different from

what Britton [1975] discovered). The students from one inner-city
school remembered years in which copying from the blackboard
was the only writing they did; this was different from the extended
writing assignments that their counterparts in the same city's college
preparatory high school were doing. Carlos, Sonia, and George
remembered writing "little" stories. George "hated" them because
he would have to read them in front of the class, and Carlos had
been told that they were "wrong" because they were too short.
Though they remembered doing little writing in comparison to
what successful students remembered, I could not interpret their
lack of recall as lack of mental acuity. They engaged my intellect.
Each seemed to have what it should take to succeed in school. I can
suspect only three things: (1) that they remembered little because
they wrote infrequently and irregularly, (2) that they remembered
little because what they did lacked meaning for them, and/or (3)
that they remembered little because they would rather not remember
their lack of success. Forgetting might have been a form of defense
for them. Carlos had begun in the interviews to make sense of
whether he was "dumb" or just "behind," but the others were
defensive when I began to ask them, "Why do you have difficulty
with school when I can see how bright you are?" Sonia responded,
"Isn't nobody gonna tell you they dumb, but I'm lazy. I probably
have some disease or something makes me lazy." But Sonia recounted
a social schedule that seemed exhausting to me; school work took
low priority in her life. Zac played basketball and worked a factory
job twenty hours a week. Orion worked at a restaurant, farmed, and
spent hours roaming in the woods. Etcetera. The basic students
were no different from others in the busy tenor of their lives.
Laziness didn't explain their lack of success.

   Orion and George said they didn't care about writing ("It's
boring"), but they had cared very much in their earlier years. Zac
had cared a lot when his teacher made him sit under her desk
because he couldn't form the C in his name correctly. George had
cared when students laughed at him as he read the monster story
he had written. "I just kept stalling, and lagging, and stuttering, and
mispronouncing words." Thereafter, he found ways to get laughs at
the expense of the teacher instead of himself. It was clear that by
eleventh grade all but a few of the basic writers had stopped caring
about writing. Writing received low priority in their lives. George
"conned" his mother into doing it for him, and then he copied it
over. Orion said: "I go outside and run around with the goats, or
out in the woods running around. . . . I'm out there, and I should be
in there doing that. I don't put it off; I forget about it."

   "I'm shy," said Zac as he explained why success came hard,

and indeed shyness in front of peers had kept Zac and Carlos from getting the help they needed, but Zac was not shy with his team members on the basketball court. Sherry too reported a sort of shyness: "I had a lot of hard time reading and writing. It's like you need help, and the kids are teasing you. I'd sit there, and I wouldn't ask for help because I felt so stupid." Was this shyness constructed so that their peers would not find out how poorly they were doing in school? Zac was shy; therefore, he said that until recently he hadn't wanted to do particularly well in school, "just passing." But when we knew each better, he dropped his shy defense and with some shame and a bit of anger told me what he thought was the real source of his lack of success—back to laziness. "Lazy . . . I coulda done it if I really wanted to, but I ain't going to do it, like that."

Perhaps the simplest defense that Carlos and almost fifty percent of the others had used to keep from feeling bad about writing was to refuse to do it for periods of time. Carlos saw the reason for his refusal more clearly than others: "Why should I write when it's always wrong?" In *Lives on the Boundary* (1989), Mike Rose puts the defensive stance of the unsuccessful student into words and also describes the price it exacts:

> Fuck this bullshit. Bull shit, of course, is everything you—and the others—fear is beyond you: books, essays, tests, academic scrambling, complexity, scientific reasoning, philosophical inquiry.

> The tragedy is that you have to twist the knife in your own gray matter to make this defense work. You'll have to shut down, have to reject intellectual stimuli or diffuse them with sarcasm, have to cultivate stupidity, have to convert boredom from a malady into a way of confronting the world. Keep your vocabulary simple, act stoned when you're not or act more stoned than you are, flaunt ignorance, materialize your dreams. It is a powerful and effective defense—it neutralizes the insult and the frustration of being a vocational kid and, when perfected, it drives teachers up the wall, a delightful secondary effect. But like all strong magic, it exacts a price. (Rose, 1989, 29)

Even the defensiveness that Rose describes doesn't keep students in school. A large number of Zac's friends and most of Carlos's siblings had dropped out of the school, avoiding daily reminders of their inadequacy. Leaving a school where they felt continual humiliation and lack of control was the basic students' final refusal and final defense.

Thus, the defenses that basic students built to protect themselves from their own feelings of inadequacy became the strongest bar to their success. It was better to misattribute that lack of success to laziness, shyness, apathy, or even recalcitrance than to feel the shame connected with appearing "dumb," the only other explanation they saw as possible.

Lack of Fluency

The second source of discrepant data that I came upon was the outcome of the composing-aloud exercises. I had expected all the basic writers to struggle with multiple concerns while writing as Carlos did (see Figure 1–3). Carlos, Zac, and the community college "basic writers" that Perl studied (1979) were more fluent than the other basic eleventh-grade writers in this study. The others seemed to have to concentrate so hard on spelling out thoughts that this process was all-engrossing. Whereas Carlos and Zac used recursion (the act of backtracking and rereading that which is already written) and in-process editing, the others could do little more than reiterate the words they were putting on the page. They seemed to have to keep it simple or it was overwhelming. Furthermore, the others seemed to care so little about writing that dealing with the overwhelming was not worth it. George, the sit-down comic of this study, said:

> If you're on a roll, all sudden you get to a word that you don't know, you gonna sit there and think, try to sound it out. You gotta wait a couple a seconds and try and write it. You just sit there; you're writing, and then you like mess. You make a mistake, and you gotta erase it. And you write, and then you erase it, and then you just get so frustrated that you want to rip your paper up, and say you quit. At home I get my mother to do it. In school you get in trouble; that's how I always feel. . . . Yah, it's too quiet. I guess I can't handle that or something. That's the perfect time in the classroom when they're all doing their work. So you go, "Hey!" . . . crack your joke, the whole room will laugh.

In the composing-aloud exercises, students like George attended to spelling, to ideas, to punctuation, and to syntax. They developed a useful tunnel vision that permitted them to get words on the page, and it is likely that until they become automatic at getting their thoughts into written words, more sophisticated concerns will have to take a back seat. Yet Mr. Fog (Zac's, Sonia's, and Iris's teacher) told me, "They are moving on to paragraph writing for the first time; I couldn't let them write paragraphs before they could write a grammatical sentence." All of these students had been "remediated" for their bad "grammar," and that very remediation had kept them from getting practice. George described his eleventh-grade English curriculum:

> In English class mostly all they taught in there was vocabulary, spelling, exercises, and every once in a while they'd put in

punctuation, something like that ... till the competency test. A week before they'd start essays. Supposedly they think you know it, that you learned it in middle school. This year I hope I passed it. I better. My mother wrote it on a card for me to take in secret, but she did that last year too, and I failed. You got to pass to graduate.

The writing that most of these students were doing kept them from the more abstract thought involved in reading and writing. To establish fluency they need to write for interested teachers who delay word- and sentence-level correction until the last draft (see Collins, 1979).

Parental Expectations and Role Models

The basic writers had little sense of how skill in writing is inextricably linked to status and financial gain in the workplace. Their parents had not had the advantages that would permit them to model that information. In the last interview, I asked Sonia what was important to her in her life. She told me that she wanted a high-paying job as a "business lady, with my own car, and a job which travel to other countries." Then I asked her how writing might help her get what was important to her. "You asking what was the most important thing in your life to me," said Sonia, "and I told you. Now how would writing get in with what's important?" Most of these students had yearnings for status and earning power that were connected with jobs that demanded academic credentials beyond a high school diploma and which were predicated on the ability to write effectively. Sonia wasn't alone in her unrealistic expectations of a high school diploma. Carlos wanted to go to acting school at Yale. George, standing at 5'3" and enrolled in basic classes, wanted to go to the University of Pennsylvania on a football scholarship.

There were no basic students in this study whose parents had graduated from college, and many would be the first in their extended family to graduate from high school. For most, the biggest goal was to pass and hence to graduate. "If it's passing, it's okay," said Orion. "My father doesn't want me to drop out of school. I would be the first to finish." Students were anxious to do well enough to meet their family's graduation expectations, but they didn't value writing as important to their career goals.

I asked these students what kind of writing they saw their parents doing. Iris said:

The only thing my mother can do is make an X. It don't only happen to her. Other people be making X's also. My mother could write her name, but it would be all sloppy. She got no further than third grade. My father went till sixth grade; he write to his mother, or like if he goes to the unemployment office, he has to like write his names, information of where he worked before.

Iris viewed writing as necessary for conducting family business, communicating with the family in Puerto Rico, and taking care of financial matters. Iris's mother, though capable of signing her name, didn't want to because it was "sloppy." When these students talked of their parents' writing and of writing in general, they were often referring to handwriting. Orion mentioned that his mother wrote well. I asked him how he knew; Orion replied, "'Cause I see it. She writes letters in cursive all the time. My father can't even read his own writing. He writes invoices though." Their parents' needs for writing were fairly simple. The accord given to neatness by the parent seemed to affect the attention given to it by the children, and many of them based their success in writing on the basis of neatness. Pride in well-formed letters was more apparent than pride in making their meaning known.

The parents of the unsuccessful students didn't always know how to work for their children's success, yet parental care and concern for that success in school work and life were evident in the stories of these students. Orion's parents took over some of his farm chores as graduation seemed possible and as passing became increasingly important. Zac's mother told the principal that she would beat up Zac's third-grade teacher if she continued to put Zac under her desk. Sonia's mother monitored her homework time. Sherry's mother bought her a typewriter even though money was tight. All cared, but that care wasn't always evident to teachers who missed them at school functions. All cared, but they could not give the daily help that was important to success in school. George had his mother prewrite his competency test, and he still failed. Mona said, "They try, but they're not that good because they got their education in Sicily." On the other hand, most students with college-educated parents told me that their parents helped them with homework (proofing papers, answering the request of "Quiz me on this, Mom," talking over writing ideas at the dinner table).

Basic writing students have less chance to get what they say they want in life because of: (1) the limited models their parents are able to set for them exemplifying the purposes for writing and the priority it needs, (2) the expectations that their parents have for them to get passing grades, and (3) the lack of skills their parents have for helping them. How ironic it is that these students' own families, families who sincerely care and want to help, can't provide an opening in their invisible cage.

Peer Pressure

I asked Zac if peer pressure made him work less:

> It's both ways. Sometimes I be shy to keep from asking a stupid question, but like I got an 80 on this test. Mr. A., he say: "Zac got an 80 on his test." He keep talking 'bout me front of the whole class. "Zac, tell everybody how you studied. Tell everybody how you read the book." I say, "I don't do it really." I in trouble. No good to let kids know you do the homework. You hear it later. . . . But there's Victor. He a senior on the team. He going to college. He tell me to [go to college]. I say, "What they say if they saw the ten "E's" on my report card in tenth grade?" He say, "Well, they see that in tenth grade you was messing up, but they say if you keep it going in eleventh grade and twelfth, you keep improving, like that, you be okay." So I decide I got to do it.

Zac dealt with two forms of peer influence. There was strong peer pressure for Zac not to excel in his basic class. In a way his upward mobility was jeopardized by peer pressure. He and Sonia talked about treading a narrow line: to do well enough not to appear stupid but not so well as to be accused of "cuddling up to the teacher." Basic-class peer solidarity, a buck-the-teacher attitude, does not serve Zac and Sonia in meeting their goals. Zac said, "My mother want me to work behind a desk." Zac may get peer pressure to just get by, but senior basketball player Victor gives him peer support to work toward college. After talking to Victor, Zac went to his counselor to get into a standard class. "I was talking to my counselor, and I told him I wanted to be in the regular group class. He say Mr. Fog got to recommend me, so I asked Mr. Fog about that because he said you have to be on some list. Mr. Fog said if my name is on the list, he will recommend me. I got to get on the list." Zac may have bucked the peer pressure not to succeed, but in looking for a way to break out of his cage, he encountered another bar—the tracking system, the list.

The Tracking System and Consciousness

Successful students were conscious of the social stigma connected to tracking and were conscious of its potential, should they be moved down, to limit their lives. Advanced student Elana said, "If I got put in a standard class, I'd be humiliated. I'd be worried about what would happen to me." Standard student Lisa said, "I guess I felt really bad because, when you're in a lower group than other people, I guess you naturally feel stupid." Most basic writers, however, were less conscious of the stigma. They were either oblivious to the difference tracking might make to future possibilities, or they had blocked out the thought because thinking about it would aggravate a well-hidden view of themselves as inadequate. Connell said, "The streaming and selective structure of school convinces lots of these kids, just as schooling convinced their parents, that they are dumb" (Connell et al., 1982, p. 167), but it is not that simple. Iris seemed more oblivious to tracking than aware of its potential to brand her as stupid, and her caring mother had neither the savvy nor the command of English by which to intercede for her. Iris said:

> I guess I'm one of the average, but I was chosen as secretary of the junior high. Whatever class you had you would try to get out for the meetings. I went another level down. I wasn't picking the easy classes; I was picking the teachers who would let you out [for the meetings]. This year my teacher put me down lower. I was the only Spanish girl up there, but I just figured was they changed me because it was overcrowded with people.

Iris did not recognize the long-term consequences of her choices. With the exception of Carlos and Zac, these students did not understand how low placement in school could affect their future.

As teachers of these students, there are things that we can do. Students in the lowest track need some help in matching their career aspirations to the preparation that is needed for them. They need a realistic view of what they need to do, the belief that effort will pay off, and encouragement along the way. Students might well interview people in the community who have jobs that interest them. In their reports they could relate what academic skills the jobs demanded, including reading and writing, and what kind of education the student would need in high school and beyond to be hired. This might give students information that their parents couldn't always give; they could begin to make more realistic decisions. When students felt humiliation in being in the lower track, at least that made for a visible bar. For Iris, the lack of awareness of the long-term implications of tracking was an invisible bar, and it was in her lack of consciousness that we see the encircling of the bars and the imminent closing of the cage.

Abstraction and Consciousness: Closing and Opening the Cage

Though the basic writers I met would be considered literate by many standards, they were not schooled in a way that promoted the ability to think abstractly—an ability that is, however, valued by their schools and by the middle-class society that offers (albeit controls) financial rewards and status. Abstraction is a connection among multiple concrete experiences. It allows people to make sense of the world around them. In interviews it was clear that these students did think deeply about questions they had in their out-of-school lives. Their logic in dealing with what was removed from the academic was laudable and resembled that which Labov (1972) described in his study of nonstandard dialect speakers.

Yet as eloquent, useful, and logical as their oral language was, it was not that which was valued by most of their teachers. Furthermore, in making decisions about their schooling, they were handicapped. Spunky and bright Sonia wanted to be a "business lady" who traveled abroad for a big corporation, yet she decided to stay in a basic class because there was less homework. Further, due to hours of watered-down, segmented content, Sonia and her peers were not challenged to use abstraction. Except in Mr. O'Neill's conferences with Orion, I rarely observed dialogue between teacher and student or among students about ideas connected with their reading or their writing. A writing curriculum of exercises limits practice in abstract thought and oppresses those it should serve. It keeps them in a reactive and defensive stance in the academic world.

Conversely, making connections among the concrete experiences of one's life leads to consciousness of one's world. Zac and Carlos were verging on awareness. They were beginning to glimpse groups of bars in their cages where before they could see only one bar at a time. Carlos had taken some initiative in arranging to return to the Upward Bound Program for the summer. Yet he was still naive. Yale seemed possible. Nevertheless, some of his dreams were realizable; he saw them as such and pursued them.

Zac, too, was taking steps to act for his future benefit; he saw a route and looked for a path to the next track up. "Well, I'm looking to college now, so I figure to myself they might give me a paper [to write] if I go. You got to do it, and I can't sit there and say, 'I'm not going to do it,' 'cause it's a waste of money, so I do it, like that." Zac saw some of the realities of his world. He knew that "I don't care" or "I'm lazy" couldn't work. But even when Zac showed signs of reflection and direction based on that reflection, he needed an advocate to get his name on the list and one-on-one help to standardize his English. He needed a Mr. O'Neill and a Mary Sue.

Teacher Advocacy and Response

After thirteen years of teaching and several of research, I began to see the cage and the importance of teacher advocacy. I was only supposed to listen to these students and observe them, but there were a few times when I felt compelled to slip out of my researcher role. Mr. Fog wasn't going to actively seek a way to get Zac's name on *the* list, so I talked with Mr. A., who had shown interest in Zac. Zac had difficulty being an agent in his world; he didn't understand the rules. He needed Mr. A.'s help in dismantling the cage he was in — to get on the list.

As Connell writes about social inequity produced by school systems and about the bind of working-class students, he too talks of the cage:

> Our image of person and society becomes that of a flea freely hopping around inside a cage, and though that may produce fine dramas about fleas, it isn't very helpful if our concern is to do something about the cage ... for the cage is composed of what people do. (Connell et al., 1982, p. 78)

As teachers we're not in the business for the money it brings us. The large majority of us teach because we want to make a difference — "to do something about the cage" — and though we can't always feel it, we're powerful in the difference we can make simply in the way we respond to students' writing.

When well-meaning teachers at the training school criticized Carlos for the mistakes that he made, he became a recalcitrant writer. "Why should I write when everything's wrong?" The teacher response, initiated to improve his writing and bring his language closer to standard English, actually killed his intrinsic motivation. And if poor grades always resulted from his endeavors, extrinsic motivation was also gone. Though students in higher tracks did not remember criticism of their writing in elementary school, all the basic students in my study recalled such periods of criticism. Orion, who devised ingenious schemes to "get teachers off my back," said:

> Miss Bothell'd tell me to come back and write papers over and over, and after school 'cause of "not too neat." I used to write in big letters. I don't know what was so bad about it. Then I decided to write small, so small teachers couldn't read it, so they started giving me B or something. Doesn't bother me. I could care less what other people think about it. To Hell with them. I don't care.

For these students, writing became an act that was resisted, refused, or done with the minimum amount of effort to appease the authority or to pass. Willingness to revise was dependent on how willing the students were to prolong a process that was anathema to them.

By the time we meet these students in their secondary years, it is hard to remember that the recalcitrant students really want to feel competent, to feel good about what they do. We often have to compensate for years of criticism that these students have endured. Yet attention to standard form and standard language is essential. As Freire (1990) advises, "It gives them power over the dominant dialect. It puts inside of the student's body the feeling that they are capable of being correct." But attention to correctness can be a late step in the writing process. If writers have something they want to say and an audience they want to say it to, the last step should be one of pride.

Every basic writer said that it was easier to write about things that they knew about or experiences that they had gone through. If writers are to value writing as a mode of expression, three things must happen: (1) they must stop spending time on "remedial" exercises that are disconnected from their actual writing; (2) they must find subjects and audiences that draw them to the act, increasing intrinsic motivation, and (3) as Collins (1979) says, they must concentrate on getting across meaning as a first step. They must be urged not only to reflect on their experience but to explain it and expand it in order to feel satisfaction in making sense of their world through thinking and writing.

Carlos noted a time when motivation due to feelings of competence in writing returned. He talked about the apple-plant teacher who had taught him how to grow an apple tree. When the tree died, the teacher had him write to make sense of that experience. The apple-plant teacher demonstrated how nonstandard dialect students can bring their strength to writing when she said, "Write down what you can and what you know." The excitement Carlos felt in making sense of his experience gave him impetus to engage in writing. If our job as writing teachers is to teach students a skill that they may use after graduation, then it's ironic if the major role we play is as purveyor of criticism. We may teach the skill, but we kill the students' desire to use it in the future, making the act of teaching futile.

As writing instructors, there are things we can do to pry apart bars in the cage. We've looked at many of these things, but we haven't looked at what the students themselves say they need from teachers. Sherry says she needs time and help — help given in a way that doesn't humiliate:

> I've got to spend a lot of time on writing. It takes me a long time to get my essay really good. Like one person can sit and write with just a couple of mistakes. . . . I have to sit there for hours. But that

time helps. Teachers that help you makes you understand the subject. Teachers that do not help get you lost and confused. Ms. Blue, she'll go around the class and she'll see everyone is doing okay. She explained what doesn't sound right, and why it doesn't. She gives you a sheet, and you got to get four key ideas, and then she checks it off when you get your ideas. Then you go and start on your essay. Mr. Mott, he sits there at his desk. I mean if I go to him, he'll look at my statement, he'll turn it around like totally opposite what I wanted to do. And he cannot walk from his desk in the back of the room to help me. I don't want to be a teacher, but if I do, I'll offer help—go around. It's hard to ask for it.

Students like Sherry who have felt the humiliation of being laughed at by the class for asking what were deemed stupid questions have lost the willingness to make themselves vulnerable to that humiliation even for help.

What this all boils down to is that basic writers need a special kind of help, and they need more help, and they need more time in school and at home for writing. Further, most of them must get this help if they are to keep their frustration down to a level where they will stay in school and keep writing. As teachers, time is our most precious commodity. Class size must be reduced, or tutors need to be provided so that these students can get the attention they need to catch up. Our students need help as a part of the curriculum in sorting out what they want in life and how to go about getting it. They need help in seeing a purpose in switching to standard English for their writing and in seeing that their home dialect serves them well for many other purposes. And these developing writers, who are behind rather than dumb, need to perceive themselves as such, need to see the real reasons they have difficulty with writing. We need time to attend with interest to our students' ideas before attending to correctness of expression; we need to understand how our response to students' work affects the view that they develop of themselves as writers and thinkers. Above all we must give these young people our time and our advocacy; intervention (the younger, the better) must be given priority in school curricula. Our schools must dismantle cages, not build them.

Chapter Three

Elana
The Success Trap

Like Tracy in chapter 1, Elana was among those who were on the top of the academic pile. Her teachers had placed her in the advanced writing class of a suburban school where maintaining advanced student status wasn't easy. Though I will profile Elana in this chapter, we'll also hear from her classmate Chris, the school's NCTE Achievement Award nominee, and from other students who generally felt good about themselves as writers and who were deemed successful by their schools in that they were placed in standard and advanced English classes. Elana wasn't one to mince words. Her brown hair swung back and forth seemingly in time to the emphasis she put on words and thoughts. In listening to her, we can see how her struggle with writing differed from that of Carlos.

A Profile of Elana

The first word I remember writing was my name ... with a backward *E*. I remember being very proud when I wrote then. I was writing things like cards to my family. If it was to my sister, I would probably get my mother's help in writing "Happy Birthday" or "I love you," but they were words. I was never very uncomfortable with having to write anything; it was kind of fun.

I loved my kindergarten teacher, Ms. T. I still talk to her. We made this recipe book; I did cinnamon toast. That was pretty advanced stuff. I remember writing down the recipe, frustrated with abbreviations like "1 T." My problem was the gaps. There is a big space, a huge waste of space on that side with a recipe. Until this day I am stubborn about margins. I push up to the line and press it. I was in love with my second-grade teacher. She was so happy, very, very patient. I think the reason why I don't remember writing [for her] was because there was nothing that really stood out as upsetting or frustrating. I loved penmanship in third and fourth grade because my teacher always told me that I had nice handwriting; I put all this energy into it. I love looking at pieces of work that my mom saved. At the time I'm sure they made perfect sense. I like the way I was taught to write. In fifth grade I remember a writing assignment that I really loved. I invented my own invention. It was something that you put on the wheel of your car, and it analyzed your breath. If you are over the limit, the car won't start. I thought that was a brilliant idea! The class thought it was a good idea [too]; it was one of the things she hung up. Another good memory would be group activities, the sharing of ideas. And at camp we played a game: you go around and write a sentence, and each person would add, and we'd come up with some of the best stories.

Assignments, particularly in elementary school were made to really trigger off the imagination, so that kids really want to write. You come up with these really good ideas and write them. That's true today, that the papers I write better are the assignments I enjoy. If I get an assignment from the teacher that I'm just not into at all, then it is usually not my best-quality work. My writing ability is above average for my age. I'm an *A/B* student, in advanced social studies and English. I'm not in the top ten in the school, but I am in the top thirty. With advanced students I am about average in writing, with other students I am above. I don't ever remember being scolded at for mistakes in writing. I was blessed with some of the best teachers.

In elementary school kids are pretty much at the same level, so there isn't very much competition. I'm not exactly fond of their whole standard, basic, and advanced system in high school. I think it is lousy; it causes distance between kids in school. You rarely see advanced students hanging around with basic. Most of my friends are not the intellects of the school who you find in the computer room all day, but most of them are advanced students like me. I do have some friends that have some basic classes, but not many. They certainly are not stupid. I don't choose my friends over how well they can write a paper. If I was in all standard classes I would be embarrassed, humiliated, like I'd let myself, my future, down. I did go from advanced chemistry to standard chemistry, and I was like hiding, but that faded away when a lot of other people from the advanced class were drifting into the standard class.

I'm a good reader, ever since I learned to read milk cartons. I didn't mind reading so much when I didn't have to work from it; I liked Dr. Seuss. In school when you have to read up to chapter eight by Thursday, there's a certain kind of resentment of that pressure that really made me not want to read. I loathe reading. I can enjoy the actual material, but the act of reading bores me to death. What I get out of it I enjoy. I more enjoy the act of writing — sometimes, not all the time. While you are reading a book, the next word that you read is not up to you; it is written right there. No control. But I like the way all these ideas are in my head all mumbo jumbo, somehow when you put them on paper they are organized, and I control what the teacher is going to have to read. Revenge.

I remember thinking in sixth grade that it was really neat that once you thought in writing, it didn't disappear, vanish. I had been going through this cupboard that I had just shoved papers in over the years and thought: "Obviously I was thinking this once upon a time; you can write this thing down and die and what you thought is going to be around. Something from your hand becomes permanent."

I don't like being told what to write; I like assignments that you are free to expand the way you want. Sometimes the teacher has very definite guidelines what they want you to write, and I resent that. I think kids would write better if they could write the way they wanted. Obviously you have to have some restrictions and guidelines; otherwise, kids wouldn't learn. If there were no guidelines, I think some kids would stare at the blank page for hours, and I think others would write and write for hours, like me.

In ninth grade, we read a book by a young black girl. It had to do with racism, but I compared her story with *The Diary of Anne Frank*. When I was writing that paper, I was thinking: "How do I write this without making it seem like people should feel more guilty for this girl, but at the same time that this girl was done an injustice?" I remember writing that paper and really getting involved, in a very personal way. I did well on it.

My hardest class in ninth grade was my social studies class, [with] Ms. C. Ms. C. is probably the hardest teacher in any school system. She is a witch — an excellent teacher, but a witch. I knew from day one that there was no way that I was going to get better than a *C* in there. It was lousy to write for her. It has always bothered me that when you think you have written a very sound, complete, solid paper, they take an icicle, and they just chop it all down. They turn it into tiny pieces, and take a little oil and put it

in a salad, and they can do whatever they want to it. I wrote a
biography of my grandfather, which was a great biography, and she
gave me a C−. I wanted to kill that teacher. I worked so hard on
that, and my grandfather had sent me all these photographs and
report cards and letters, and all kinds of things. I worked so hard. I
learned so much. She had all these criticisms that were primarily
for mechanical things, like long paragraphs and five-line sentences.
They were all justified things, but my God! It was the ideas that
were the important thing. It was demoralizing. Well, what the hell,
if I'm going to try to think of what the teacher wants from me next
time, that's all they'll get. I try to do what they want, and I resent
it because I'm the one who is supposed to be learning from it.
There are many teachers in the school that are very good at
making you feel like shit. Just by the way she'd talk to you: "Huh,
you didn't do your assignment," and loud enough so that all the
other kids could hear. I had a pretty strong core, so I didn't let her
get to me as much as the others.

My parents were in the process of divorcing, and my dad came
in with me and let her know that I was having some problems,
and she suddenly turned into this nice person. "You know, my
parents went through a divorce too, and I know exactly what
you're going through. It's okay, and you take the time you need."
I'm like, "Why can't you be this way all the time? Why can't
teachers be people?"

In tenth grade I had "Argumentation and Debate," and the
assignments were very, very safe. She [the teacher] was working
with you. And Mr. O'Neill was a great teacher too, really knew his
stuff. But even though he was great, by then I was a procrastinator.
Half of my homework is reading, half of it is writing. Sometimes I
have a lot, sometimes I don't have any, sometimes I have a lot but I
don't do any. I bring it [homework] home, but it doesn't come out
of that bag. I do a lot of rationalizing. "Well, I can just do the
outline tonight." Or: "I know it is due Thursday, but she said we
could have till Friday. Maybe I could get an extension until
Monday. Oh, no, I'll write it right now." But then there are all sorts
of things I have to do in my room, a good song on the radio, and I
have to dance when I listen to the radio, and suddenly I haven't
hugged the cat in a long time.

Sometimes when I get started, I feel like, "Okay here it comes,
they [ideas] are starting to flow," but sometimes even when I'm
writing, I have my ideas all stopped for awhile. In Mr. O'Neill's
class you'd read a play, and he'd give you a choice of about ten
options to write. That was good, but sometimes if it was a difficult
play, I would be full of anxiety. I would sit in front of the paper for

an hour, nothing on it. I'd want it to be good, and I would feel like an asshole for leaving it to the last minute again. Then I would picture me handing in that paper tomorrow. I might even know what I was wearing to school that day, and I'd close my eyes and see myself in whatever I was wearing, putting the paper on his desk. I liked him, and that would always give me some assurance because I realized that I was going to finish the paper. I may not finish until one o'clock in the morning but making that picture in my head sort of gives myself an assurance that it's going to happen, so I do it.

I have two older sisters, we're Jewish, and the older is going to school in Israel now. I've been going to camp connected with my religion for eight years. My mother is an administrator, and my father is at the university. My older sister was straight *A*'s, honor roll, dean's list, extremely bright and studious, more so than I would ever care to be. She spent her life in her room. My mother says I am an underachiever. My younger sister is also an underachiever. I think I am the medium between them.

This year we've had a topic that we are responsible for writing all our papers on. I chose Zionism because I belong to a Social Zionist Youth Movement. I knew very little about Zionism, so I thought I would really learn something from it. I haven't resented most of those papers—the teacher, but not the papers. Class this year is extremely boring, very frustrating, and at the same time, not safe, because Mr. Shultz doesn't tell us what he wants; he makes us fish for it. I don't really like doing work for him. Right now I rarely write in class. It is hard to concentrate in there. Nobody writes in there. I think people are so tense that they want to get out of that room. I've had to write a satire paper about Zionism, and I had no idea what I was going to do. It is such a hard thing to satirize because it does mean something to me, and I was having lots of trouble with it. I asked my sister and my mother about it, and I didn't like their ideas. Finally I just said, "Elana, write something about it." It took an hour and forty-five minutes to write the first draft.

It was a paper on kibbutz life with an occasional one-liner, which really is not what satire is all about. I really did not have a satirical tone in my paper, but at the time I was writing it I didn't care. My grandfather just died this weekend. I was feeling stupid because I had four days to do it, but I really didn't want to write that paper . . . at all. I resented doing the paper, about a subject that was hard for me to criticize. I wasn't getting anything out of it for myself, and it was just making me more upset, frustrated, and angry. I changed about three words, copied it over, and handed it in. In writing my main concern is getting it done. Lots of other kids will stay up to four o'clock. But if writing is upsetting me so much, I'm just going to write it and not toil over it. A paper for Mr. Shultz shouldn't take more than three hours to write [especially] if I am in pain while writing it. When it is painful, I don't really want to put the extra oomph into it. If I put more priority on school, I put more priority on pain.

I don't write on my own free will now. I think about writing all kinds of things, but I don't do it. I doodle, while I'm on the telephone, words and pictures, and it is interesting after to see what I've done when I wasn't thinking, but that is the only thing that I do with my pen unless I'm assigned. Oh yeah, except when I was mad at my sister. It was October and I was furious. I wrote a whole page, I saved it, but she hasn't seen it. That doesn't happen a lot because usually I will tell her directly, but this time I had such overwhelming feelings, I wrote.

If I'm given an assignment, and I think the assignment stinks, I'm not creative. If the teacher says you have to make three pages, and you have to have this and this and this and this, I want to go, "You know where you can stick that paper." It doesn't make me want to write it, so it is not my strongest work. I resent it because I then have no power and no control in it. I think of writing as revenge sometimes, that I control what they have to read, but when I do what I think they want, even that is gone. The littlest thing will distract my attention when I am doing that writing; I'll get completely off base. I have no control over my own ideas, because I know what they want me to say. But other times when a teacher gives an assignment, and it's a good one, I can have a whole bunch of ideas, and I find it's easier to write. I can just fly along. I mean the ideas are flowing, they are coming, they are going from my brain, to my hand, to the paper. I'm going to write; [if there's a] twenty-eight-hour nuclear holocaust, I'm still going to write.

I'm sort of putting this together for myself right now. Take grades. Take the paper [my grandfather's biography] I wrote back in ninth grade. When I got back that *C−* on it, I was angry, but it didn't really stay with me very long because I thought it was a good paper. Believe me I didn't go "Yea!" But if I truthfully thought the paper was good, I'm going to try to think of what the teacher wants from me next time, but then I lose control. I'm the best procrastinator that you will meet. I should be getting angry at myself, because I leave things to the last minute. I'd say that 90 percent of the kids in my class leave their writing to the last. I tell my parents that, but they don't believe me. I could start it three hours earlier, I could start it three days earlier, but I choose not to. I know ahead of time that I am not going to do it until the last minute, and I create this kind of pressure. I don't know if it works well for me. If I don't have the pressure, sometimes I think my paper wouldn't be as good. The logical thing is that it would be better because you spend more time, you go away from it, you come back to it. When you do this last-minute kind of thing, you write it; you like it; you type it. Once I wrote three drafts for a paper, but the other times I write the original, make some corrections, copy it over, because who needs to waste that time. I don't procrastinate with people, but they are more important to me than anything that I am doing in school. It wasn't always that way.

I'm going to college and graduate school, and writing is going to be a crucial element. It is also going to be a pain. I don't need writing to make me happy. Happiness is going to come from success in life, but then writing is going to have to be in there, to get there. I mean writing has been part of my life because it has had to have been.

When Elana talked about her preschool greeting cards, her "Cinnamon Toast" recipe, and the alcohol-sensitive car, there was an excited child in her voice. Like Tracy and the other "successful" writers, her satisfaction in her early writing was full-blown, and she shared it with appreciative teachers, parents, and peers. But when she began to talk about ninth grade, her voice changed. By ninth grade, she began to feel challenge, which was positive, and pressure, which was perhaps inevitable, and loss of ownership and motivation, which was certainly regrettable. In ninth grade she wrote for two teachers: Ms. M., her English teacher, and Ms. C., her social studies teacher. In Ms. M.'s class, Elana still was engaged and challenged in writing a paper about Anne Frank: "I remember . . . really getting involved, in a very personal way." She was also engaged in her grandfather's biography, which she wrote for Ms. C., but it was through this assignment that she learned she had lost ownership of her own writing, a sort of loss of her writer's innocence. From the grading and response to one beloved project, she became aware that pleasing the teacher was necessary if she was to get good grades.

She met this sense of loss with anger and a rhetoric of rebellion. "Well, what the hell, if I'm going to try to think of what the teacher wants from me next time, that's all they'll get." But her anger turned into a form of self-defeating and passive resistance — procrastination. "I am the best procrastinator," Elana said, trying to make light of it, but, in fact, procrastination was a response to writing that had lost its meaning and that, when exacerbated by any other pressure, engendered deep struggle.

The Process of the Successful Writer

Of course, no two writers go about writing in exactly the same way. The forty different writers in this study used forty different processes. Nevertheless, I began to see connections in their approaches to writing that will be useful in our search to understand why Elana and most other successful writers found writing to be either boring or distressing by eleventh grade. I took a close look at four aspects of the successful writers' processes: (1) idea generation, (2) organization, (3) drafting, and (4) revision/editing.

Idea Generation

Successful writers took more time in finding ideas for their writing than did the unsuccessful writers. Each successful writer made time for collecting ideas, and many considered this process, along with writing the first paragraph, to be the hardest steps in the process. Elana searched for ideas by thinking (probing and contemplating what was stored in her long-term memory), by reading, by talking to teachers, parents, and friends, and finally by rethinking all this input and making "a list on a piece of paper." Her approach to gathering ideas was representative, though several students did without the "list" until they had written their opening sentence or paragraph. Many teachers organized brainstorming or freewriting to get students started on a paper, and students responded well to that. Kathy said: "I found that writing has improved with the brainstorming thing. Whatever comes out I just write down, and then I can just translate it into something more meaningful to people who don't follow my train of thought." Further, students didn't take the first ideas that came. Meg said:

> One half of my brain is brainstorming about ways to react to the assignment and how to approach it, and the other part is sort of sitting back and evaluating each brainstorm and then [focusing] in on the one that I think is most effective and that I can most easily deal with.

The few students who didn't give this stage of the process adequate time often struggled with overload. Portia tried to write without separating idea generation from transcription. "Introductory paragraphs are the worst; they are so hard, and it is hard to predict for me what I am going to say if I list. How can you figure out what you're going to say before you write it?" Portia had found out that you can find out what you think while you write, but because she attempted to write her papers in one draft, too much thinking and organizing had to occur simultaneously.

Students talked about having difficulty when they concerned themselves too much with what teachers would think of their ideas while they were trying to generate them. Perhaps potential teacher criticism took up so much room in their conscious attention that solidifying ideas was difficult. But when students felt that teachers were interested, not critical of what they would say, this stage of writing went more smoothly. Others joined Portia in making the following kind of statement contrasting the good and bad times:

> I like to call it writer's block 'cause that's what the professionals call it. Sometimes it gets bad, hard to look at a blank piece of paper, and darn, it happens a lot to me. This year it's been different; for some reason I've found something that I've always wanted to say, things I think the teachers won't mind hearing. I don't know, maybe the difference is that there are teachers I want to say it for this year.

In their interviews and composing-aloud sessions, students often spent anxious time selecting a topic and generating supporting ideas that would meet teacher approval. Students looked for clues as to what the teacher wanted from them instead of searching for what they wanted to say. Elizabeth said: "I'm almost timid when I have to write those 'anything you want' papers. It doesn't tell me what the teacher wants. When I'm given choices, I can write. I know what the teacher expects."

Writers became less enthused about their topics and ideas when writing became less of a relationship between themselves and the material (Seidman, 1982) and more of a balancing act between what they wanted to say and what they believed the teacher wanted them to say.

Organization

Unlike the less successful students, successful students were able to give quite a bit of conscious attention to organization during the writing process. Often idea generation and organizational planning were not separate processes, and like professional writers, the successful students often spent up to half their writing time in preliminary planning. In most of the schools, organization was an important focus of the assignment and hence the primary focus of the writer's endeavor. Ideas were generated with the assigned format in mind. Though there were exceptions, the most successful writers considered organization throughout drafting and revised their plans often as they went along. Hence, many students found it frustrating to have to hand in iron-clad outlines prior to writing. Two reported that they were penalized because they didn't follow the outline in the paper they finally handed in.

Most writers followed the teachers' organizational guidelines without enthusiasm or complaint. "You just organize it as they say you should," said Tracy. "No use arguing," said Matt. "You just do it. That's the way it is." However, Elana and Chris found more dissonance between what they wanted to do and what the teacher had assigned. Chris said: "I worried about trying to make what I was saying apply to the guidelines of the paper." Elana said: "When you get an assignment that the teacher has very definite guidelines about, I resent that."

Formulaic writing (writing according to a tight, teacher-prescribed organization) was a widespread expectation for the successful students, and most of them managed it. In two of the students' schools the formulas were quite complex. In one school, students were even asked to overlay two organizational strategies (termed a "doubleton")—for instance, interpretation overlaid with an advantage/disadvantage format. In another school, the format was laid out so tightly that students were told what sorts of sentences to use and where to use them. Peco said:

> We even have to use special procedures for a particular paragraph, like: "use the diction packet and the thesis paragraph for the short prose analysis and include the two sentences: one about the tone of the author and the other about its effect on the reader, and use a general purpose of the author to guide your writing." Of course you get to pick part of it, but most of it is that iron-clad, the so-many paragraph essay that we've had since ninth or seventh grade. There is no reason to vary from that style. You've got this pressure on you that if you try to somehow vary what you're doing, you're gonna kill your grade. "This is well written, but I'm gonna give you a B or C because it's not what I asked for." Kind of hypocritical, telling us to write it like this, and then they have us read excellent authors and say this is so well written, yet those authors aren't sticking to the formal styles that they taught us.

Students were able to meet these complex expectations, but there was a cost. Though many students fulfilled expectations, they did so without enthusiasm or, like Peco, Elana, and Doug, with resentment.

In studying the processes that these students used, I noticed a pattern. Students were most engaged in writing when a topic that interested them was the most important facet of the assignment and when teachers took a backseat in the organizational process. This was rare in the experience of the advanced students I worked with. Mr. L., Kathy's social studies teacher, was a teacher who provided a process by which his students could come to their own sense of what their organization should be without his dictating it.

> When we first started, we did the focusing statements. We had to write questions about our topic, and I had about twelve questions I was gonna answer. And he just wrote, "Whoa! This will be a mammoth paper." I had to cut it down to about three, but because I had so many questions about it, I was getting so excited about it. Finally I took just one of the questions, and [even then] I got a paper that was forty-two pages long. It was very good to have to narrow it because it was a way of finding out what I wanted to say. You had a goal to get toward, however far away it was, and it sort of entailed all your information. Every time you looked at information, you'd say, "Well, how does this apply to my question? How will I fit it in?" And you'd be working on an outline without even knowing it.

Portia, who had this same teacher, was not accustomed to organizing ahead.

> Usually I just write it out and write it out, and then I would go back and divide it up and move it around until it seemed right. I didn't really have a process. I would just rewrite it until it worked. That worked with the three-page papers, but thank God Mr. L. had a way to get us to get from our topic to the outline, 'cause thirty pages written over and over wouldn't have worked.

For Portia and Kathy the primary objective was not to organize in a prescribed manner, but to answer real questions that they had about a subject. With Mr. L.'s help they evolved an organization that would help them report the results of that pursuit. Students whose assigned organization was their primary focus during writing were making organization instead of making meaning. Hence, the writing meant less to them.

Drafting

Successful writers could attend to more complex considerations than could the less successful writers while drafting. Examination of the composing-aloud data in Figure 1–3, p. 19–21, shows that only rare attention was cast to spelling, handwriting, syntax, punctuation, or textual conventions. (Tracy was an exception, as she was still consciously attending to substituting standard English verb forms for the black English forms that were more automatic for her.) Unlike the unsuccessful writers, the process of transcription was relatively automatic, and their minds were freed to attend to other aspects of the writing task.

Even decentering (Graves, 1983) — making sure that the written word would be understandable to an audience — was quite automatic, unless that audience was distressing. Students rarely had to stop and think about how to say something for their intended audience. Recursion occurred in bigger hunks than it did for Carlos and Zac. It was normally used to review what they had already written before starting a new section, to revise an earlier plan, to choose better words, or to get going again when they were stuck.

Each writer had a different cluster of concerns that interrupted focused attention during the drafting process. It was clear in linking composing-aloud sessions with interviews and observations that students were most often interrupted in their drafting by concerns that past or present teachers had urged on them. Many of these concerns might have been attended to more efficiently after ideas were on paper; as early interruptions they impeded progress. They were further indications that the teacher was eminent in the conscious attention of the writer. Doug worried about vivid details and active constructions; Tracy worried about length and verb endings; Chris and Elana worried about colloquialisms; and every successful writer worried about word choice.

Elana said: "Finding the words, that's the worst that happens to me. If I could get over that, I think I could write more efficiently. When I'm pushing for time and I get flustered, it's worse." Kathy described the frustration:

> There's this faint glimmer of light in the back of my head, but I just can't draw it out with the right words. And sometimes I'll go up to somebody and say, "How would you say it?" and I sort of garble out what I'm trying to say, and they rephrase it. I don't think I'm lacking vocabulary; it's like you're in a blind room, and you just saw the coffee cup on the table, but you can't find it. You know it's there, you just can't touch it.

Striving to use what Elana called the "five-thousand-dollar words" was perhaps the most common symptom in the please-the-teacher syndrome. In the middle of one protocol, as she was trying to find wording for a thought, Elizabeth said, "I just don't know if the teacher will like this." We'll see in the case of Elana and Chris how such concerns could turn into counterproductive worries which interrupted drafting so often that focused attention on the task was impossible.

Writing was most engaging when students were enmeshed in the act of making meaning for themselves. Then they could write, even (as Elana said) "[if there's a] twenty-eight-hour nuclear holocaust." This deep concentration came only when their present and past English teachers were not sitting in the corners of their minds.

turn around in their view of themselves as writers—if the grade was indicative of competence in some area. Joel was feeling bad about himself as a writer, when to his surprise, "Mr. Shultz asked me to put it in a poetry contest. I began to write songs for a friend's rock group, and then I just took a poem to the writing magazine." Joel began to take the risks necessary for him to grow in other writing as well. When a teacher recognized even one area of competence, confidence was often restored.

The writers in this study had a lot to say about two symptoms of overbearing extrinsic motivation. They labeled them "procrastination" and "perfectionism."

Procrastination. When extrinsic motivation for writing far outweighed intrinsic motivation, writers had trouble keeping their attention on the assigned task. For Peco, procrastination was calculated and calm:

> Sometimes you're just doing something else, and you get this nagging feeling that maybe you should be doing your essay because what happens if you don't finish it on time. You're doomed. But ever since this year, I don't worry, probably because last year what my English teacher liked in a paper was just pure regurgitation. She didn't really care about critical thinking. I guess that's where it started, just gave me this lackadaisical mood. And that really starts to worry me because now it feels like I simply can't get any productive writing done until the night before. I simply have to have a sense of deadline before I can get myself to write. We had a movie to make just last week, and we got on it just like that. It was a topic I liked, and we had a lot of creative ideas. From there I just plowed right on through. I put off a lot of things to do that.

But for other successful writers, procrastination took the form of a struggle, which was more intense before they sat down to write than when they were actually writing. Portia said:

> Peace of mind is gone when I have a paper to do. It's getting myself to do it. I'll be enjoying something and then get this nagging feeling, almost like shame. It's euphoria when I hand it in, and then she'll go and assign another paper.

Other students experienced the struggle with their own lack of inclination to write both before and during writing. The cost of this procrastination was that there was rarely time for multiple drafts, in which ideas or organization could be reconceptualized. Portia said:

> I honestly can't do it until the night before. It's agony, and I'm sick of staying up the night before. I can't think of anything; I get so

frustrated, and I'm really up late. I get this pressure, and then I think, "I'm going to write it and get it done. I don't care what kind of grade." Why I can't just start earlier and get a good grade, a couple of weeks in advance.

For these writers, procrastination was a process by which they revved up anxiety until it became strong enough to overcome their inner disinclination to complete a task. By eleventh grade, most had lived with the disinclination to write for so long that they had learned to cope with the struggle it engendered.

Perfectionism. Perfectionism is a more complex manifestation of heavy extrinsic motivation. As five of the writers told of their experiences with schooling and writing, it became apparent that their confessed tendency toward perfectionism was, in reality, an internalization of the very high teacher and parental expectations which they struggled to satisfy. For Doug, it perhaps started as a complex response to: (1) a favorite baby-sitter who rewarded him when his letters were perfect, (2) an early elementary school teacher who told someone within his hearing that he was a slob, and (3) a mother who had very high expectations for him.

For Doug the process of writing could be painful. He felt the burden of the audience in several aspects of his life but had maintained extrinsic motivation to please. When he strove to perfect his part in a play, perfectionism served his thespian self well, but it caused him a certain amount of agony when doing writing which he didn't really want to do.

> I can't just pour it out. I'll write one really nice sentence and the next ones'll be choppy—piece of crap. They won't make any sense, and I get really upset with myself. It's just because I'm a perfectionist. If I'm in a drama class and we're preparing a skit, and my friend's not ready, I'd much rather not go on than make a fool out of myself. I've come to realize that everything I do is this big performance. Same with writing. I write lots of drafts, over and over and over again. I just look for everything. My writing hasn't been fantastic, but she can't say anything about it, you know, "Oh, it's messy," or "It's not well done."

As the pain mounted, students either found strategies to deal with perfectionism, or began to care less. Kevin said:

> I was a little perfectionist in fourth grade, like book reports; I would spend an hour and a half on just a little report going over it with a fine-tooth comb, making sure everything was perfect. If I really botched it, then my class would harp on me for the day, but most of the time it was just my own perfectionism. I don't care as much anymore.

Kevin wasn't alone in caring less in his high school years. As teacher approval got old, as he cared less, the power of the teacher to make him want to write impeccably decreased. Nevertheless, grades remained paramount because they held a key to these students' futures, and they knew it.

When Threat and Overload Cause Struggle: The Case of Chris

Criticism comes late for successful writers. None of them talked about receiving criticism from teachers until they reached junior high. Ironically, criticism arrived at the same time as their adolescent self-consciousness, and hence, by junior high, prolonged criticism was often devastating. Mr. Shultz had been a committed teacher for many years, doing what he thought was best for his students. But Mr. Shultz was, with the best intentions, critical and inflexible, and those characteristics posed a threat for both Chris and Elana. We'll take a close look at Chris's writing process and at the interruptions Mr. Shultz's prior criticism brought to his usual deep concentration. Chris's first protocol took him forty minutes, and in that time he generated the following twelve sentences of a "doubleton" satire/ speculation paper:

> In history class we learn that technological advancement and historical change are closely related. New plows prompted an agricultural revolution, and Gutenberg's printing press put religious and political matters directly into the hands of the common people. The entire feudal system might never have developed without a single implement, the stirrup. Without this simple piece of twisted iron and leather, the mounted knight would not have been able to dominate the masses. The nobility would not have been able to demand that the peasants provide them with labor, goods, and sundry luxuries in return for protection. A millennium of Western Civilization would be erased from the black boards of our European history courses; our entire heritage obliterated in a cloud of chalk dust. In its place, a different social order would have risen in the place of the feudal system.

> The stirrup may be a simple implement, but it gave the opportunists a means of subjugating the common people. Before the stirrup, cavalrymen could not strike blows from the saddle, and simply hurled arrows and spears, trampled their opponents, and vanished in cloud of dust. With the aid of the stirrup, the mounted knight could deliver a vicious blow without being unseated. With a sword and armor to complete the ensemble, knights dominated warfare. The peasants contracted the knights to protect them from the barbarian hordes and brigands that had destroyed Rome.

Looking at what was in Chris's conscious attention as he wrote this draft gives us a better understanding of his struggle. In Figure 1–3, p. 21, we can see a listing of the instances that have interrupted his drafting.

As Chris composed aloud, he made a brief list of ideas and considered the double format he had to use. During drafting, idea generation and planning were not interruptive. He probed for new thoughts in a sort of brainstorming manner, and when he found what he wanted, he wrote it down. Other thoughts relatively unrelated to his task popped into his conscious attention, such as: "Karl Marx wouldn't have lasted long in the middle ages. They would have cut him in half as soon as he said 'class struggle.'" These thoughts came and went and didn't shake his concentration. They seemed to entertain him in this bout with writing, and they certainly entertained me during the task of data analysis.

But there were worries that did interrupt his concentration. His searches for better words went on long enough for him to have to backtrack to regain his direction. Nevertheless, none of these interruptions was as distracting as those heralded by the image of angry Mr. Shultz. His image became the harbinger of a "block" as Chris describes it. This occurred three times during the first protocol, and each time there was a substantial interruption in his concentration.

> He can't stand colloquialism . . . . like hand in hand . . . It is not a personal relationship anyway . . . . Let's try this . . . . . I can see his correcting pen all over this . . . . new . . . . plows . . . um . . . . starting,   creating . . . begin . . . sloppy . . . . there is a mental vacuum. There is absolutely nothing in my head . . . . wait for a word to pop out . . . .
> . . . .

And Chris is finally back on track. Another time he talked of "burning my fingers on colloquialism" and followed with "bad time when you get something in that class and then apply it to everything; can't escape it . . . being unseated . . . I can see Shultz's face hovering over me. . . . " And the final block began. When Chris came to the end of a page, he said, "A whole page? It took me hours to write one page the last time I tried." Apparently this session at composing aloud was only a mild version of the struggle he had been having.

Chris said several times that Shultz's criticism triggered in him a self-criticism that was even "more devastating." This was evident in a protocol of a short story that he began after his last final exam. It was about a young man who retreated to "the solitude of the hill tops" to "silence memories of endless exams and draining assignments." At the beginning of this protocol, he tried to talk himself out from under the penumbra of Mr. Shultz. "This is not a school assignment. No need to put my name on it. Titles I can do without. I'll have no margins. No margins, no comments." But Mr. Shultz was internalized, his internal critic held court. "A terrible introduction." "Archaic language again." "Another word. The word is hovering. I can't take this again. I don't believe it. Oh no! I'll think of it twenty minutes later." During twenty-five minutes and seven sentences, he interrupted himself ten times with self-criticism. Searching for words, avoiding colloquial and "archaic" language, criticizing his logic, and blaming himself for unoriginal language were all the subjects of his self-deprecation. Each instance interrupted his concentration. Chris was struggling.

Before analyzing Chris's composing-aloud sessions, I thought it was his endeavor to change the "archaic" style that had brought him to a state of overload. However, it was clear that emotion linked with Mr. Shultz was interrupting and disrupting his command of attention during the writing process. (And Chris was sensitive to something that was real. Mr. Shultz sought me out in the teacher's room one day to tell me that he thought Chris's work was "overrated" by other teachers.)

One would think that one critical voice in a chorus of approval wouldn't be enough to shake Chris's belief in himself and his writing, but he was "down on himself" for other reasons. Chemistry wasn't going well either. Further, another teacher mentioned that he had gone to a prestigious college with Chris's father and that he hoped Chris wouldn't lose his ability and drop out of school as his father had in his sophomore year. "I still have to do the work, but I don't have the confidence to do it." Chris started feeling bad about himself as a writer and a student and said to me in an interview that he wondered if the onset of this feeling was hereditary. The pressures converged. In many respects he was active in analyzing his "writer's block." He saw the parts of the whole struggle but was just beginning to see that the whole was composed of the parts. At first no one thing seemed serious enough, yet each component added to what made inroads into the conscious attention that he had available for writing. A final component that exacerbated his struggle with writing was peer pressure, but I will save his perceptions on that, as they are particularly poignant and relevant in the context of what other writers have to say about peer pressure.

Peer Pressure

Every student is affected by peer pressure, but successful students seemed to feel a special kind of pressure. Peco describes it:

You're pressured to be the ultimate achiever by parents and teachers,

and then there's this social pressure that you shouldn't be intelligent, especially in high school. I have this ability to pick up
ideas a little quicker than everybody else, but you don't let everybody else on to that. You make it sound like you either did a lot of
work, or you go "Oh this is so horrible," because deep down
inside you, you know if you come off as too smart, there's gonna
be social ostracism. If you can be cool and smart, that's probably
where it is. When I get a good grade, I don't mention it. I mumble
something if someone asks me what I got, or "just not that good."
You can't be too organized, and the thing can't come too naturally
to you. It sounds better to say you're lazy to your peers. "I'm into
time management" sounds nerdy. I know some people who put
the word "like" between every other word just to give this appear-
ance as if they're stupid. I get this feeling girls think it's better to
act dumb than to show their intelligence; that to me is the worst.

Very successful students faced a unique kind of peer pressure
that had a way of complicating their lives and exacerbating any
writing struggle they happened to be dealing with. Peco had perfected
the strategy of being "cool and smart." But for the students who
were designated brains, this pressure could be vicious. Kevin said:

Seventh grade was purgatory. Once you get into junior high, you
don't have this shelter that you get under the teacher. It's more
your peers, and they were not so happy with me. Your writing has
to be perfect or they'll make fun of you, but if you're perfect then
they're going to make fun of you because of that. It was like a trap.
At lunch I had to sit with these two kids that were the worst; I sat
with the destructors. Here are people whose values are completely
different from mine. I never knew what to expect. I was a brain, so
I was set aside.

Elana was in a different place, in the middle of the top of the pile.
And for her, fear of mediocrity (for instance, having to go down to
standard chemistry) seemed perhaps more distressing and humiliating than it would have been to be taunted as a brain. Part of this
had to do with the very academic school she attended. Elana didn't
have to sprinkle her language with "like's" to survive.

Students who had been on the lower end of the success scale
felt pressure to raise their views of themselves and would go to
lengths that even they saw as self-defeating to make themselves
look good. I asked Joel if he ever felt competitive urges connected
with writing. He quickly responded, "Not at all." And then with a
sheepish grin he said, "Yes, I do. I try to finish fast a lot, giving me
a feeling of superiority that I finished first. I used to do that on tests
also, but I realized how stupid that was." When I observed Joel write

an in-class essay, he worked with great concentration, seemingly oblivious to the chattering around him. He was the first finished with a draft. When he asked if anyone was ready for peer editing, he was in his moment of glory as he received impressed stares from all those still writing. If he had been in a basic writing class, the stares might have been hostile. If he had been at the top of the pile, he might have been seen as pompous, flaunting his abilities.

Peer pressure actively affected topic choices for writing. This is particularly true for students who felt vulnerable among their peers. Joseph said:

> It's been hard because I didn't know what my classmates would accept. The popular ones were really relaxed; I wasn't. I had to worry what I was gonna read in front of class. I'd worry about sounding awkward. I tried to stay away from jokes. I didn't know what kind of joke would work, and I'd get embarrassed if they didn't laugh. I usually tried to stay in the middle of acceptable. I wasn't really writing it for something that I would like. It was more something that they would like.

As a high school teacher I'm afraid I was insensitive to the precarious position of the successful student. Constructing a writing curriculum so that students weren't competing with one another would be a sensitive way to make our most proficient writers more comfortable. After being persecuted by "the destructors" in seventh grade, Kevin began to learn some of Peco's strategies and told of one his teacher used as well:

> The people that persecuted me in seventh grade, I get along with now because I know how they work, so I can move between groups as long as I don't flaunt it. Last year when we had to do writing it didn't affect me as much because my teacher was good about whatever you do is between you and your teacher. You could circulate it to your friends. It was more like working with your peers than against your peers.

Downplaying competition might also temper the "distancing," as Elana calls it, that seems to occur between students of different tracks. Chris was particularly sensitive to this;

> Some of my friends are in standard classes and have seen me as this great student, saying, "Well, Chris, you're going to go to Harvard; I'm going to community college," and they're giving me this all the time. We had a little award ceremony, and they say, "Oh, you're going to win ten awards," a vicious little circle of humor that's designed to cut. They're putting more pressure on me. I mean, my friends telling me I was better than them because I

had been a little bit more successful in school. I never thought it
made me a better person. And so, my friends having those school
problems in their lives made me separate.

Chris was not alone in talking about friendships that were lost
because of competition and resultant discomfort between the
successful and the unsuccessful students. Elana, Joseph, Peco, and
Kathy commented on it as well — the loss of a friend, the guilt of
"distancing." Distancing puts those who best handle standard English
in one group and then keeps the ideas that transfer among peers
separated, segregated, until one group knows less of how another
group thinks and feels. Does high school become a microcosm of
our stratified society, with its separation of classes, or does it per-
petuate it? Distancing did not seem to originate in students' disdain
for those who did less well; it seemed to arise from the discomfort
both groups felt from the complex dynamic of competition. (For
further discussion of peer pressure and writing, see chapter 5.)

How Students Coped with Struggle

In adolescent years, struggle in writing most often started in the
world that surrounded developing writers, and it intruded on their
inner interest and confidence in the writing process. But the
successful writers in this study were clever in inventing ways to
cope with the struggle they felt. Their biggest challenge was to
maintain control of their flagging concentration during the writing
process — to command their own attention.

One of their biggest obstacles was that the world around them
commanded more attention than the writing topics or audiences
that were dictated by assignments. Kathy talked of lack of interest
in topics:

> It's grudging, hard work in general, but there are other times when
> it's been really exciting, and I think that when it's been hard work
> is when I didn't have interest in the thing that we were writing
> about, some sort of mental block where I couldn't express what I
> was trying to say. I see myself often getting those.

Kathy was one of the few students who figured out that if she
could somehow connect herself with every assigned topic, it would
be easier to write.

> When I don't like the topic, I have to push myself. It's like I'm
> forcing myself to sit there. So now I try to get excited about topics,
> brainstorm, anything that I can think of, however remote, that sort
> of gets me closer to it.

Many students talked to me about the game of "psyching out" the teacher. Kevin said: "I'll see if the part she liked matches the part I like, so in the future I make sure and try to do that kind of thing again." When they saw it as something they did to get some control in the situation, a game in which they could be a winner, then they weren't so frustrated with writing for the teacher.

Teachers who encouraged helped. Once Elana began procrastinating, she had to work hard to keep her attention on her work. Her visualization of herself handing in her completed paper to encouraging Mr. O'Neill helped her when she was bogged down. We see another side of this coin, however, when Elana was trying to write for Mr. Shultz; she knew that the image of Mr. Shultz wouldn't inspire confidence, so she didn't even try that technique for his papers.

Making a distinction between "pleasing the teacher" and attending to audience may be important here. Expanding the conscious attention to admit viewpoints that are not what Piaget would call egocentric is an important part of development in a writer; nevertheless, if a student's own viewpoint is continually subjugated to that of the teacher, negative consequences ensue. Attending to their audience, learning ways of making their ideas accessible to their audience, was not what Chris and Elana were learning from Mr. Shultz. If Chris and Elana were learning anything from him (for instance, his attitude about colloquialism or style), it was through adversity. Teachers needn't be that weighty in the writers' context.

When Meg met rigorous teacher Ms. C., she began to use defensive strategies to get beyond her unaccustomed discomfort with writing:

> When I was writing, I was always aware she was going to react to the paper. I think fifty percent of the time I turned in a note at the end: "I wasn't sure about how to go about this assignment," or "After you have graded this can we talk about other approaches I should have used in writing this paper?" Total insecurity, but [those notes] it let me get the paper done.

She used defensiveness to feel control in the situation. Peco, like Elana, used a sort of revenge to maintain some feeling of control in his writing:

> I really dreaded eighth grade because we had a very horrible teacher. She had this overbearing attitude that wasn't gonna help us any at all. She was forcing topics on me, and then I just can't stand writing, so I'd put it off until the night before. I think that's affected me. And she gave an essay about a personal experience, and you wouldn't feel comfortable giving a personal essay to this teacher who runs her class as if she had a whip and chain. I did

one story about my friends getting into a root beer fight 'cause I figured this would really get her mad, or you'd write about some shallow experience, like "I went to the beach" or something just to pull it off. A past teacher had talked about never having a story end as a dream, so I would intentionally do that just to bother her. I'd keep up my vocabulary scores and test scores, so I could still get an *A* in the class even if I turned in shoddy writing, and she couldn't do anything about it.

Peco's and Elana's revenge was the most negative way that students learned to claim some control and ownership in their writing and to command the attention that they needed to get on with their work. It was negative because students were working without the benefit of a teacher; they were on their own, working against the teacher, in spite of the teacher. But in doing so, students still had some control in the situation, and, most important, they were conscious of what they were doing and why they were doing it. This consciousness was important.

Consciousness and Command of Attention

Successful writers were more conscious than were their unsuccessful counterparts of how context, teachers, parents, and peers caused them to struggle with writing. They were more likely to be angry than defensive, and they were more likely to make conscious decisions about what to do. Chris said, "I wasn't used to criticism." But when he felt it for the first time in eleventh grade, he was highly aware of its effect on him and was active in trying to figure out what to do about it. After my first interview with him, he told me that I had come along at a good time. "Here's somebody who actually wants to listen to me talk about my writing just when it is troubling." And as we worked together, he was active in making sense of what was happening to him, in seeing connections between what at first seemed disconnected. The writers I worked with needed to be conscious of what was going wrong for them in order to make changes. And unless criticism was long-term and unless it affected their self-confidence and self-esteem, they could pull themselves out of the mire of struggle when circumstances changed.

Chris, who had internalized Mr. Shultz's criticism, needed help in recognizing that he had done so. He needed to recognize that Mr. Shultz's voice lingered in his consciousness while drafting, so that he could have power over it, so he could dredge it up to use only when it was useful — in the later drafts of his papers. He needed help in seeing that he could suspend the voice until it served him.

Unfortunately, the teacher who sits in the corner of the student's consciousness is often an accumulated version of all the past teachers and an extension of the parent. Talking with students about our own writing process and about the ghost of teachers past that still sits on our shoulders, interrupting our attention when we need it the most, helps them to be conscious of what goes on for them during writing. Having students keep process journals (see Perl and Wilson, 1986) in conjunction with their writing will help them with this also. In addition, I tell my students: "Don't let my nagging teacher voice, or that of teachers past, be heard when you are thinking up ideas or writing your first draft. If you want to call it up as you revise and edit, I, as one of your teachers or past teachers, would be most pleased to be permitted into your mind." This seems to help writers to reclaim command of their attention.

One thing that successful writers were very conscious of was that there were two kinds of writing: the writing they wanted to do (which they didn't find themselves doing too often anymore) and the writing they didn't want to do. We've talked a lot about the writing they didn't want to do, so I'll end on a positive note with the writing they did want to do. Developing writers wanted to write when they felt some ownership in the process, in the content and in its form. They wanted to write when they could maintain command over the attention they needed for writing. By eleventh grade, Meg was recovered from her ninth-grade experience with Ms. C.

> I think despite all my gripes, I really do enjoy writing when it gives me an opportunity to pull some thoughts and ideas together, and I honestly do think that it serves a purpose. In this "Death and Dying" course and in Psychology, when we have to write papers, it served a much greater purpose because I was working through some things that were going on in my life. Even though it wasn't real creative, it was to a degree, but it was also analytical. It's still a struggle, but it's the more creative struggle, one that probably comes whenever you do anything artistic or creative.

Perhaps this chapter is ending just where it ought to be beginning. We have analyzed the problems, the struggles of the successful writer, but have only dealt peripherally with what needs to be done about them. At the end of the book, we'll examine the forty writers' good experiences with writing as a way of exploring writing curricula and teaching methods that engage and excite students.

Chapter Four

Elana Continued
When Life Gets Tough

The student's life affects all facets of the writing experience. When permitted, it gives pith and shape to the writer's material, and forms the voice that permeates the product. And when students write from their own uniqueness, we can be grateful; otherwise, we become mired in boredom as well as papers. Sometimes, however, the life outside school that shapes the writer, and hence the writing, may be connected with intense emotions and overwhelming pressures. As teachers, we need to understand what happens to writers and their writing process when life gets tough.

I had already done my three interviews with Elana when I met with her to do her last composing-aloud session. She was planning to write a summary of a book about Zionism for Mr. Shultz that had been due earlier that day but which she hadn't completed. In the first few minutes there were long silences, groans, and frantic pencil erasures. I watched with some concern over the next five minutes as things got worse. Seeing her distress, I turned off the tape recorder even though the researcher in me sensed I would be missing a good example of emotional disruption of writing. Relieved, Elana attempted to make sense of her struggle, and as she began to sort out the reasons for her distress, I turned the tape recorder back on. As she said, it all started with the death of her grandfather and ended in a serious writing block.

A Profile of Elana: Continued

It started with the death of my grandfather. That started triggering off these feelings that I have about me, and my parents, and Zionism. The [older] people in our [youth] group will be going to Israel. It started me thinking about my going to Israel in two years, and all of a sudden I got very frightened. And one of the persons choosing to [go] was my sister who I'm very close to, and the idea of me not seeing her, and of me having to make that decision in a few years. . . . it was really scary. It was very difficult for me to do a satirical paper on this topic. Everybody who critiques my paper says, "This is a very hard topic," and they don't know the half of it. I mean everyone else is doing something that's separate from them, but it has something to do with them, like fashion or computers. It's not something that they really have to put themselves into. I wanted to know more about Zionism, but I had no idea what I was getting myself into. He didn't let me change the topic when I told him.

If I am feeling terrible, I get distracted. That's why it's so easy to put the paper off, because the people come first. I'm thinking about something else, and I'm not thinking about the paper. Or if I have other work that is stressing, like a math test the next day, it is very hard to write a paper when you have a test the next day. I have real problems just focusing, and what happens, I get so preoccupied with trying so hard not to be preoccupied with these other things that it gets to sort of spaghetti, and it gets awfully messy, and it is a royal pain. When I don't care about it, I just want to get it done, not put that energy into making it really good.

There are kids in school who can separate their life from their work, and I admire those kids incredibly. No matter what problems they're having, they're still capable of sitting down and doing what needs to be done. But I can't do that. Whatever else is on my mind is a distraction. Technical stuff like chemistry and algebra are easier to do than stuff that I really have to delve into because when you do math, you have one formula, and you do multiple problems with the same formula. You don't have to think about it. But when you write something, your mind has to be constantly flowing, coming up with new ideas, new structures, not just to write them but to do it in an attractive creative manner. And you have to be thinking about all those things at once while you're writing. And it's hard work. And when I have some other things on my mind, I absolutely cannot write. I tried to write a paper for Mr. Schultz last night; the book summary was due today. It took me quite a while to read it, and I didn't even remember most of it when I was done.

After about five lines of writing, I stopped and said, "This is terrible! This is a terrible piece of writing. Okay, Elana, start again." I was preoccupied. It was a very busy, rather upsetting weekend, and the youth movement that I belong to is crumbling, losing people. And my summer is crumbling with it. Many people that I thought were going to be there are not going to be there. That will leave me with an awful lot of responsibility, some that I'm not gonna want.

I tried writing on the bus on the way back but gave it up. It wasn't because of a moving vehicle. I did it when I got home, but then it started happening again. It has never happened so that I've been so preoccupied that I haven't been able to write a paper at all; it might take me longer, and it might not be the best, but it never got so I couldn't write a word. I tried to do it. I get frustrated because I can't write which makes me unable to write even more. I'm so preoccupied, it doesn't come. I know I can do the work, but something is preventing me from doing it. I mean I have difficulty starting, but never before like this. I already resent the teacher, and it makes me resent the writing. So I said, "Elana, just put it all behind you, don't think about it, and just do the assignment." With Mr. O'Neill I would try to make that picture in my mind of handing it in. I didn't even bother with Mr. Schultz. I know that I'm a good student, and I'm a capable student, and first quarter I got a B with him, but by now my relationship with Mr. Schultz has deteriorated.

I want to talk to him so there can be an improvement, so I don't keep falling behind. I want him to understand that I'm not doing so hot, without his feeling that I am taking him for granted. I want him to say, "I understand; take the time you need." I don't think he's going to believe me, and I don't want to ask my mother to write him another note. She wrote him a note — it was over a week ago — explaining what was going on, and I was glad. But now I wish I could just explain to him what's going on. He would have to listen to me and believe me. He's going to be thinking, "You're bullshiting me; you're taking me for granted." He's going to say, "No, I gave you time, and you obviously didn't use it wisely, and I'm not gonna help you get out of this, and your grades are going to suffer."

I have these two little antennas sticking out from my head that pick up feelings around me. Sometimes I like those antennae, and sometimes they get in my way. Maybe I'm underestimating [him], but my antennae tell me it won't be that simple. Maybe it's my imagination, but I don't like the way he looks at me. I wanted to talk with him, but I didn't want to cry, and I was afraid I would. He doesn't call you "stupid" or "irresponsible, adolescent little brat." He doesn't do that, but I just really feel like when he looks at me, he's saying those words to me with his eyes. It makes it hard. He just looks away or nods, or makes a sound, like I don't know whether it's a yes or a no. And I have to go, "What was that?" And I feel stupid for having to ask. I only have four weeks left in this class, and I need to make it a good month. He was understanding when I told him the first time, with the note. I didn't expect it, but I have been avoiding talking to him again, and I have to. I don't want to get out of the work, I just need a little time, and it would help if I could change the topic.

Elana finally got the nerve to ask if she could change her writing topic again, but her antennae hadn't deceived her. Mr. Schultz wouldn't let her change her term topic from Zionism — "No exceptions." She continued to block in attempts at her assignment. She finally received a failing mark for the writing that she couldn't complete. Thus began a bout of writing struggle for Elana.

A Focal Look at Command of Attention

Elana felt pressure from three directions simultaneously. First the *topic* she was locked into writing about caused her distress, and it was linked to feelings of loss and distress in her *life situation* (sister leaving for Israel, grandfather's death, and the "crumbling" of her youth group). Further, her *audience*, Mr. Schultz, also brought her distress. She would have been able to concentrate on many things with room left over for her writing if it weren't for that "bottleneck" of the conscious attention. Emotions connected with her "preoccupations" disrupted her concentration not once but continually as she tried to accomplish her task. She lost control of her own attention. As Elana said:

> When you write something, your mind has to be constantly coming up with new ideas, new structures, not just to write them but to do it in a creative manner. And you have to be thinking about all those things at once while you're writing, and it's hard work. When you do math, you have a formula, and you do multiple problems with the same formula. You don't have to think in the same way. When I have some of these other things on my mind, I can't write.

Many of the forty students described "bouts" of having to write when life was distracting, and they all had that one symptom in common: constricted, belabored, distracted, overloaded conscious attention. It was important to requote Elana because she says what other writers only alluded to: writing is harder to do when you're upset than many other school activities because it's such a complex activity, one that needs focused attention. It's important for writing teachers to understand the dynamics of what goes wrong when someone is upset and trying to write.

Students talked about deaths in the family, about romantic problems, about being angry at friends or parents, or about disappointing them. There was only one group of writers who didn't seem to experience this kind of struggle while they were writing. The large majority of basic writers simply lent no importance to writing if things were falling apart in their lives. Iris said, "I just not gonna write if I'm upset. I just don't care enough 'bout writing." Aside from Carlos and maybe Zac, who gave some priority to writing in their lives, writing received slim attention when basic writers were troubled about things that *were* important to them.

The Distressing Life Situation and Writing Struggle

Brief Stress, Brief Struggle

Sometimes writing struggle is fairly short-termed and easily resolved. Doug said:

> At this private school, I would sit down and write and . . . get upset about the flack I got today. . . . We were writing a paper on *Nectar in a Sieve*. That paper took me longer to write than anything else I've done in my whole life because that day I had gotten a lot of trouble from seniors. The funny thing is I really cared what these seniors felt about me. I'd gotten thrown in a trash can, and then trash dumped all over me, and then thrown into the pond in the back. [They were having all the fun, and] I was just really upset. I went home and I sat and I tried to write that [paper]. And I wrote a sentence down, but I would stop and think . . . and would go, "OK what would be a good word to start off with that sentence," and I'd start thinking . . . zoom off to what happened. It was just beyond frustrating that I couldn't get it done, that I couldn't block it out. But if you have a lot of good friends and feel comfortable at school, and you're not hassled every day, you're not gonna be going home worrying about that while you're doing your homework.

Because Doug's distress had nothing to do with the topic or the audience for writing, attention for writing returned when he changed schools. That isn't to minimize the struggle that he went through at the private school. He was easily distracted from his writing. Before one composing-aloud session, he told me he didn't know if he was in the mood to write because he had lost his wallet containing the

$200 that his parents had given him for food and expenses while they were away. I asked him to give it a try, and he was right; that event did have an effect on his command of attention. A portion of his protocol:

> The introduction will have more than this minimum, but these sentences will ... great ... let's get this down. Attitude and effect .. s .. on the reader down first ... um ... on the reader. Ok ..... attittude desperation effects on the reader create sympathy ..... effects .... desperation .. (groan) ...... *I wish I was back on the beach with my girlfriend and wallet right now* ... um, effects on the reader .. desperation and how to check .... and attitude ... can't believe this ... have to have ..... oh my god. I have to ..... twelve ..... forty .... effects on the reader .... effects on the reader .... um let's see .... tone and attitude. I'm just sitting here giving the same thing .. hm ..... Well I saw someone that was desperate .... sympathy effects of the reader sympathy ..... and ..... and a new knowledge .. of . the .... lifestyle .... Hm .... *I wish I hadn't lost my wallet.* I really wish I hadn't ... hm ...... huh ok ... first sentence.

And on Doug plodded, managing three sentences in the half hour before he asked to end the session. We have all had times when we couldn't concentrate on something due to strong emotions linked with something very different from what we were trying to accomplish. It's very upsetting, especially when important deadlines must be met. Nevertheless, the effect isn't a long-term one. Reversal of this form of struggle happens when the problem causing it is resolved. When Doug met me for the next session, he announced that someone had returned his wallet and money. He had regained command of his attention.

Serious Distress Due to Topic or Audience

Struggle is more apt to persist if the emotion is linked with the writing topic or the audience. If Elana had been able to change topics, to write about something far from the source of her distress, far from the term-long topic of Zionism that she had chosen, she might have been able to focus her attention on the subject. Other students reported times when both the topic and the audience they had to write for were distressing, threatening. Kevin had been asked as a representative of his youth group to deliver a speech to the congregation about a proposed split in his church; his father was the minister in that church.

> I have had upsetting experiences, but then when I sit down to

write, I can usually shut everything else out so that it doesn't interfere. As soon as I put the writing away then I'm back upset again. But this one time it didn't work. Our church was having a split up. I had to write a five-minute speech. About two-thirds of them [the congregation] were attacking my family and criticizing them. I felt like two-thirds of them hated me. I was terribly upset. I would write and tear it up and throw it away and start again, over and over and over. . . . I would just reach a block and get absolutely terrified. I wasn't thinking clearly and so that didn't help. I had to say everything just perfect or they would turn it around. I had to write it and then weigh it for its impact on each audience and see how they would take it. If it didn't [work] then I had to go back and reweigh the whole schmear over and over and over. I turned off my lights, and I had to work by the light that was coming through my window just so I wouldn't have anything at all distracting. Even having the radio in the background was grating that day. I wound up turning everything off and just shutting it all out. Nobody was gonna come into my room because I was being a holy terror. I just started writing like a robot almost.

Kevin had to find a way to command his attention, so he could get beyond the specter of the angry two-thirds of the congregation that had been silencing him — a discipline that Elana and others envied.

With Elana and Chris, a critical teacher entered into the mix, causing both of them to begin to feel bad about themselves as writers. This was a new feeling for both, and no doubt it was further complicated by what was going on in their lives. When Elana was feeling good about herself in ninth grade, Ms. C., another critical teacher, didn't upset her. Her father had let Ms. C. know that Elana's life was a little rough at the time, and she also felt she was operating from what she termed "a pretty strong core." Elana said, "I didn't let her get to me as much as [she did to] others." Meg was one of the "others," and her situation was parallel to Elana's: the same critical teacher, Ms. C., and the same pressures that occur when parents divorce. Meg said:

In eighth grade I had Ms. C. for social studies, and that name strikes terror in the hearts of so many. She taught an excellent course, extremely challenging, quite a change from the previous year. I learned a lot, and I did well in class. Then in ninth grade I had Ms. C. again. Something drastic occurred. We were doing a different type of writing, and I was getting C's from her when I was getting A's [last year]. She came up to me one day within the first month of school and said, "Are you getting bad grades now because you didn't like kids hassling you for getting the A's before?" She just wanted to know what was going on, but her comment totally devastated me [because it wasn't the kids].

I can remember just breaking into tears after she left. See, my dad left and mom was totally devastated. So I held her together, and then in ninth grade she started to pull herself together, and it was okay for me to fall apart. I managed to be absent an entire month after that, a solid month. The longer I stayed away the harder it was to go back. I wasn't functioning. After that I had "Ms. C. Sundays" working on papers with a parent. It was the first time I was seriously challenged. I don't know whether it was worth the agony that it caused my parents, me throwing temper tantrums, screaming, bitching at everybody. My emotions were all screwed up. I couldn't think clearly about my mother and father. How could I start straightening out my thoughts on the writing that was half as complex? To write a good paper I have to get into the mood and mean what I'm saying. So I think my mind was all jumbled, and I wasn't really able to get down and concentrate on writing.

Often students could handle one stress at a time, but when more than that hit, writing was caught in the middle and struggle ensued. Though in ninth grade Elana managed with her "strong core" and different kinds of support, Meg had her "strong core" depleted the year before. But when life got tough for Elana in eleventh grade, her resilience wasn't there. Other eleventh-graders told stories of the "challenging" Ms. C., but they were able to perceive her assignments as just that, challenging. The state of the writer's "core" (the state of self-confidence and resilience) seems to be the fourth variable that interacts with the extent of distress produced by disturbing life situation, audience, and/or topic to determine whether a writer can concentrate on a writing task. If only one of these variables was stressed, the writer seemed to be able to keep at a task, but if two or three things caused distress, then more serious struggle ensued.

Lilly, a young Vietnamese refugee, wrote about a painful subject and wrote for a distressing, though ironically sympathetic, audience. Lilly's teacher knew that language was still difficult for her, so she asked Lilly to write about something that she knew about—a wise approach for the teacher to take because it lessened the chance of cognitive overload by allowing Lilly to write from her own experience. She asked Lilly to write about Saigon before her departure, but each time Lilly tried to write, she thought of her last few minutes with her father. The topic, Saigon, took her mind irretrievably in that direction. Finally she resolved the problem by writing about the incident to which her mind automatically went. She described her leave-taking from her father as he put her on a bus to "join a boat of people to freedom." She wrote this fairly easily, probably because it focused on what her attention directed her to anyway. Her teacher was struck by the strength of the writing, and with the very best intentions, read her paper to the class. Lilly described the experience:

> She read it out loud, and everyone kind of feel sad, and girls crying about it too. It touch feeling inside. I don't want to hear that paper again. I started crying. Girls have feelings sad, trying to reach out and comfort you. No. I really don't like it. I don't want to cry in front of anybody. The boys said, "Good paper, congratulations." Girls have soft feelings, say, "It was really good paper, Lilly, but it was sad."

For months thereafter, Lilly was caught between wanting to write about what she knew, her own experience, but being upset about the possibility of exposing herself again in front of the class. Before the public reading, Lilly had overcome her first obstacle by writing about the source of distress connected with the topic Saigon. When she focused her attention on what was disrupting her concentration, the writing came easily, like a catharsis. Had Elana been able to write about why satire was distressing (for instance, in a process journal) or about the death of her grandfather, to a trusted audience (for instance, in a workshop or similar setting), her struggle might have dissolved.

"When There's No One There But My Notebook": The Cathartic Moment

> Sometimes I'm in these moods, when my emotion's exaggerated, something teenage, and I get really inspired. Things come into my mind. When there's no one there but my notebook, I pick it up and write it down, and it's like there is someone there. I write a lot of poetry, believe it or not. Not fantastic, but it's kind of an outlet for some emotions, not necessarily upset, but just when my emotions are going, when my adrenaline's pumped up, or when I'm very angry, when I'm very happy ... very something.

Like Doug, half of the successful students that I worked with used writing to their benefit when emotions became too strong to handle. Fred was the only basic writer who reported using writing in this way—a one-time poem.

> My girlfriend and I got departed. The next day, I think, I wrote that poem. It was about feelings of togetherness, what happened, and about it. My best friend is going out with her. That's why I wrote the poem. It would have been harder to just go out and tell her this. She liked it, but it didn't matter. She just said it was

sweet. But now the hard times are over, don't have to think no more.

The writers who used writing to deal with short-term distress were often taken by surprise with the urge to write. There seemed no other route open to them to cope with anger, depression, sadness, loss, or confusion. They wrote with a sense of urgency, on whatever was available, and reported that it brought clarity and a sort of purging.

Many successful writers wrote unsent letters as Elana did to her sister, but most of those letters found their way to the scrap basket, their purpose served.

I asked students what gave them the idea to write when they were upset, and most answered that they had done something like it when they were doing journal writing in school. Many, however, reiterated what Kathy said: "I couldn't write anything too personal in those." Nevertheless, journal writing seemed to become a model that was very useful in later years. It was a time when students were given license to write about their life and its events. Though most students who used this cathartic sort of writing reported it as a rare occurrence, for several, writing had become a habitual way of making sense of upsetting things in their lives.

Writing to Make Sense of Life

Of the forty writers, Heidi, Vance, Portia, Kathy, and Tom used writing over extended time to deal with events in their lives which they needed to understand or get control over. Kathy started this when she was very young:

> In third or fourth grade we wrote journals. One of the reasons I was ridiculed in that school by the kids was because I was too open and personal, and that wasn't always so good. Like I wrote about how I was unhappy with those kids. It's like I exposed myself. I started not handing it in, but kept writing it. If I'm trying to write something down about myself, I can look at it and say well this is why I'm like this. Writing helped. I got better — writing became the friends I didn't have. Now I know how to talk to friends instead of the pen and notebook. It was like practice.

Unlike Kathy, the other students who used writing to deal with life stress didn't begin doing so until adolescence, but like her, most of them had picked up the habit as a result of journal writing in school. For some of these students, writing was the only help they received.

As Heidi began to tell me of her history with school and writing, and as the tale of her school changes and life upheaval spilled out, I was amazed at her equanimity and clarity. Her life reminded me of two soap operas, one in the North with her father and another in the South with her mother. Writing was the one tool she had to make sense of it.

> Sometimes you just can't depend on people to tell everything to, and sometimes they've got problems of their own to tell, but there's always paper and pencil out there that you can turn to, it helps you out of a lot of anxieties. I keep a sort of notebook for all the poems I write and a journal. It's not like a daily journal, like I got up this morning and brushed teeth, not like that. It's like if I'm really upset or something like that I sit down and I'll write everything that's going through my mind — the thoughts and stuff about how I feel if I got into an argument or something like that. I would sit down and write about whether I thought it was fair or not. When my boyfriend and I broke up, I wrote a couple of poems. I write short stories in it about things in the past, change them a little though. I wrote a short story in it about my mother and when I was seven, that was really hard. One night she came home from work and a man came. I don't know who the man was, but it must have been some man who was crazy about my mom. I remember waking up and hearing her screaming at him and telling him to get out. When I came to the front room, she told me to go back to bed. The next morning when I woke up my grandparents and everybody were there and the police. I didn't know what had gone on then. She had taken five lethal doses of sleeping pills. It got too tough for her. She was in a coma for three days. I was sent North. In the story I had her die, but I kind of wish I had wrote it the way it really happened because I think it's neat that she made it through and could show her strength. When I write the personal things that have happened to me, I don't stop because it's all in my head, and I want to get it out. I notice that you don't have to carry the weight inside you anymore. A lot of people scream and yell, but I like to write and get it out.

Every English teacher is aware of the controversy that goes on over the personal nature of journal writing, but after listening to the writers who used writing to deal with the upheaval in their lives, I see that encouraging the use of writing as a way to make sense of life might be one of the most important gifts that we can give our students. Privacy can be promised by allowing students to write a certain number of what I used to call "Private Entries" amidst other journal writing they might be doing on a variety of self-selected topics. Students were allowed to staple or tape pages closed, to put a star on the top of the page so that I wouldn't read it, or to show me the page from a distance so that I could see that they had been writing and could give them credit for the writing before they took it home.

Journal writing should be one of many kinds of writing that we encourage our students to do. Portia's experience will make a useful conclusion to this section because it shows us both how academic writing can be tough when a student's mind is elsewhere and how personal writing can be useful for making sense of life.

> Freshman year was about the worst year of my life. That was the year my father died. In the beginning of the year he was diagnosed, and then he was getting worse and worse, plus that had to be the year that I was really insecure. I didn't fit in. All those things just piled on top of this one year. When I tried to write, I would feel like I was just babbling on, and it wasn't making any sense. I'd get really frustrated, and I wouldn't want to go over it for mistakes. I just didn't want to deal with it. I just hid out in my room. I was in advanced placement classes, and it was really hard. We read a lot of good stuff, but it all bothered me so much. I had a really hard time writing stuff 'cause it was hard to get down the ideas that I had. I could analyze it, but I couldn't say it on paper. I only got a *C* on a *Lord of the Flies* paper 'cause it just wasn't right. I probably put it off until the night before. Every paper I wrote was really bad. I liked the class, but I just couldn't handle it. I remember wanting my father around. He was an English teacher and had always helped me, and I missed that. So like on *The Lord of the Flies* paper and others, I guess I just avoided them. I hid out in my room and missed a lot of school. I would come like maybe one day, and then I was just so depressed and so out of it, but I made it through. My cousin gave me a journal when my father was declining. I really didn't understand a lot of things. She says, "Just write anything in it that you want, and it will help you." And it did, 'cause most of the time there wasn't anyone to talk to 'cause they were so occupied with my father, so I just kind of talked to this book. I still keep it. I write something in it just to get it out, 'cause I want to see it down on paper.

The Teacher's Role When Life Gets Tough for Students

> My teachers were really kind. I remember my social studies teacher. When I was going one day a week, he said, "You gotta get your act together, just start going to school." He wasn't yelling at me, but he wasn't saying it in a passive voice either. "I know it's really hard, but you've made it, your father died, but you're still living. So kick yourself in the pants and just get going." Nobody else had done that to me. It didn't work right away, but it started to. And I got through.

Portia's social studies teacher did two things. He let her know that he cared about what was going on for her, and he let her know that he trusted her to find the strength to pull herself out of it. This combined with her journal made all the difference. It would be nice if there was a teacher available for every student when life gets tough.

If students feel that a teacher is approachable, they will usually come forth with solutions to the distress-related struggle they are having with writing. Perhaps Ms. C. and Mr. Shultz couldn't see ways to be flexible and approachable while maintaining their applaudable high expectations. Let's look at some tactics teachers can use to help students get beyond distress without jeopardizing the standards they wish to maintain and without letting students lose their writing confidence.

First teachers need to be able to identify distress-related struggle, and that isn't always easy because the symptoms can be similar to those of recalcitrance. Missed deadlines, worried looks, grumpiness and irritability, groaning and moaning, absences, and/or grades that drop may be clues that something is going wrong for the writer. In the end we can only depend on instincts before asking: "Is there something going on for you right now that is making this writing hard?" or, depending on the student, less intrusively, "I notice that you're having trouble concentrating on your writing. Let me know if you think of a way that I can help you get beyond that. I might have some ideas for making it easier for you. I'll be in my room during sixth hour or after school." Parents can help pave the way for students if they recognize that times are tough. Perhaps teachers should request that parents let them know if something upsetting is going on for students as a regular part of the "Back-to-School Night" ritual.

One of the things that impressed me the most about the forty students that I talked with was that they seemed to have a sense of what would make writing better for them, and usually it wasn't to get out of work. With the exception of con-artists George and John Doe, students understood that teachers needed to make them accountable; in fact, most of them felt more control in their lives if they knew how and when they needed to be accountable. They just needed to find a way to get beyond the time pressure, and then they often knew strategies that would permit them to fend for themselves.

In a writing workshop setting, where students can make their own decisions about topic and audience, distress-related writing problems often resolve themselves. Some students, however, described traditional teachers who were willing to negotiate deadlines, topics, or audiences so that they could manage the distress connected with their personal lives. When teachers were willing to do this, students were able to write without struggle once their distress was resolved. When teachers were not flexible, a longer-term struggle often ensued. Writers began to feel bad about their inability to get the work done by their usual standards. With lowered confidence, students often began to see the teachers as a threat, setting off the chronic kind of writing struggle that pursued them through subsequent years.

Given the distractions and stresses that adolescents have to deal with, teachers take preventative measures when they make sure that students write about things that interest them. Alice said:

> I just can't think of a lot of things at once. I have to set my mind on one thing and do it, and then I can go on. That's a reason why it's hard for me to write papers sometimes, 'cause I'll have to write them, but my mind will be thinking of something else. I can't think of what I'm writing, and I can't get a lot of expression in it because I'm not really thinking about it right then. I want to be thinking about something else, not what happened in World War II or whatever the paper I'm writing about is. It's easier to write on a topic I like because it is easy to fix my mind on an interest and keep it there.

As in Elana's case, students may need to be allowed to change their paper topic, or in severe cases like Portia's they may need to negotiate changes in what is expected of them until they have the concentration to return to what the rest of the class is doing. Other students may need to be allowed to write for a different audience than they are presently writing for. In the next chapter, we'll see how Lisa had trouble writing for an audience of her peers. Teachers might check to see if audience might be the problem: "If you want, you can write this paper for Mark (a peer whom the teacher guesses the student will trust); he can make sure that you've done it and that you have proofread your last draft. Then we'll talk about who will read the next paper." If students usually work in groups, we might ask a distressed individual to select a group of students that will make up a comfortable audience. Or we may be willing to have them write for a limited period of time being graded on quantity rather than quality, just showing us a certain number of full pages of writing. For most students these can be very temporary measures. In traditional classrooms, a contract like the one shown in Figure 4–1 might help in this kind of negotiation and might help the student become more conscious of the circumstances that are getting in the way of writing. Raised awareness will lower the chances of the long-term struggle with writing that Daly (1975, 1978, 1985) terms "writing apprehension."

Figure 4–1
The "When Things Aren't Going Well" Contract

If your present assignment comes at a particularly difficult time for you because of upsetting things that are going on in your life, let's set up a contract. As your teacher, it is important to me to make sure that you have a comparable writing experience to what your classmates are having even though you aren't feeling like writing. You may vary two of the following three aspects of your assignment, in case those are adding to your distress. Remember, try not to put the deadline off too far because we'll be doing other writing that may back up on this assignment. A delayed deadline may be just what you need, but then again it may add more pressure in your life instead of diminishing it. If you can think of something that will help you write that I haven't suggested, we can talk about it. In any case, we'll confer on this before signing.

New Deadline:

New Audience:

New Topic:

Because it's important to me that you help yourself get beyond what's bothering you, I want you to try something for me in exchange for my willingness to make this contract with you. Often when people write about what's upsetting in their lives, they can come to terms with it or decide on some active thing to do to reduce that distress. I'd like you to try this out. Find a time in class or wherever when you can think and write nonstop for ten-minute blocks. Find a time to do three such sessions. You can do them one after another with a quick break in between, or you can do them whenever or wherever you can fit them in. In the first session, ask yourself, "What's causing this writing to be difficult for me?" In the second: "What's going on for me that distracts me from the school work that I have to get done?" In the last ten-minute block, ask yourself, "What can I do about it?" You need only flash these in front of my eyes (unless of course you want me to read them). After I have seen that you have done these three seven-minute free writes, you may either destroy them or put them in a private journal.

Student Signature: _____

Teacher Signature: _____

If it's any consolation, teachers have it easier than the parents who live with adolescents who are in distress. Kevin described himself as such a "holy terror" that no one would have entered his room, and Meg talked about throwing temper tantrums, screaming, and bitching at everybody on her "Ms. C. Sundays." As a parent of two adolescents myself, these students' statements bring up memories of my own. (My daughter once had to write a paper proving something that Emerson wrote, using quotes from Thoreau. It was due on the day after the girl that sat next to her in algebra had committed suicide. I certainly wasn't isolated from her agony.) And if the cause of the stress is connected with the family, parents are under tremendous pressure themselves. Portia's mother had a heavy burden: a dying husband and Portia curled up in her room with the agonies of adolescent insecurity, with grief over her father, and with a paper on *The Lord of the Flies* due the next day—all the more reason for the teacher to intercede.

I would like to conclude this chapter with Vance's description of his basketball journal. My guess is that something very similar to Vance's basketball journal might have been just what Portia needed to write in place of the *Lord of the Flies* paper. Vance wrote and read on a subject that obsessed him. I imagine some guided reading and writing would have hastened Portia's recovery and restored some of the self-confidence that she lost during that stressful period (she dropped out of AP English for the rest of her high school career).

One of the values of qualitative research is that it often offers up discrepant data. When Vance started talking about his basketball journal, I knew I was hearing something I hadn't heard before. When students did cathartic writing, they often dumped emotion on the page. They didn't ponder it unless they read it later, sometimes years later. When the heightened emotions were spent, the purpose for the writing was over. What was remarkable was that Vance extended the use of this genre even though it wasn't required by school—and he took it another step.

Writing can be a source of relief, like I do with basketball. I don't care for poems too much, probably 'cause of the macho image or whatever. I keep a sort of diary, not a diary, but I write down, kind of mental preparation for the game. And when I do bad or play well, I write that down. Then I can look back at it and say, "Hey, I don't want to do that again." I use that a lot. I usually do it after a game, so I'm feeling really good if I played well—that's the good part of it or if I played really bad. . . . I just kind of sloppily write it down and date on a piece of paper. I have a folder with that and all kinds of memorabilia, rosters, and stuff like that. I remember last year after one game when a boy was just getting me frustrated, I'd just write down what happened or something. I look back at it and say, "Hey, that was not enjoyable, that situation," and I write to figure it out. I can see the situation clear later. I've had a few things to say about my basketball coach, too. Right at the time I write, "Hey, this guy's out to get me," but I usually don't write emotion stuff too often. Maybe again 'cause it's not the man thing to do, but for basketball I take a different approach because it hasn't been easy for me. I love the game so much, 'cause I love to play, so right now I have to mentally figure out what I have to do next year to play. I write down my goals, plans. I read about basketball too, like the guys in pro-basketball, how those guys get so tough. I don't know if they know what they are doing, but I can see how tough it is for somebody to play like that ... a lot more mentally than physically. There is going to be a really good team next year and there is not going to be that many spots, so you have to work physically and work mentally by writing stuff down. Like priorities. The coach says family first, religion, beliefs, your school, and then basketball. I'm not sure where it is in my priorities; I do well in school, but I would rather play basketball than go to school.

Though others reported emotion-based writing, or "getting it out," Vance went further. He combined cathartic writing with reflection and analysis. Perhaps he has taken the journal genre to its origins. One has to stretch it a bit to compare Thoreau's *Walden* to Vance's basketball journal, but there are parallels. Vance used it to defuse emotion, to ponder what he saw around him, to reflect, to analyze past occurrences, to formulate theories about life and priorities, to plan for the future, to be proactive instead of reactive in his life. This is close to but a step beyond the useful, though limited, cathartic writing that others reported. The basketball journal may be a missing link, a way that teachers can encourage students to combine strong purpose, thought, and voice-shaping emotion while letting them write about what is very important to them. Most important, this kind of writing empowers students at the deepest level. This is a genre that schools might and sometimes do encourage, a kind of writing that can truly have an important place in some students' futures.

Chapter Five

Lisa
The Powerful Presence of Peers

Peers—they matter more than we think. Or at least they matter more than I thought during my years in the secondary classroom. In starting this research, I wanted to believe that peer groups were the answer, the answer to finding a compelling audience for student writing *and* an answer to the writing teacher's work load. After talking to Lisa and the thirty-nine other developing writers, I still believe that peer involvement in writing is an answer, but I found that structuring it must be done very carefully. When Lisa and others were comfortable with peer involvement, they showed increased motivation and increased willingness to take risks, but when peer presence was threatening, young writers stopped taking the risks necessary for growth. I'll start with a worst-case scenario: Lisa will help us understand the potentially damaging power of peers in the writing classroom. From there we'll look at how peers can be both inspiration and audience for compelling writing, both in and out of response and editing groups.

When I first saw Lisa, she sat in full cheerleader's regalia, chatting animatedly with three friends in the back of Ms. M.'s writing classroom. Each successive meeting with her defied that original peer-confident/cheerleader stereotype. Lisa was clever in keeping her vulnerability hidden, but it was there and it profoundly affected her writing.

A Profile of Lisa

I didn't used to write very well, but I'm getting into it now, and I think that is making a difference. Back then [in early elementary school] I wrote what I liked and I drew pictures. In first or second grade I was writing something, and I wanted to erase it, but we didn't have erasers, so I crossed out and kept on writing. It's funny because I can remember saying to my friend, I can't remember who the friend was, but I remember I was mad because I couldn't get the eraser to erase it and make it look nice. I liked the teacher; she brought a goat in one day. We had to write some lines for *Alice in Wonderland*. We got to write one scene in our own words. And I found dolphins really interesting, so whenever we had an assignment to write about anything, I would always write about a dolphin. I knew a lot about them, so I could.

I guess I wasn't a very good writer in later elementary school. The teacher told me I could read fast, and so I said, "Why am I not in *Dimensions*?" And she said because I didn't have good sentence structure. I could read as good as the people that were in *Dimensions*, but I couldn't write as well as them. It was the highest reading group. I was practically in the lowest. I wanted to get up there, but I couldn't. I felt really bad about writing then because when you're in a lower group I guess you naturally feel you're stupid. That had a part to play in my feeling bad about writing. We had to write sentences or answers to the workbook questions, and I would just answer the questions but not in correct sentences.

Then there was a competition thing. We had about a month to write it. They paired me up with a boy I didn't even know. I just started writing about a turtle, which wasn't anything, so at that point I decided I wouldn't hand it in. The person with the best paper would go into the newspaper. I wasn't good enough, so I didn't even try. I found out what day it was due, and that day when I woke up, I told my mother that I didn't feel good. She didn't make me go to school. That was the only time that I really played hooky because I really felt uncomfortably about writing. Other people were going to decide whether mine was good enough to go into the paper. Right now I don't mind if someone else reads it, but back then I did because I was more unsure of my writing. In sixth grade my penmanship was bad, and so I started out in the second-to-worst penmanship group. We were put into three groups. People who were very neat . . . people who were okay, and people who were sloppy, and I was in the okay. By the end of the week I was finally in the neat group, and I felt good about that because all my friends wrote neat. In seventh grade, my first year in the big school, I wasn't a very good writer at all. I had a teacher Ms. Josephs. I did not like her. One time we had to write a poem, and I really thought it was good. I was really upset because she didn't. I could tell that she didn't like me because everything would be wrong. I was talking about how the coral reef wasn't there because of pollution. There was always a "You're not doing this right." I didn't really want to work on it, so I stopped and I got a D+. She didn't like anything I was writing about. So I guess I sort of rebelled, and stopped writing. So whenever I got a paper back, that was proving I was a bad student. I would feel really bad because everyone would be asking me what I got, and it was really embarrassing to tell them the grade. In the beginning I was trying to do good, but after that I got a D+, you would say, "Well, I didn't really want to do it anyways." I guess I know now why I don't like it when people criticize my writing.

I did better in eighth grade because I liked Ms. Dussel, and I learned a lot from her. I had C's and a few B's on book reports about Anne Frank, so I was doing better. And I got a B+ on a paper for social studies. This year was when I started being really serious about writing. I'm doing really good. My grades are going up, getting prepared for college. I want to be a marine biologist and study sea mammals and how they pertain to human life. And I want to write a book about the sea. I guess I'm learning that I'm going to have to use it [writing] when I'm older.

I was going through my drawers and cleaning them out [a few years ago], and I said why am I keeping this poem, the one that Ms. Joseph hated, if it is so bad? I threw it away. This summer, I was trying to remember some lines from it. I was with "my brightly colored angel fish, floating by the coral," and then I said something about now there is no brightly colored angel, there is no coral reef left. I was really happy writing back then, and I was thinking about how good a grade I was going to get on it. I was happy other times when I was writing about dolphins.

This year I had a fight with my best friend, so I'm much more into my studies. For the first half of the summer we had a job, but when we came back to school we weren't talking or anything. I would talk to my mother about what was happening. I guess for the first week she listened, but then she said, "Why are you letting this affect you?" I started thinking, "Why am I letting her rule my thinking?" I didn't know what I was upset about, so I went upstairs, and I just started writing why that had happened. I felt better about it. I reread it and I saw that was probably partly my fault. I guess that was a good idea to write it down. I never got a chance to tell her because she was always with her [new] best friend.

I'm a cheerleader, and she's a cheerleader, and her [new] best friend now is a cheerleader. I began to do more school work to get my mind off five years of friendship not anymore. I started getting into grades and doing really well. I guess I'm sort of feeling better about myself because she did worse than me in algebra. I found out she had a *C* for a quarter grade and I had an *A*. And she always did better than me in school and in sports, so it made me think, I am not that dumb, so why feel so bad? This year I have changed. I'm more open. I was always letting her talk. Now I'm the only one—no one else is going to be saying this for me.

In Ms. M.'s class [this year] I get to choose about what I want to write about, but what I want to write about I can't in that class. I can't write about the sea because she makes you read it out loud, and I'm embarrassed because I don't think people have the same views as I do. I guess I'm embarrassed about something I like. This year I've learned different ways to express my thoughts better, so it's easier for me to write a paper. Before I didn't even know how to put words together, and I hated writing. [Now] I pass in a paper and wait to see what I get for a grade, and I didn't start dreading it when teachers would assign a paper. Before I didn't know the difference between papers, but now that there's different types of papers, and ways to write them, it is easier. If I have a topic I know I want to write about, then I can, but if I don't, I can't write about anything during that class. I'll either talk to my mother or my friends about a good topic, or read a newspaper. Then I [can] go back and write in class. It's hard to think of a topic when you only have forty-five minutes and then start right in. I keep starting papers, and I don't like the idea so I'll either crumple it up and throw it away, or I talk to Barbara or Marie or John [my friends that I sit near], and then if they can't [help me] figure out one, then we'll just talk, unless they're writing. Ms. M. is wonderful. She sometimes helps me on my rough draft, but if I can't get her because she's helping a lot of other people, then Marie, or John, or Barbara. I'll ask if this is good, or if I should switch it around.

When you have to read your paper out loud, and I think I've written the paper well, then I'll volunteer, but if I don't think it's good then I won't volunteer. I volunteered to read a literary criticism because I thought I did a good job. I'm not that good of friends with everyone in the class, so I get embarrassed having to read it. I feel like they're thinking, "She can't write." So my face'll get really red, I'll start moving my feet, or bouncing up and down or something, or else I'll start hiding my face, or laughing, or talking really softly. It's happened this year because we've had to read them out a lot . . . Oh God . . . I can remember now, I read something, but I don't remember the paper it was, and then she started giving hers [criticism] and then people were putting in theirs, and then I started to get a little embarrassed. I started agreeing with everyone's decisions just to get out of that situation. If I'm sure of what I'm doing, I'll start asking questions, "Well, should I have done it this way?" or "Should I change this?" What I most hate is when someone will read their paper out, and it will be really, really good, and then she'll call on me to read mine. I'll have so many corrections to do while other people don't.

But then . . . God, I remember the paper . . . it was a paper that I did on Killer Whales, and she had me read that one out loud. I was very embarrassed because I thought people would think I was weird or something for talking about whales. She'll call on you, so I had to read it, and when I was reading it, I was reading it so they couldn't . . . I was leaving out words so they couldn't tell I was talking about a Killer Whale. So no one understood what I was reading, and I just got more embarrassed, and I just said, "I'm not reading out loud." I don't know why I've liked them [whales] so much because most animals people like are not with the sea. When I go to Maine, I'm there to pick up shells or to look at the ocean. They'll say, "Well did you see any cute guys?" and I'll say, "Yea!" It's hard for me to explain to them that I was really into the ocean. They won't understand the way I feel and think I'm weird for doing a paper on that type of animal.

[Yesterday] she said, "Lisa, you will read your paper tomorrow." I guess that's what made me not able to write it. Then I didn't have anything. I guess it is when I know I have to read it out loud and share it with people that I am intimidated and afraid. I don't want to talk out loud in that class because some of the people in there, well one of the people in there, some of the people in there I don't like, and others, I don't really know anyone in that class at all. I don't mind in my short-story class, and in other classes I am more willing to speak out. When I understand, like I can write in almost any atmosphere, so it's not like I have to have a quiet room or a noisy room. Like, if I was writing a paper on the sea and the dolphins. I know how to put it in words. But if I'm writing about something that I don't really know, then I really have to think a long time what to put where and how to form the sentence and everything.

We can't use the word "got," and we can't use colloquialisms, so you got to avoid them. It takes longer and everything 'cause you have to find the appropriate word, the correct words and the grammar. I'm not very good at grammar. I'll read it over and over, and if I see that I have the word "got" in it ... This is going to sound weird, but I've gotten more conscious of how I'm talking 'cause I'll look around, and I'll hear people using words like "adamantly opposed" or something like that, and then I'll start looking for other words.

The opening paragraph has always been the hardest for me. If you're doing a paper on a sea animal, then you have to watch what you're doing. As you're reading it out loud someone's going to say, "That's a weak hooker." I don't like people criticizing my writing. So I guess it's from that time in seventh with Ms. Josephs. But my attitude started changing. Now in Ms. M.'s class it's really changed. I guess I've started to feel better about myself and my capabilities. And sports has changed me also. I'd tell my father, "Well, what's the sense of me trying to race her when I know that she's going to beat me," and he said, "Well, how do you know that she's going to beat you if you don't put your all into it?" So how do I know if I'm not going to get a good grade if I don't put my all into it?

I've felt stupid a lot, I guess. I noticed this yesterday at Student Council meeting. The way I was talking, it was so people could understand, you know, not ... "I feel that my position on this is ... " This school seems so different than other schools and more high class than other places. The people that talk that way are the brains or they have money, and I'm not a brain, but I'm not poor. At Student Council meetings I felt inferior. I have been focusing on my words and then theirs. So I just said, "Well, I'm just going to say what I want to say and that will be it." But then I was thinking how they're going to say, "Well, she knows what she's talking about, but she's not saying it in the right words." It made me more reluctant to speak out again. If you don't know big words, then that's other people's problems, not yours. I'm trying not to let things like that bother me. I used to ask my ex-best friend who had advanced classes everything about a paper, but now I have to pick my own topics, and I have to write it by myself. So it's me now, not her and me, her and my writing. As you get older, you become more your own person.

I guess I'm coming out of my shyness. I'm growing up and seeing that you're going to have to say your opinion. There is always going to be somebody who is going to do better than me. I can say I'm doing better than my brothers which is helping me. I haven't failed a course at all, and both my brothers have in junior high school and high school, and in college I think, but not me. So I guess I'm not as dumb as I used to think I was. I'm real serious about my studies; that'll pay off for me when I want a career. My job will mean more to me because it will be something that I wanted, not something that was the easiest major and the easiest thing to get a good grade in. I'll be able to write my papers in college. I think I'll do fine. It's like a chore, but maybe when I get older, it will mean more. Because when I'm thirty or forty, I'm going to write a book. I guess really one way to get fame or to be known is to write a book. I'll be living somewhere near the ocean, and I tell my mother, "Watch, I'm going to make something out of myself."

As Lisa and I walked down the hall to our last interview, she directed my attention with a silent nod toward an attractive young woman in cheerleader garb. After we passed, she said, "That used to be my best friend." The ex-best friend was engrossed in conversation with another cheerleader whom I recognized as the student who sat in the front row in Ms. M.'s writing class. "Was she talking with her new best friend?" I asked later. Lisa grimaced assent. All of a sudden I understood Lisa's painful self-consciousness in her "Exposition" class. She had said, "I don't want to talk out loud in that class because some of the people in there, well one of the people in there, some of the people in there I don't like." I was struck mid-hall with the strong effect that the presence of peers, even one peer, can have on a student's writing process. Lisa was a peer-conscious, audience-conscious, self-conscious writer. We'll examine what can happen with a student's writing—with Lisa's writing—when audience becomes too much of a concern during writing and then look at what the rest of the eleventh graders had to say about the powerful presence of peers.

Lisa and Her Audience

Though by eleventh grade Lisa felt much better about herself as a writer, her self-consciousness often returned unbidden to cause struggle. A brief but characteristic glimpse of her "thinking aloud" as she wrote what she termed a "gothic" for the short-story class (a class in which she felt comfortable) will help us see this more clearly.

> He beckoned her in . . his frantic beckoning . . . no his frantic calls
> to her made her run up the . . . made her run . . . frantic . . . calls
> . . . . made . . her run up the . . . What? . . . the sidewalk . . . no
> they're rich . . . stone . . . path . . . yes, the stone path to her
> house . . . and she . . . When she arrived at the door . . Amin
> . . . Aminadab . . . was blocking her view to the inside . . . No . . .
> Mrs. Arkus, you may not go in there, you mustn't . . . .

..... That's stupid ... [disgust in voice] .... I ....
... I can't think of what to say .... stupid paper .... oh
God! I don't really like anything I've written ....

Three things are apparent from this small section: that standard writer Lisa, unlike most basic writers, is fairly automatic at transcription; that she can think, plan, and write simultaneously (see Figure 1–3, p. 20); and that she has an inner critic at work when she writes, an internalized representation of past critical audiences ready and waiting in her conscious attention to pounce on any slip of the mind or pen.

Audience factors affect Lisa's relationship with her material. I have found that the extent to which audience will affect the writer is at once a function of the writer's self-concept and a function of the development of a writer's ability to put thought into written words. Very young writers' sense of self is egocentric. Donald Graves describes the gift of self-centered confidence the beginning writer has.

> The child will make no greater progress in his entire school career than in the first year of school simply because self-centeredness makes him fearless. The world must bend to his will. This child screens out audience ... the child centers on a very narrow band of thinking and ignores other problems in the field. (Graves, 1983, p. 239)

As the simpler aspects of writing become more automatic, children become more aware of audience and take it into consideration during writing. As children round the bend into adolescence, the way they feel about themselves begins to be largely reflected from peers instead of significant adults. If peers are actively present in the writing environment, writing will assuredly become a relationship among the writer, the material, and that peer audience. Though each of the eleventh-graders in this study evidenced some audience awareness during the writing process, only the writers who were adept at transcription seemed to have enough conscious attention available during composing to worry about the particular whims of an audience. Most basic writers did not consciously consider audience during composing; perhaps they had to concentrate too hard on other facets of composing, or perhaps they didn't care enough to consider what their audience (almost exclusively the teacher) thought about what they said.

The inner monitor that signals the need for revision is a potential asset. "How will they know?" Lisa said as she tried to decide if her readers would follow her line of thought in the "gothic" short story. Even though she was beset with self-doubt, she still benefited from the internalized audience and completed her story.

At times, however, Lisa's audience awareness crippled her attempts at writing. I observed her "Exposition" class the day before her "interpretation" rough draft was due. She listened to the teacher intently, took notes during the description of the assignment, worked quietly at her desk with brief consultations with the peers who surrounded her. Right before class was dismissed, Ms. M. said, "Tomorrow we'll work with the drafts of those who have shared their work less frequently, like Lisa." Lisa told me what writing the paper was like that night:

> I'm sure that if she didn't say [yesterday] that *I* would have to read my paper, I would have gotten it done. It was so hard I didn't know what to do, what kind of topic. I had a pad of paper, and I would write something, and I'd say, "No that's not good," and I'd try again. It was something that had to be done, but I couldn't do it. Then I didn't have anything. It was awful. I guess it is when I know I have to read it out loud and share it with people that I am intimidated and afraid.

Lisa was silenced, made "dumb" before an audience that she did not trust. She was fluent enough to have room in her consciousness for critical audiences to loom great. (Emotion linked with a distressing audience interrupted her attention and redirected it toward potential derision from her next-day audience.) In many ways, Lisa is a worst-case scenario, but she is definitely not alone in having her writing process negatively affected by fear of peer criticism. We'll work our way from other worst-case scenarios to the best-case scenarios as we consider how we can use peer presence to enhance the writing process.

The Adolescent Peer Mirror

To a large extent, the view that developing writers have of themselves as students and writers is reflected from the response they get to their work. Elementary school children attend carefully to how teachers react to them, and they compare their progress with those around them. They count stars and smiley faces or the absence of them. It's rare that children are oblivious to their reading-group level, and they often take measure of themselves on that basis. Teachers assist in comparison by giving formal and numerical renderings of comparison and by setting up the "ability" reading groups that so upset Lisa. Grades and group status were the most destructive criteria by which students compared themselves to others. Standard writer Jessica's self-comparison with her peers challenged her, but continually mediocre grades set her into a period of self-deprecation.

> I couldn't write or do good on a paper. Like some of the papers she'd read out loud, and I'm just saying, "How could someone write like that, and use all these fancy words." Then I would compare it to myself. And that made me push myself more, but it still got me way low. I pushed harder, but I just went down the drain. I had C's, but then I still had C's across there [in the grade book].

For Jessica, it was the unrelenting C's, the scourge of mediocrity, that seemed to send her down her own drain. Grades are powerful in the packaged comparison that they permit in the classroom.

Language was another medium by which students compared themselves. Lisa began to feel better about her writing, but she remained troubled (simultaneously angry and ashamed) by her awareness of the potential unacceptability of her word choice and sentence structure in her writing and speaking. Her concentration during drafting was interrupted thirteen times in one fairly short composing-aloud session as she struggled to find acceptable words. In many of these instances she lost her train of thought through the interruption.

Frank Smith says, "None of this word-generating is conscious. Words come, they are shaped, as James Britton says, 'at the point of utterance,' on the tongue, the pen, or in the voice we hear in the mind if we rehearse them mentally" (Smith, 1982, p. 108). But for Lisa this word search was conscious because she censored the words that came to her unconsciously as too simple or incorrect. This, along with audience awareness, made her agonize over writing.

Comparison with peers affected the way students viewed themselves as readers and writers, but reflected response to their performance also formed their view of themselves. Almost every unsuccessful writer that I talked with remembered humiliating responses to their very early reading or writing, and these responses caused later struggle in writing. David said:

> Even though I am great at math, in first grade I was really slow in reading. We'd go around in the group and read out loud. It was awful. I can read alone fine now, but when I read in front of class, I still fumble, get really nervous, and I start to sweat. I had a lot of frustration with writing in first grade too 'cause I was slow. I used to never get my work done. One day I finished my work, and that time the whole class stood up and clapped. It was like they were making fun of me. The principal came in and said, "What's going on here?" The teacher said, "Well, David finally finished his work for the day so we're showing him our appreciation."

In early adolescent years, David became a closet writer. If a peer might see it, he wouldn't write it.

Adolescents go to great lengths to avoid negative responses from peers. Erik Erikson noted that an adolescent would rather act "shamelessly in the eyes of his elders, out of free choice, than be forced into activities which would be shameful in his own eyes or in those of his peers" (Erikson 1968, p. 129). Basic students will go to extreme measures to protect themselves from a public display of incompetence. They will act out as George and Orion did, refuse to write as Carlos, Zac, and others did, or sit or slouch silently in the back row. Mona was one of the silent ones:

> I proofread myself. I could always just like go to a friend, but I don't like doing that. I'm just not good at writing. I just feel weaker or just lower than they are. They don't need my help, and I feel stupid asking the teacher when everybody else knew how to do it. Whenever I talk in class, it's like I see everyone's staring at me, and I just shrink. The words won't come out. How am I going to ask about writing assignments when the word won't come out? I had to do it over three times 'cause I couldn't ask.

Adolescents begin to see themselves in the reflected light of peer responses. This peer mirror makes them vulnerable, even desperate at times. Lisa defended herself from public criticism by refusing to engage in writing, by playing truant, by saying she didn't care, even by risking one humiliation (risking a confusing reading) to avoid another (admitting that she had written about whales). When she discontinued writing about sea mammals, she lessened the chance of appearing foolish in front of peers, but then she had to deal with subject material in which she had neither investment nor prior knowledge.

Though standard writer Lisa threw up defenses in late elementary school, basic writers like David reported doing so even in early elementary school. By the time the participants were in junior high, even the best of students feared exposure that might make them look foolish in front of their peers. Mona planned early-morning visits to her teacher so she could avoid asking her "stupid" questions in front of the class, but even advanced writers like Doug found it dangerous to ask certain questions in class.

> If you don't understand she gets really upset. I try and listen to her, but she mumbles. I am afraid to ask a question in that class because she's gonna ridicule me, and my friends'll look at me and make fun of me, and you look dumber and dumber and turn all red. So I avoid asking questions. I asked her what passive was, but she rambled on in a quiet voice, and I didn't get it, and I asked again, and she said, "Well, maybe if you'd listen." Of course you

can't say, "Well, maybe if you'd talk louder." Then last essay she said, "Great, not a single bit of passive." But I didn't know what I did.

Like it or not, we as teachers are tremendously powerful in our roles in the classrooms. Unknowingly and with the best intentions, we sometimes orchestrate situations in which destructive peer comparison and peer response occur. Because Ms. M., a very sensitive and skilled teacher, didn't know about Lisa's vulnerability, she put her in a situation that made her struggle and fail in her attempt to draft her interpretation paper. And herein lies a teacher's dilemma. As teachers, part of our job is to encourage writers, speakers, and readers to go public, but past experiences have left some writers, speakers, and readers with such deep humiliation that fear of audience leaves them effectively silenced. They need to be eased back into trusting peer audiences. After listening to these forty developing writers, I found myself developing a rule that I'll use from now on: *Never, from kindergarten through college, have students read aloud or read their writing aloud in front of the class unless they are willing to do so.* If it takes more than a nudge to get writers or readers to go public, the effort may well be counterproductive.

Teachers also play a powerful role as assigners of grades. As we have seen with successful writers and with unsuccessful writers, grades probably do more damage than good in the writing classroom. Grading sets a limit on the number of winners, and in the end the winners and the losers lose sight of their own reasons for writing: to make sense of their world, to act upon their understanding, and to develop skills that they see as important to their future.

Peer pressure that occurs because of grades is another reason to de-emphasize them. We've seen that peer pressure moves most successful and unsuccessful students toward peer-acceptable mediocrity. This pressure is exacerbated by the public and comparative nature of grades. Derision from classmates fosters both fear of failure and fear of success. The writer's attention becomes focused on audience response rather than on the process of writing.

Does that mean that I advocate no grading of writing? Absolutely. The second rule I've made for myself as a result of this study is: *Remove the onus of grades and their implied praise or criticism as much as possible from the writing classroom.* It would be ideal if writing were graded on a pass/fail basis so that students might feel more ownership in their writing, so that the primary relationship in the act of writing might be between the writer and the material and the secondary relationship between the writer, the material, and the audience. But, of course, some administrators and school boards will not be convinced that grades are destructive to growth in writing. We'll explore the issue of grading in the last two chapters, but for now let's look at how Ms. M. graded Lisa, who often felt good or bad about herself as a result of how her grades compared to those of her ex-best friend and her brothers. Ms. M. seemed to be following the "subjective grading" strategy that Tom Romano describes in *Clearing the Way*. When she saw low self-esteem but honest work on the part of a student, she did not destroy a valiant effort with a *D*−. For students like Lisa who felt bad about themselves as writers, a spurt of better grades to match a spurt of obvious effort turned around the way they saw themselves as writers. This seemed to be the only positive effect that grades had on writing. Grades became for Lisa an indicator of growing competence.

Developing writers don't need potentially destructive grades as an impetus. They do not need praise or criticism. They need an audience for what they have to say, they need feedback to help them find the best way to say it, and they need help in seeing and setting goals for the next steps in improving writing.

Although Ms. M. wasn't aware of Lisa's fear of her peer audience, she was aware that Matt was one of the silent slouchers in the back of the room and that he lacked writing confidence. Matt had been writing without caring and feeling bad about himself as a writer since an experience in ninth grade. "Writing is like scrubbing the bathroom floor," he had told me one day. Ms. M. asked Matt's class to write persuasively in order to get the board of education to agree to a proposal they might make. Matt cleverly fulfilled this assignment by proposing that sexual passion be made an applied part of the physical education curriculum. An adept science student with pre-med aspirations, he made a convincing clinical argument that sexual passion was a more valid physical exercise than those offered in gym class. His arguments were couched in medical jargon about aerobic capacity, endocrine systems, and cardiovascular health. Although concerned about the content, his teacher recognized his proposal as the first piece of writing he had cared about in some time. She told him the argumentation was superb and told the class that as well. She added she couldn't send the paper off to the board of education, but that he had mastered the art of argumentation so well that she was sure he would have no trouble writing a replacement paper before the next day. She added that she couldn't keep Matt from letting a few friends see the paper. I observed the class as I saw the paper passed from cluster to cluster of students who, after reading his paper, congratulated him on his "superb argumentation." Matt sat puffed up in the corner and lost no time getting down to writing another compelling proposal. Ms. M. subtly permitted Matt feelings of competence and permitted a positive view of himself to be reflected from peers in his classroom. My third rule: *Identify the most self-conscious and distressed writers in your class and help them rebuild confidence in themselves and trust in classmates.*

Student Perspectives on Structured Peer Response

There's no doubt that the forty students saw benefit in working with peers on writing. Every one had positive things to say about at least one aspect of peer involvement in writing. Students reflected on effective group strategies they had used.

Jessica felt that exchanging papers helped her to internalize editing and revision strategies, and she learned as much from reading others' papers as she did from the advice that she received:

> When we exchanged papers, people were really honest; they weren't just saying, "This is really interesting." They'd also say, "This doesn't make sense." "What are you trying to say here?" "Maybe you could do this." It really helps you out. I read this one paper, and it really babbled on, and the next time I read my paper I kept thinking, "Well this sentence isn't necessary," and I'd cut it. I started to look at mine as someone who didn't know what I was saying and that really helped a lot. We had our student I.D. numbers on them so I didn't have to feel embarrassed.

Tom told of a process by which peer-editing groups sharpened his skills:

> We all get into a certain group, a group for sentence structure, grammar, punctuation, spelling; then she passes out the papers to each group, and we do our certain job. When my group is finished with marking the spelling, we pass it [the paper] on to the punctuation group. When you read them, you get ideas of how the others laid it out and how they did their introductory paragraph; you get a lot of ideas 'cause everyone writes differently. And just when you get good at finding spelling, she changes you to a different group. Then she gives it [our paper] back to us, and we can take it home to rewrite.

Alice learned to be more open to advice from others:

> It mattered more if there was a student reading my paper. I would like more to write that paper because I wouldn't have to worry about it yet. I think I look at comments differently because it's a student's, more seriously. It opens my mind more. And I'm more happy to get it because it's someone my age giving me suggestions rather than the teacher. What they say doesn't put you down grade-wise, and you may actually think of things you haven't thought of.

Vance benefited from feelings of competence and found reason to redraft:

> Our writing groups help me if I forgot something or what it sounds like. I put these new lines in a story to make it more exciting, funny. I don't know if it came off humorous or not, so I read it to the others and they laughed. I knew my plan had worked. I couldn't figure that out on my own. It made me work harder on it . . . more than once. Now if I think it's good, I like to hear the whole class's reaction. Unless you know it's good, you could be really embarrassed.

These students knew what they liked, but they were equally clear about what was distressing to them about peer involvement in their writing. Like Lisa, Elana valued individual peer response, but she didn't feel trust in the larger class, especially if she felt her draft was weak:

> I actually critiqued their work. Not only is it good for them, but it really helps me to find the flaws in my own work. To let the whole class critique it, it has to be a good paper. If I get across the point like cream, then it doesn't bother me at all. If I think it is a weak paper, it bothers me a lot.

Doug felt writing groups were valuable only if his sense of purpose and ownership in them was strong and if he felt comfortable with the members:

> The only time I really push and try to discuss in these little group things is when I really want to know. In the back of class today with Joey, we were talking because we both wanted to know what each other thought about the paper topic. That was just want-to-know and a need-to-know. Instead we have to get in our groups and do this brainstorming, a big waste. We could be talking about pasta as far as she knows. These girls I'm with started talking on as if I wasn't there. I was excluded.

Students' openness to support or advice was related to their past experience with writing and groups, to their confidence in the piece to be reviewed, to the size of the group, to the extent of their desire to know what others thought, and, most important, to the trust they felt in the group members. The most confident writers were open to criticism from the whole class. I observed Elizabeth's class one day when they were given fifteen minutes to try their hand at satire. She wrote a full page and was the only one willing to read her piece to the class. She seemed unbothered when they examined it to see if it was indeed satirical. "I like to have mine done in front of the class because then I know where to take it from there. Half the work is done." Confidence was the key.

Students cared most about who was going to be in the group, and everyone had different opinions on what worked well. Some, like Lisa, felt most comfortable with sharing their writing with friends. Kathy said:

> In fourth grade I'd open up in writing, and I'd get ridiculed for it. I was vulnerable. Now if I'm with someone I don't know, I don't know if I want them to read it. If I'm with good friends, I trust their judgment and won't feel defensive. I know their thinking processes. If I'm writing on a project with people I don't know, they might not care about the project. I'll just sort of listen to what they're saying. I wouldn't bring any radical ideas up for writing. I think with friends I would work harder and concentrate more on the stuff.

Jessica and others, however, felt that friends weren't the best responders:

> I think groups and evaluation sheets help, but it doesn't help out if they're friends of yours; friends mark down it was a great paper. It helps if there's someone who you don't really talk to much, and they can tell you how they feel about it. I think, "Hm, that's totally different from mine, but she did a good job." If someone has the perfect paper, maybe I'll get ideas from their paper, but I don't feel I'll always be able to help them. They might have mistakes in there that I don't realize because I have it in my own paper. If I find mistakes then I have some ability to correct things. That makes me feel good.

What it really came down to was trust. Forty different students, forty different criteria for comfort, and forty different constructs that might lead to vulnerability. Our guidelines for group membership must be set up, however, with vulnerable students like Lisa in mind. Hence I made a fourth rule for myself: *To maximize trust, permit students some say in the way they are grouped and in the audiences to which their work is exposed.*

In workshop settings (see Atwell, 1987; Romano, 1987; Murray, 1986, and Graves, 1983) groups often self-select, emerging and changing quite naturally as the year progresses. Other teachers permit students to select groups using preset criteria: "Form your own groups of three, making sure that there is a male and a female in each group." Neil Witikko, a teacher in Hermantown, Minnesota, forms ongoing groups by having students turn in confidential group-preference lists. Each student writes down three peers with whom they would like to work and, if necessary, the name of one person with whom it would be difficult to work. Witikko tries to accommo-

Figure 5–1
Handout for Forming Semester-Long Writing Groups

We will be forming writing groups for the semester. These will be made up of three or four students who will give one another feedback for the writing that we will be doing in and out of class. I would like you to fill out this form as I think it will help in making these writing groups work well. First I would like you to let me know how group work has been for you in the past, and second I would like you to give me some information that will help me in assigning groups.

I. Could you answer the following questions on separate paper and hand them in with this sheet? Write in full paragraphs.

   A. Would you write about a time when you liked working in groups?
   B. Would you write about a time when you didn't like working in groups?
   C. What advice do you have for me about the way groups might be run in this class?

II. I would like you to list the names of eight people with whom you would feel comfortable working. Most people find it best to work with people that aren't their best friends; others feel comfortable only with people they know quite well. That is for you to decide. Don't forget to put both males and females because the groups will be mixed. I will try my very best to make up groups taking your list into consideration, but it's very likely that you won't have everyone on your list in your group. If you have serious concern about working with someone in the class, please talk to me, or jot down a note on the bottom of this sheet where it says "concerns." The concerns blank is for other concerns that you have as well. This sheet is confidential. I will not leave them out on my desk, and I will destroy them as soon as I have formulated groups.

List:
1.   5.
2.   6.
3.   7.
4.   8.

Concerns:

P.S. Groups may be changed at my discretion if problems arise, but this will be a rare occurrence. It is very important that you work hard at getting the most out of these groups. Do confer with me, however, if your group isn't functioning well. We all will have a lot to learn about how to make these groups work.

date their requests. (See Figure 5−1 for a variation on Witikko's worksheet. Students can fill this out to help you assign groups. You will want to revise it to meet your particular class's needs.) Witikko keeps groups small enough (three or, if necessary, four) to promote trust and just large enough to permit a diversity of opinion. If a problem group surfaces, he works with the group to raise trust or changes membership to solve the problem. Lisa would have felt good in his groups.

The Peer Underground: Informal Peer Response and Help

In Iris's first interview, she told me: "When I gets stuck, I will catch on with somebody else." It wasn't until I observed her writing in class that I became aware of the peer underground.

Desks were lined up and nailed down for silence in Iris's inner-city school, but when she didn't understand something, she wrote notes and passed them along with whispered questions every time Mr. Fog turned his back. The silent and recalcitrant ones slouching in the back were too frightened or too jaded to seek peer help in writing, but those who were still trying got it any way they could. Zac was caught by Mr. Fog whispering to his neighbor. "I'm just asking for spelling," he griped to Mr. Fog and added an under-the-breath expletive for the benefit of his neighbors. Mr. Fog never provided a structure that encouraged peer involvement in writing, yet it went on.

Observation of writing classes showed me how highly interactive the students were. This was encouraged in most of the writing classes I observed. Students helped one another in thinking of ideas and in figuring out how to align those thoughts with the designated format. They also reached out for support on particulars. "How do you spell . . . ?" "What's a word that means . . . ?" "Something's wrong with this sentence. What is it?" "I need another example for this point I'm making." In Mr. O'Neill's basic class, Orion and his writing buddy, Jason, chatted back and forth during the class period, dreaming up ideas for each other's adventure stories. "Save that shock till the end; that'll leave 'em shivering in their Nikes." These less confident students sought this kind of support from friends whom they trusted and who knew them well enough to know that they weren't stupid. Having choice in seating encouraged this.

Perhaps the most gleeful writing that occurred for peer audiences was the rather contraband note writing. Every student in the study reported that they had done it. Chris recalled (with amused tolerance at his youthful silliness) "The note" that he and his advanced friends compiled.

In ninth grade we started this note, and the note eventually became "The Note" and stretched to about five hundred pages. We would start stories and then give it to someone else. Most of it was really ridiculous humor, but you didn't have to please any teacher. One of my friends still has it.

There were other variations on the note practice. When June rolled around, in-class yearbook signing was just as engaging and clandestine. Using an alternative surface to the page, Orion took great pride in notes he wrote on his desk to those who sat there in other periods. He kept up running dialogues with unidentified correspondents. Even Zac succumbed. "If somebody in school write me a letter, I write back." Iris had trouble writing a short paragraph in English, yet I saw her write two pages one day to her friend Rosa, and when I asked her about it, she said, "I do it at least every day." The participants from Mr. Fog's class had gotten more practice in transcription through note writing than they had in the skill/exercise type of writing that they had done in their English classes. This writing was peer-inspired, voice-laden, and meaning-driven. It provided practice and permitted students to become more automatic at the simpler aspects of writing so that they might have more room in the conscious attention for more complex writing tasks. It was free of constraint and was never reported to be troublesome to the participant. This kind of writing was a mutual getting on in adolescence that teachers couldn't have prevented if they'd wanted to.

Additional informal peer help with more complex school writing also went on outside the classroom: in the halls, lunchrooms, and study halls. Kathy said: "We'd say, 'Let me see yours.' It made me work harder. We could look over each other's thesis and major supports. I could see hers were a lot better than mine, so I worked on mine." Doug said:

> My friend asked me to proofread her essay in study hall. She had all these blank spaces that she had filled in with big words from the Thesaurus. They had a different meaning than she was trying to say. I said, "Not so flowery; just say what you want to say." This was intense for me. I was giving somebody advice on writing! The only thing I had learned about writing, and I could tell her.

And most important, peer-inspired writing went on outside the school building — at least through junior high.

The Creative Current Revisited

Tom Romano (1987) reports that peer-inspired creativity, which he terms "The Creative Current," runs through his classroom, nourished by the workshop setting. The forty students that I talked to didn't say much about a creative current in their classrooms. Outside of school, however, writing for peer audiences and for peer-related purposes did continue for some students. Letter writing abounded when out-of-town romances and friendships ran concurrent with low budgets. Every female participant and some males wrote in journals at some time during their adolescence, though few still did so by eleventh grade. And as we've seen in the previous chapter, emotional upheaval in students' lives engendered writing for the more successful students. Unlike assigned writing where concentration was sometimes interrupted by peer and family problems, this cathartic writing allowed writers to make sense of the upheaval in their worlds.

Peer involvement in the writing classroom is one of the ways we can return the creative current to the classroom. Designing writing curricula so that adolescents are writing for peer audiences that they trust, utilizing a workshop model, and structuring writing tasks so that peers can work collaboratively toward common goals all foster intrinsic motivation in adolescent writers. But, as we have seen, this peer involvement must be handled with care.

Though students reported examples of peer-inspired creativity in the late elementary school years, the creative current was close to extinction by high school. I was astounded when John Doe, a student who vied with George and Orion for being the cleverest at avoiding writing, told me of the last time he enjoyed writing:

> See we had this fort in this kid's garage. I came up with the idea, "Let's write a movie, short little movie." This other kid goes, "Ya, let's do it." We sat there and wrote, and we didn't think of the time. You just kept writing, cross things out, keep going. And then pretty soon we turn around, it's dark outside, ashtray's full of cigarettes. Seven hours, and we didn't even realize it. Just a stack of papers with cross outs. Must'a been an inch thick. We had a projector and everything, and we were gonna make this movie. This before he got sent to the juvenile center. We were gonna do it, no time, blew it off. Tell you the truth, still like to do that movie. We even had the house picked out for it, a friend's old house I'd always been scared of. It was something with my friends. Wasn't for a grade, or to make a teacher happy, or parents, to do better in school, just for something to do. It was our ideas going into it.

John Doe's script writing occurred in eighth grade, Kevin wrote for a friend when they were rained into a tent on a family outing, Sonia wrote stories "back and forth" with her cousins, Elana wrote "shared stories" at a girl's camp, Orion and his friend Jason wrote their "little adventures" in late elementary school (and then they stopped until they happened to be together in Mr. O'Neill's class again in eleventh grade, where the creative current returned for a brief stand). Almost every student had such stories to tell, but only Joel, Heidi, and Portia among the forty shared nonschool writing with peers in high school years. Joel began to enjoy poetry writing in high school when he found that he could write lyrics for a friend's rock band. Heidi wrote poems to her friends for their birthdays. Portia and a friend exchanged short stories. Otherwise, the creative current had dried up.

After taking a look at the circumstances and experiences of ESL writers, we will look carefully at complex reasons why the creative current dried up and at curricula that will return the creative current to the classroom.

Chapter Six

Jenny
Second Language Blues

As a high school English teacher, I never felt confident that I was doing the best I could with the ESL students who were mainstreamed into my classes. I'm writing this chapter with them in mind. Actually, I hadn't intended to have ESL students in my study, but two slipped into my minority participant pool quite by accident. Matt, who immigrated from India at eight years old, was placed in the pool of minority students because his teacher thought that he was black. Though I wondered about his accent, it wasn't until I started hearing about his past experience with school in India that I understood my mistake. Iris, who came to the United States at age four from Puerto Rico, entered kindergarten without speaking any English. After I began to talk to Iris and Matt, I started to value both my mistakes. I had been seeking diversity, got more than I had counted on, but became fascinated with the immigrant experience and how it differed from and resembled the experience of other minority students whose language or dialect was not standard English. I included more-recent immigrants in the minority pools, and though this chapter will concentrate on what writing was like for two different groups of immigrants, I'll bring a third group into this discussion later in the chapter because they, too, did not have standard English as a first language. The three groups are:

1. Immigrants who entered American schools between eight and thirteen years old, who were literate in their first language though they knew little English, and who had a parent or an adoptive parent who was college educated. This group includes Matt, who immigrated from India at age eight, Jenny, who came

from Korea at age ten, and Lilly, who came from Vietnam at age thirteen.

2. More recent adolescent immigrants who were hardly literate in their first language because they had recently come from Vietnam and had great gaps in their schooling. This group includes Patti, whose first language was Chinese and who came from Vietnam at age fourteen, and Tony, who came from Vietnam at age fifteen.

3. Students who entered kindergarten in the United States and who learned English in the streets and in the schools. These two students, Carlos and Iris, were of Puerto Rican heritage and spoke a low-status dialect of English in their eleventh-grade year. They were not so different from those students whose first dialect was black English or working-class English.

The challenge that speakers of English as a second language pose to our educational system will not go away; fortunately, the cultural enrichment that they offer won't go away either. The new wave of immigrants is here to stay, and the number of minority students for whom English is a second language is increasing and will continue to do so. Indeed, in some urban areas students whose first language is not English comprise more than 50 percent of the student population (Johnson and Roen, 1989). As teachers, we need to be ready for these students who will be mainstreamed into our classes. Teaching composition to these students is part of our responsibility, yet we aren't given much guidance in how to go about it. Though they are but a few of the many ESL students in our schools, Jenny, Matt, Lilly, Tony, and Patti offer perspectives on second-language acquisition that are important for classroom teachers to hear.

Jenny and Matt were the most articulate in the first group of immigrants, and though the choice was a difficult one, I have chosen Jenny to tell you of her experience with American schooling.

A Profile of Jenny

I was ten years old when I came here. So first and second grade was in Korea, starting seven years [old]. There I remember just writing little papers: "Spring is wonderful. Spring is spring showers." I don't know why I can remember. There you go to school four times a year. We go for the winter, then we get a week or two break. So I guess I had to write a paper when I came back. The language is like

Japanese. I just know how to write my name in Korean now. School was stressed a lot because in Korea my dad didn't want us doing manual work. In Korea girls don't go to school, but my father had made sure my sister went to college. She was still going to school . . . when my father died. My brother, he was still going to college; he wanted to come here, but we had no way of bringing him. So school was one thing that was stressed; he didn't want us to rely on anybody else. That was one thing my father said, "You have to go to school."

When my father had died, sometimes I couldn't go to school because my younger brother was not in school yet. My older brother was already in school, and my older sister was in school, and my mom had to go to work in the city and stay with her sister. My younger sister just wouldn't go to school. We had two different schools, so I didn't know about her skipping. So I had to go like between lunch break, make sure my little brother was okay. So if I didn't come back [to school] on time, you got hit on the head and stuff. I remember my teacher being really mean. By then it was kind of hopeless, everything was jumbled up. I don't think I went to school not even half the time. I was afraid, not enough money for materials, so the teacher'd get all hyper, so I was afraid he might do something to me.

My mom wasn't going to put me up for adoption, but I asked her to. She had told us: "You'll get a good education. You can go to school. You don't have to worry about [being] a girl." I decided then. I told my mom that I would study hard and become a doctor, and I'd come back there. So I'm still going to be a doctor, but I'm not going to go back there. I think because I saw so much sad things. That's why I told my mom I wanted to be a doctor because she had told us all these things. Before we left, we had gone into the country to see our grandma. That is the last time we saw the family and were together. That means an awful lot to me. I brought two books from Korea. They took one on the plane, and I was pretty sad about that. It's weird, but I can still remember the story, about this old man who had this little daughter who was going to get married. I stopped in Washington, and a couple days later I was going to school here. My younger sister came too, and we have another older Korean sister, not biological, who was adopted.

When we went to school, I was so scared. I was so scared I was shaking. But it was a small school, and they knew that I was scared. I had a friend who helped me an awful lot. She would explain everything to me really slow. But when you go into a room full of kids, and you don't understand what they're talking about. The first word I ever learned was Mom. After that English came pretty fast.

We had a big dollhouse on the patio, and my American mom would try to make us speak English. We would say, "How do you say this in American?" and she would say it really slow for us. After that period we could play with the dolls in English because we didn't want to be different, embarrassed.

I went with the ESL teacher. I had a hard time with *th*'s and *r*'s and *l*'s. And still if I don't watch out what I'm saying I get the *r*'s and *l*'s all mix up. It's terrible. I have to think about what I'm going to say. I don't want to make a fool of myself, so I talk slowly and think about what I'm saying. It came after practice, over and over. I learned to spell by sounding it out, and it doesn't sound out. My spelling was terrible. Anything I wrote my [American] mom would correct it. She said, if you don't get good grades and have a good education, then nothing else is important, so right away she had us writing. I remember summertime; my mom would say you're going to have school now, and she'd give us words and we'd have to sound them out. We had a board, like using the word *at*. She'd put a *b* in front of it, *bat*, and *c* in front of it, so it all rhymed. So the next day she'd go over the same thing, and give us a new word, like *ight*. I think I learned more in the summer than I did at school. I went to summer school and took all the English classes, and then I went to this program where you put on a play. It was close-knit, so they helped me.

My mom decided to put us in a Catholic school in sixth grade; she thought it would be a better education. The first day we got to school, we had to write about how we spent the summer, and I didn't know how to write. In the Catholic school we'd get more attention. So I go to her and say, "I don't know how to write this." I never had to do a paper before. So she explained to me how you have to put it in outline form. As a class we had to take a fairy tale and put it into modern time. I had taken Cinderella and tried to put it into nowadays. In seventh and eighth grade we had to do a lot more writing. It was great, but I always had run-on sentences. I just put everything all at once, and she said, "What you have to do is get a subject and a verb in one. So then you can start dividing them up and cut out the *and*'s and put a period and a capital letter there." So I think as I grew older I learned to use words right. Because my vocabulary was better, I could put more depth into one sentence than just jumbling on and on about nothing. In high school and in Korea, they didn't really care whether you got an education or not. At the Catholic school they care. When I'd get a bad grade, they care what's happening.

When you start to speak the language, you start to lose the other. After we had lost it completely, my mom tried to get us to speak it again. I don't know how I could have lost it so fast. If I heard someone talk I wouldn't know if she was speaking in Korean or Japanese. My mom tried to bring us back, but our interest was gone. All the Koreans who were adopted got together. It was no good because we didn't want to speak Korean. You'd think it would be in the back of your brain, but it's not. It gets me frustrated 'cause I really would like to speak Korean now. I don't know how to spell it or say it. It's not like I'm ashamed of being Korean, because I'm not. My Korean brother knows English, so he writes to me, and I write to him once a year. Last Christmas I didn't write. I don't know if this sounds selfish, but I haven't seen them for nine years. How am I supposed to feel about people I haven't seen for nine years. Every year I write the same thing. Kind of sad. I don't like to think about it. One of my friends, it's harder for them to learn English because they came as a whole family. It was easier for me to catch on 'cause I was surrounded with it for 24 hours a day.

It is so frustrating when you don't know how to do something, and you have to do it. Each year we have to write a bigger paper. Gimme a break here. But the teacher knew that she'd have to help me, and she helped me a lot. When teachers were understanding, it was easier 'cause they didn't expect you to get it right away. So she give you time. "You think about how you can get one idea into this sentence."

When I was in grade school, I was afraid everybody was going to laugh at me for writing something that wasn't exactly what everybody else's was. We'd just have to write out little sentences. In seventh grade I wrote papers about general things, not about me, and in eighth and ninth grade we had to write about what we thought about. But when I went to high school, I figured out that by then nobody didn't laugh at you. When I get an essay, I think about what I am going to write, how I can relate that back to me. If I have to write on a subject, but I don't know what it is about, it's hard for me. Now I can use more vocabulary words, and I know what they mean. And I have more to put on paper. But I can't just begin writing sentences because that doesn't make sense. My friends laugh 'cause they can just write anything, and it makes sense. Mine doesn't. I get mad at myself. I have to go through three copies of what I'm doing. My friend just writes it in one. If I don't plan, my paragraph is all a jumble-idea stuck in all different places. But planning doesn't help me with other stuff. It's so frustrating. They've probably had to write since they were in first grade, and they know how to speak the sentence the right way. I had a different way of writing.

One teacher wasn't understanding in ninth grade. She didn't

like me. I know she didn't like me because I sat in the back of the room, and I never volunteered answers 'cause I was still shy. I didn't want to raise my hand and make a mistake and have everyone laugh at me. She would always have so many kids around her desk, and I didn't want to go up there. That's one year I did bad in English class. I knew how to write, but I didn't know how to write in-depth papers. My mom helped me, try to explain it the right way. The teacher would say, "You should know how to do this." I just said, "Fine, I'm not going to ask her anymore." And I just didn't bother to. But that was the only grade that I felt that my teacher wasn't understanding.

English is good for me now. I used to put it off until the last minute, then I'd panic. If I don't plan, then my paragraph is all a jumble, ideas are stuck in different places. My mom will look at it and say, "What is this?" and she doesn't know what the heck I wrote. It took a while to learn to do. The first teacher said to jot down everything you know so that you don't get 'em mixed up, and then you take things that are similar and put in one group. Another teacher taught me about the topic sentence and an outline using complete sentences, and then another teacher said, "Just write a couple words down to give you clues on what you are going to be writing." As years went by I took a little bit from each teacher. That doesn't mean it's easy. Knowing what to write, that's the hardest thing. I have to get supporting evidence, items that I know about. I put it into groups like A, B, and C, then one idea into one and another idea into another, and then I get supporting sentences. So after I just put down the idea and split that idea up, I make a whole sentence outline. And then I combine them together with whatever words that needs to be put in between to get all the sentences all together. Others can just flip it off. Sometime I think it's because I'm afraid. I usually miss articles like *the* and *a*. When I write I don't worry about all the nouns and articles and stuff, but then if I have to write for someone where that's what counts, then I better look at them all over again.

Last week I had to write a paper about a play we read. And I had the book in front of me going over it, and then I had to have a dictionary 'cause I had to understand some of the words. I had everything written in two paragraphs, but he wanted it in six paragraphs: introduction, closing, four paragraphs. I just wanted to drop everything and pretend it was not there because it was too frustrating. But that's not the way you solve things, so cooled down after a long time. I asked some of the other kids. This girl just writes the whole thing down, and she's got it done. Not at her, I'm mad at myself, "Why am I not able to do this? C'mon, Jenny, you can do this." Maybe in grade school she had to write more papers than me. I've been here ever since I was ten years old, so why can't I write, and she can write. So I started again, six different pieces of paper so I wouldn't get confused. So I just kept on waiting until the last night. My mom's going, "You should have done that a long time ago." But I tried to tell her, "I've already got it done, but it's not enough paragraphs." So slowly but surely I separated those two paragraphs into whatever ideas I needed. I went back into the book and got more examples until 12:00.

When I got that paper back I got a B because he said it wasn't my own ideas, it was from the book. I just wanted to quit. I don't like to write, that's for sure. In test essays I start off with the sentence outline, and I always take a lot of paper. And then I put in the couple of words that need to be in to combine all the sentences, I forget the "ed's" or the "ing's" or the "s's". I could just write a jumble of sentences, but that's not what I want.

People say English is the hardest language, but I'm taking French now. I think English is a lot easier than French will ever be. French class has helped me an awful lot. Because then they'd say in English class, "need a helping verb here," and when I did it in French I'd finally have to first know it in English, so my French class was kind of like partial English and French. I could just rattle 'em off [memorize verb conjugations], but in French I have to know what it is in English. Like "I am going to the store." "I am" in French is "*je suis*," but if I didn't know what "suis" was, I couldn't write my sentence 'cause there is "I am going," "*je vais*." "Am" is a helping verb in English. I learn.

When I first started to write you had to think about the capitals, the periods, the spelling, and if you have the right format. Now you have to go into deeper what you're writing. It's not easier in one sense, but I'm not afraid to write anymore. I don't want to become a writer or anything, but I don't get paranoid like before when I had to do a research paper. I don't mope. Another thing is as you grow older you understand more things, and you have a wider idea. Therefore you can put more stuff into it.

Writing is expressing yourself. I don't like to tell my problems, but I can write it all down and look at it. Then the next day you read it and go, "That was really stupid. Why did I think that way?" I've done that many times. I was going through my diary a couple of nights ago. I guess I was mad at my mom 'cause, I mean, it was the dumbest things I had written down. The thing that's weird is that I can sort of understand both sides.

I just know that my goal is to be a doctor if it goes as I planned. If you know how to write, you know how to do reports for different things that'll help you. My plan is partially what my [Korean] mother wanted. That's where I decided to become a doctor to help the poor. So after I get to be a doctor, I'm going to join the Peace Corps, go to different places to help others. My Korean dad was like a perfect piece of the apple out there. That's how I remember him. He said, "What's the use of hurting someone when they're going to be hurt enough as it is. So you've got to go out of your way to make sure that everybody is having a good day." So my idea is to put everybody's ideas like into a bunch. My mom now, she said, "You can be anything you want to as long as you do it to the best of your abilities." So that's what I'm going to do. My dad and my mom from Korea, they wanted me to be good and to help others, so I'm going to do it to the best of my ability.

I believe that Jenny will do it. She's a determined young woman who entered school knowing that she needed to do well for herself and for her families and knowing that she was capable of doing well if she worked hard. The kinds of difficulties that Jenny and her immigrant peers had with writing were similar to those of other students, but they take on new configurations. And as their composition teachers, we probably should take a look at variations on forms of struggle introduced in previous chapters: cognitive overload exacerbated by frustration, loss of command of attention due to the life situation, threat in the writing environment, and motivational struggle.

Cognitive Overload

Cognitive overload was the most pervasive form of struggle that Jenny and her immigrant peers described. Like any writer, they had to attend to the generation of ideas, prior knowledge, word choice, organization, motor control (handwriting or typing), spelling, punctuation, syntax, textual conventions, clarity, voice, audience, and purpose. And as second-language learners they had to add a myriad of language concerns (already automatic to English speakers) to the burgeoning list of considerations which needed to converge for the finished product. Furthermore, because they had not lived in the United States long, they had less knowledge of acceptable conventions and formats, less sense of "appropriate" purpose and audience, and different experience and information from which to write. In order to write in English, they had so much to do that their conscious attention, the workplace of their minds, was overburdened.

Overload at its worst seemed to manifest itself in a stage of "languagelessness" that everyone but Jenny talked about. Lilly arrived from Vietnam with only a younger brother, who was adopted by a different family. She said:

> I was like a deaf person, just walk into school, kids talking, and you know nothing. I go to school for three months without know English. I can't talk either. If I want to go to bathroom, I look in dictionary for that word, and I write it down, and she let me go. Kind of feel like I'm not smart enough to speak. Think maybe I'm a slow learner. It's getting better English, and now I'm trying to learn back Vietnamese, but I don't want to learn it. English I can't even learn. Sometimes it drives me nut. I get frustrated. Trying to spell, I mean I don't even know how to spell Vietnamese now. Someone ask me how to write Vietnamese letter, I don't know how. If I can't find something in American, I ask my [adopted] mom. In Vietnamese, no one give me answer. Don't know two language. . . .

If students had immigrated without their family, or with a single sibling as did Lilly, they went through a period of intense loneliness when they couldn't communicate well enough in either language to satisfy the need they had for self-expression. This was a time when caring teachers and peers were very important. Even after this period of languagelessness disappeared, there was still depression and, of course, still too much to concentrate on. Syntax, vocabulary, and spelling were the most obvious contributors to this overload.

Syntax

The most complex contributor to overload was the mismatch of grammars between an old and a new language. Lilly said:

> I have ideas, no words for my ideas. I have an idea, and I jot that idea down, simple words, children's words. I'm trying to use new words, and it work for me, but I still don't know if they're adjective or adverb, how to make them fit in sentence. I still have trouble with that.

This mismatch of grammars continually interrupted these students. Lilly said:

> I'm not good at writing. I will read it, I stop, and put the verb in, stop. I'm not good at verb either, like past tense, present tense, *is*, *are*. I used to repeat one verb a lot, like *is*, *is*, *is*. And I'm not good at it. I'm trying to change. It is hard.

As Lilly wrote, she was continually interrupted with the need to focus her attention on the grammar rules that she was learning because she wanted her writing to be correct.

Stephen Krashen (1982) has made a useful distinction between two processes by which second-language competence evolves: acquisition and learning. People acquire language in a nonconscious way. When Jenny was playing dolls on her porch in English, she was acquiring English inductively. She was subconsciously finding regularities in the language and making use of those regularities to try to understand and to try to make herself understood. Jenny developed second-language competence in a second way as well. She was taught the *rules* that govern the use of verb endings and articles to help her learn English, and she learned French almost entirely by learning rules.

It's likely, though Krashen doesn't say this, that learned competence becomes automatic only when we have used a rule long enough that we don't need to call it up consciously. Until then, we may resort to a sort of monitor in our heads (Krashen, 1982; Jones, 1985) which interrupts us midway through an utterance or written sentence to confer over what form of a word to use, or how to order a sentence, etc. We may remember flipping through a conjugation in our minds to come up with the right verb form in a foreign language (*amo, amas, amat . . .* ; *j'aime, tu aimes, il aime . . .*) or trying to resolve the old "who/whom" dilemma midsentence. This monitoring interrupts other parts of the writing process (generating ideas, connecting them, organizing for audience) and clogs the process. Tony, the recent Vietnamese immigrant, talked about the kind of interruptions that his "monitor" made as he was writing:

> Well, we speak English, we have to change it around. Like you say "brown table." We can't say that, have to say "table brown." I always put it backwards. And like past you have to put *ed*. I always forget about it. Sometimes I don't know where should I put *ed*. We have the exact word for past, and you just put on.

Evidence of this sort of monitoring was in the protocols that I did of almost all of the students in the study. Something the teacher had emphasized in rule form would trigger an interruption during drafting. We saw how anything that smacked of colloquialisms interrupted Chris's conscious attention during transcription because of Mr. Shultz's rule, "No colloquialisms in formal writing." A limited number of monitor interruptions can be an asset. ESL students, however, had so many conscious rules to attend to that writing became a stop-and-go process. Though Chris used past-tense marker rules unconsciously because he had "acquired" them before he began school, most immigrant students were trained to make such considerations consciously. This brings up a big debate that goes on among second-language acquisition theorists. Jones (1985) summarized his own and Krashen's study (1982) by noting:

> Reliance on the monitor is not even an effective means to achieve the goal of grammatically, because the second language learner simply cannot learn enough rules. Acquisition is a more effective strategy (Jones, 1983, p. 113).

Other theorists caution that rule-learning may be important at some stages and ages. Whereas Jenny's "acquisition" of language went fairly quickly at age ten, Lilly had a harder time at age thirteen. At adolescence, acquiring a second language becomes more difficult because of differentiation of brain cells, and some learning by rule may be justified. Nevertheless, the negative effect of the "monitor" that Krashen and Jones describe was evident in my study. In analyzing the composing-aloud sessions, it was clear that ESL students were interrupted much more frequently by syntax considerations than were those whose first language was standard English (see Figure 1–3, pp. 19–21: Jenny, Matt, Carlos).

Students who spoke black English and *cared* about "correctness" were also more frequently interrupted (see Figure 1–3: Tracy, Zac). I didn't ask the newest immigrants, Tony and Patti, to do composing-aloud sessions after observing how difficult it was for Lilly. Lilly was so interrupted in her drafting that she just couldn't continue composing aloud. It's clear that the monitor that Jones and Krashen describe is a factor in the cognitive overload that these students experience. Factors other than syntax—such as limited vocabulary and spelling acquisition—are interruptive as well. The teacher needs to find means to limit what the second-language student has to consciously think about for an assignment.

Vocabulary

By the time the ESL students were mainstreamed into English classes, they usually reported having enough words to go about their day, but they didn't have enough experience with our culture or a large enough vocabulary to accomplish the writing that other students were doing. They reported that vocabulary came with time—with the listening, speaking, reading, and writing that they did—but as teachers we need to remind ourselves that limited vocabulary and experience must be taken into account. Continual pausing to search for words contributes to overload. More and simpler assignments may be best for students at earlier stages of acquisition. Time, experience, and an occasional nudge from the teacher to keep expanding vocabulary help to resolve this limitation.

Spelling

As a classroom teacher, I was unaware of just how difficult spelling was for second-language learners like Vietnamese Tony, who explains:

> Before, I say a word, I couldn't even spell it out. Now everyday I'm getting like I spell half of it, not the whole word but half. I think writing is very hard for most of the Vietnamese people. You say the word you know, couldn't even spell it. In Vietnamese when we said the word, we really spell it out. I mean every word I can spell it out, even I don't know what's *graduate*, I know I can spell it out. We don't have the long words like fifteen letters. Before I have to remember every letter, like, *she* so I have to remember *s-h-e*. It's kind of hard to remember.

Jenny talked about the hours that her "American mom" spent with her on spelling in the summers. Some syllabic languages make spelling a relatively easy process, but English has a complex spelling system, and most of it must be learned inductively by long-term experience with the English language. Jenny said, "I learned to spell by sounding it out, but it doesn't sound out." Plenty of reading and writing is one of the best strategies for spelling acquisition. Just as exposure to oral language helps the student "acquire" vocabulary and syntax, exposure to written language helps the student "acquire" spelling, and vocabulary and syntax as well. Teachers can best help second-language students in spelling by encouraging them to read and write. Focused instruction is perhaps best reserved for only the most common patterns in English spelling.

Lack of Experience: The Subtle Contributor to Overload

Though all forty students in this study told me that writing was easier if the topic was familiar and interesting, ESL students were particularly vehement about this subject. Because these students had so much that they needed to concentrate on and because there was so much about our culture that they didn't know, they could concentrate more on composing in English if they had a command of the subject they were writing about. Lilly said:

> It hard if I don't have idea, and if I don't like the topic. And if I don't know much about it I can't write — that's big problem. I don't want to research information to write. Just my own opinion; that way nobody judge me if it's wrong. If I look for information, write something wrong in there. They say, "Hey, this is wrong." I just write my own information myself, and nobody know about it. I'm not really good to research information. I read that information. I

must [be] misunderstanding. I love to write when I have so many
ideas, and the brainstorm, that makes it easy, brainstorm and
ideas. Hard topic and me hard to write it. Mostly if I have enough
information down, it real easy for me to write.

There's so much that these students must attend to while writing
that they need to write from readily accessible information and
experience. Jenny, who had been in the United States for almost
eight years, was just becoming able to do the reading needed for
research papers. Tony and Patti were so new to reading and writing
in English that trying to do research to write was difficult. "Well
kind of hard because I couldn't understand *Time*, and sometime the
news couldn't understand. They ask should woman be vice president,
couldn't understand magazine, news; just write something I think."
When Tony began to overload, he changed to a more familiar topic
and disappointed his teacher. As a classroom teacher, it took me
quite some time to figure out that when ESL students didn't follow
assignments, they were probably confused. Having them write about
their experiences allowed them to be supplied with writing ideas
from their long-term memory. If they were permitted to interview to
gather information for papers, they would probably benefit from the
speaking and listening practice as well.

Even Jenny, who was quite proficient at writing, couldn't think
about topic material and write at the same time. This made essay
testing hard:

> Everyday in American Lit we have a reading assignment; we have
> a quiz. We have to write what we think, which is really hard. I
> first have to get "now what do I think." I could just write a jumble
> of sentences, but that's not what I want. I have to write down what
> I know. I always take the longest time.

When students could bring real interest to their topic, that helped
as well. Lilly said:

> Book report . . . I like it. Sometime I copy from cover, but mostly if
> I like the book, I write pretty well in it. That kind of book I read I
> like, real interesting. But if I don't like or don't understand, I can't
> write it down: I copy.

Grasping an assignment was also a lot harder for immigrant
students; they had missed years of experience with the American
written code and with American format conventions (some being
very different from those of other cultures) and had gaps in general
knowledge expected of American students. They didn't have the
cultural knowledge about what topics were controversial or taboo
in the classroom and worried about that. Though they were anxious
to understand what the teacher wanted, that understanding didn't

come easily. Just when Jenny thought she had the "essay" figured out, she learned a new lesson: even though two paragraphs have all the information, six-paragraph essays were the only acceptable format for this teacher.

It's interesting that Jenny and Matt still had so much trouble with format. Jenny's difficulties probably stemmed from her lack of early exposure to the language. She still had to catch up on what was presented to Americans through speech and reading and living before age ten. These students held different kinds of knowledge. They simply needed to spend more time on writing, and they needed more help than others. Jenny did quite well by conferring with friends, so a teacher's individual time wasn't always necessary if peers were a part of the writing program. Jenny also found some strategies on her own that limited overload.

Strategies to Prevent Overload and Capitalize on Prior Experience

Cognitive overload, as I've said before, is not entirely cognitive. Frustration enters the mix, making writing so difficult sometimes that it's bewildering. Teachers can modify or divide writing tasks for second-language learners (or others who are having difficulty with overload) so the tasks are below the level of frustration. Guiding students through several variations of a process allows them to find their way when they're on their own. Jenny took to outlining as a way of generating and organizing ideas; Lilly preferred clustering. It's significant that separating preliminary idea generation from drafting helped both Jenny and Lilly. First drafts should focus on getting meaning across. Teachers can increase motivation and self-respect by showing interest at this point; conferring with peers may help students expand the ideas they have in their writing. *Most important*, attention to surface correctness should be delayed until a later draft, and then the teacher should sit down with the student, again validate ideas, and point out the differences between the student's language and standard English. Use of grammar and spelling logs as suggested in chapter 2 will help with that process.

Writing was especially complex for students who weren't literate in their own language. Patti and Tony, who were caught up in war-torn Vietnam, missed out on most of their early schooling. In eleventh grade, they were still learning the processes of reading and writing as well as learning English. Jenny, Matt, and Lilly were schooled before immigrating, and being literate in one language helped them to become literate in another. Nevertheless, they had still missed hours of absorbing English sentence sense, story sense, and models of the written code because they hadn't read or been read to in English in their younger years. Jenny was aware of this. When she complained that her sentences didn't make any sense, that they were jumbled, it was not because she was incoherent or that she didn't have organizational abilities. Rather, it was because she just didn't have exposure to English sentences and to English written formats when she would have been able to absorb them easily. What native English speakers know intuitively crowds the conscious attention of second-language learners.

Jenny learned to unpack the composing process through the years. She learned to separate planning from drafting to reduce overload.

> I put it into groups like A, B, and C, then one idea into one and another idea into another, and then I get supporting sentences. So after I just put down the idea and split that idea up, I make a whole sentence outline. And then I combine them together with whatever words that needs to be put in between to get all the sentences all together. Others can just flip it off. They open their books and just write it.

Jenny limited what she attended to by dividing the process into pieces so small that it would drive most of us crazy. This process kept the syntax "monitor" from intruding during idea generation, yet allowed it full sway when she wrote her sentence outline. Nevertheless, planning took an inordinate amount of time. For a composing-aloud session (see Figure 1–3, p. 20), Jenny did a letter of application for a summer job. It was a fairly simple project, but before she composed aloud, her planning was at the "ABC" stage. She wrote the letter attending mostly to syntax and punctuation. She made a few changes in her original "ABC" plan as she went, thought of some new ideas, and made some minor revisions at the sentence level during her final reading. Zamel (1982) noted that too much attention to form brings continual disruptions to the writer's discovery process, and this in turn brings on writer's block. Jenny was successful in avoiding that by putting together advice from several teachers. Unlike Carlos, she learned planning steps to use before drafting, and hence, she drafted without slipping into a simpler organization or syntax.

Writers who had less time in the United States than Jenny found other strategies to limit overload. Tony said he used a form of narration that was automatic for him: a chronological presentation. "She tell me to write about the weekend, so I just write about my Friday, and then Saturday, and then Sunday, go like order of time." Depending on where they were with language aquisition, delaying more complex formats seemed a useful strategy to limit overload.

Of course, this may pose a problem if a teacher is restricted by a lock-step curriculum; nevertheless, miracles can't be expected on the part of these students, and high frustration was causing Tony to contemplate leaving school.

Another debate that goes on between language acquisition theorists is whether students should spend most of their time becoming correct so that "fossilization" of incorrect patterns doesn't occur (fossilization of incorrect patterns had already occurred for students like Carlos) or whether they should involve themselves in any kind of language use that keeps communication going and encourages fluency and confidence, despite some incorrect usage.

Of course, in the best of all possible worlds, both should happen and, I believe, can happen. Reworking writing is a way for ESL students to identify incorrect language forms, and it's especially valuable when they use grammar and spelling logs in conjunction with that rewriting (see chapter 2 for these logs). However, practice with a new piece of writing, as opposed to multiple rewrites of the same piece, may allow students to "acquire" more and despair less, and still identify incorrect forms. Lilly said:

> You took all the things you had wrong and rewrite it, correct it. The second time I give to her there is some minor wrong in there. Go home recopy it. One rewrite, that's the way I learn. Someday I learn when I write it down, read carefully, and recopy only one time. Teacher want me to recopy many times, recopy whole paper again. Make me not want to do it.

Furthermore, these students need time for a lot of unevaluated reading and writing and speaking, all of which give them the experience with written code that allows them to become more automatic, to "acquire" instead of to "learn," to fit things together for themselves. When these students are first mainstreamed into a regular English class, the teacher may want to have them keep response journals instead of having them do formal analysis. The more automatic they become, the more they are able to attend to higher-level considerations such as format and transitions.

Matt, Jenny, and Lilly all talked about how "making meaning" in reading and in writing helped them. Lilly said:

> When I write a note to my mom I put "I go store" and I look again, my mind say it isn't right. I said "I go to the store." I have a "the" in there. That's how I started to do it. And I started reading more book. Mostly it taught my mind a lot.

Matt said: "Seventh grade I used to read these Hardy boys novels. I read twenty of his books. In eighth grade I had a 10.1 [grade level] in reading." Matt, who immigrated from India at age eight, had learned that practice and patience are central to second-language learning.

Matt's Theories on Practice and Patience

See I believe that to everything there is a trick. You just have to get it; practice show you how to get it. Like I was telling you about breakdance. There was a trick to it, every little move. I found that out by myself. Writing has a trick to it. Once you learn that, you can write. That's what I'm waiting for. It's a hard trick, but I'm going to get it. It's a matter of time.

I have this stereotypical person in my mind, like Alfred Hitchcock, Christopher Reeves, or that British man in "Magnum P.I." You know, someone who speaks real good English, just born with the trick. [My language], that's fate. I was born like that. I could get angry about it, but this I can't do nothing about. I can only do one thing, that's to get like that stereotype. I like literature by Charles Dickens. The stereotype is affected by my reading. I always picture the author who is writing. This is what gives me the stereotype. Every time I see a person, I can tell whether he is a good writer. I could tell the way he speaks if he is a good writer. Big words, formal language. I want to get that good. You just have to learn the trick. It's a hard trick. I just don't like writing, you know. I have to learn it. I just don't sit down, some idea come up, sometimes the stereotype person comes into mind. Wham! Yeah! Why don't I just do that, and the right words. If I had been brought up here, knowing English from an early age, I could write. All my ideas come up in my mind and stay there. I'm a person with ideas, and I can't write them. That's why I got to keep silent a lot. You've seen me in class. I don't feel comfortable. I'm Christian, Pentecostal. When I'm alone up here [away from the city], and if I have a problem, I talk to God, if He's listening. He's just like an older brother. You don't have to worry about what language you are talking to Him. You don't have to write to Him either! One day I'm going to talk like that stereotype when I'm a doctor. I have an intention to write well.

When Matt immigrated, he moved into the inner city where black English was the prevailing dialect. He has the double problem of not only having English as a third language but also having acquired a nonstandard dialect of English that gets in the way. But he has a lot going for him as well. As with the other immigrating ESL students, he feels good about himself as a student. Because of his success in school prior to immigration, he's confident that he will, with hard work, learn "the trick."

Life Upheaval

Life is not simple for students who have pulled up roots and come to a new country. Even those students who immigrate with their families have a certain amount of upheaval in their lives. They're separated from their larger support group and often parts of their family, they're immersed in a culture that's strange to them, and they have to adjust to a new school, often with no friend or even acquaintance to help them in that adjustment. They've immigrated with life views and ways of being that may be substantially different from those held in the United States. Further, immigrating families often find that the land of opportunity holds less opportunity than they had hoped for, and they have to live with poverty and upheaval.

Iris lives in an inner-city housing development, ashamed of being on welfare, signing checks and conducting business for her Puerto Rican mother, who is just waiting until Iris graduates so that she can go home. We know Carlos's story from chapter 2. Tony's immigration from Vietnam was sponsored by a cousin; his father was sponsored by someone on the other side of the United States; his mother was dead, and at seventeen, with little schooling behind him, he was in a strange world, relatively alone and earning his own living. Patti immigrated with her Chinese family from Vietnam to Malaysia, and then to the United States, where they are trying to begin life anew. Lilly left Vietnam with her seven-year-old brother (because "my family not have enough money for all of us") on a "boat with 137 people and a cup of water a day," survived a dangerous journey through a jungle and down a river to the ocean, and then spent eight months in a camp in Thailand waiting for a foster home in America. She, like Jenny, had no way to earn passage for the rest of her family. Jenny spent a final weekend with her grandmother and family, boarded a plane with her sister, spent a couple of days in Washington, D.C., and was in school the next day. It's easy to see how these students began their careers in American schools with a lot on their minds. Writing was low on their list of concerns.

By eleventh grade, however, we see Jenny secure with caring adoptive parents, successful in school, prizing assimilation enough to pick the name "Jenny" and to be on the school's dance line, and headed for medical school. Adjusting and assimilating was top priority to these students. The efforts of American schools, adoptive families, and church groups to help them retain their home language and feel grounded in their own culture were unheeded, though those efforts probably made the students feel a self-worth and validation that was important in their adjustment. They tried to fill the gaps in their knowledge, wanted to know how to dress and what to write about that would be acceptable.

Another problem for immigrants is that those around them can so easily misunderstand or underestimate the wealth of their linguistic and cultural background. Until I talked with Matt at length, I didn't know that he was from India, that he spoke the language of his region in India, "a mountain dialect," and English, and that he still spoke the dialect with his mother, who didn't want to speak English. I'm sure I underestimated some of my classroom students' experience on some levels and overestimated it on others. Had I been Tony's teacher, I might easily have assumed that he had regular schooling and might have misinterpreted the gaps in his knowledge; I might not have known about the great knowledge that he had about fishing and farming. As teachers, knowing a little about the students' life situations and interests will help us to help them find subject matter and an audience that will be familiar enough for them so that they might become more automatic at the other skills needed for writing.

The immigrant students were grateful for the caring approach and extra help that their American teachers gave them. These students may lead more stressful lives than many of their American peers, but as teachers we can use the same techniques to help them as were described to help American students when their lives get tough (see chapter 4). In addition, because immigrant students are trying so hard to assimilate, it's particularly important for the teacher to check with them before reading their work out loud to peers. Lilly was raised with such respect for teachers that saying no when her teacher wanted to read her Saigon narrative was difficult. At the same time, crying in front of her peers meant "losing face," even though those peers were empathetic and supportive. Nevertheless, allowing, even encouraging, students to write about what is distressing to them, as Lilly had done, will lessen this form of writing struggle and will allow writing to have a meaningful purpose.

Threat in the Writing Classroom

Peer Threat

Immigrant ESL students were very sensitive to their peers, and by adolescence, peer response posed a threat. They wanted so much to be accepted by those around them that most chose very American pseudonyms, and they were always concerned about whether their subject matter for writing would be acceptable to their American peers. Lilly, Jenny, and Tony mentioned insecurity in not knowing what might be funny, interesting, or ridiculous to their classmates. Fear of exposing themselves to peer criticism was a powerful source of difficulty for these students. We've heard about how exposed Lilly felt when her teacher read the story of her parting from her father to the rest of the class. This incident added to her struggle in writing because, thereafter, she had to be wary about writing something she would be uncomfortable having to read again in front of the class.

If ESL students work in twos or threes with their American peers long enough for trust to develop, much of this wariness of peers may be eliminated. Jenny's fear of not being like others was based on the mystery of the public junior high mass: "There were so many kids at the junior high, so you are afraid to express yourself." When the mystery is broken in the context of the small group, then ESL students begin to get what they need, the security in which to express themselves orally and in written discourse. ESL students soon figure out that their peers are more accepting than they thought, and they quickly learn the rules for what makes writing acceptable.

Teacher Threat: A Contrast Between Groups

We've seen how Carlos and Chris and others struggled with writing when a teacher continually criticized their work, when emotion linked to a threat in the writing environment disrupted their writing process. When talking about this difficulty with writing, it's important to make distinctions between the immigrants in this study who were Asian and those students who entered kindergarten in the United States (like Carlos and Iris). The teachers in America posed no threat to Asian students in comparison to the authoritarian and sometimes punitive teachers they had left behind. Lilly said:

> My worst teacher was my fifth grade. In Vietnam they grade like one to ten. If you have a ten then you aren't in trouble, but if you had nine point, you got one spanked your butt. If you got eight, you got two spank your butt. If you got only five point, you got five spank your butt. After the 1975 rule is you're not supposed to punish the kid. But the teacher still punish the kid. I never liked writing. Since first grade I start to write and the teacher is terrible, wanted me to describe basket, five pages, spank not enough pages. From that on I never liked it. I just think writing is disgusting.

Matt, like Jenny and others, described pre-immigration fear of school:

> At school they had a bamboo stake . . . whack. If you was absent,

they hit you; if you were late, they hit you. I was in second grade and there were these couple of guys and they did something, I don't know what it was, and they caught him, made him go to the principal's office. They made 'em stand up and the principal had a switch, beating them, and it went whack, whack, whack, and I was there watching it. And one day I was doing my work, and I don't know why he hit me, but he hit me.

These students were relieved and pleased to find "helpful" teachers in the United States, teachers who nurtured their self-confidence and who had high expectations of their ability to succeed. Tony said:

Teacher there really ... they can hit you. They used to hit me in the hand everyday I'm wrong. But my computer teacher [here], she is helpful. I mean everybody, every teacher, they just seem like really nice 'cause every time I ask them they always try to help me out until I'm done. Any teacher I ask help.

And the more assertive they became in asking for help, the more they received. Lilly said:

In school you can ask for help. In school you don't mind doing that. That's great because if you minded that would be too bad. I've asked what the word mean, something like that. And sometimes the teachers ask questions, and I don't know what it mean, and I have to ask for explanation. Mrs. A. is a good teacher. I like her so much. She wanted you to work really hard. First time I do a term paper, no Vietnamese ever do a term paper, it kind of hard. But [she help], and when I was through, when I done that term paper, I think it so easy to do a term paper.

Both Jenny and Matt ran up against teachers who were critical in their ninth-grade year. They didn't feel comfortable approaching them for help and so lost someone to help them with their special needs for that one year. However, they both had enough general self-esteem to get back on track when positive teachers returned.

The difference in the levels of confidence between the group of immigrants and the group of unsuccessful students (see chapter 2) who came to school speaking a low-status language or dialect explains some of the differences in the motivational and performance levels. Carlos began to feel bad about himself as a student and a writer when he was continually corrected and criticized for his errors. "When I was a kid, I was dumb, too dumb. I knew I'd be getting it wrong." Students who spoke low-status languages or dialects lost confidence in their ability. We can contrast this with Vietnamese Tony's outlook:

I don't feel like I'm smarter than them, and I don't feel like they're smarter than me, so [I'm] just like every student in my class. I been here three years. They put me in seventh because I don't know any English. Later that year I just jump up to nine. I feel really good, comfortable with school. Then I finish nine, and I go sophomore.

In contrast, Carlos resorted to refusing to write in fourth grade: "Why should I write when it's always wrong?" Because of lowered self-esteem, writing tasks seemed insurmountable and were avoided; these students weren't getting the practice they needed to limit the cognitive overload that their language difficulties intensified. Given this, the 50 percent dropout rate for Puerto Rican students who learned one language at home and another in mainland schools and streets is no surprise.

There are social issues related to threat posed by criticism and resultant loss of self-esteem. Writers like Carlos reported this struggle at an early age; whereas, immigrant second-language speakers whose language was *not* an indicator of social class rarely reported this struggle.

Jenny, Lilly, Patti, Tony, and Matt were all second-language learners who came from foreign countries, who had success in their previous (though sometimes limited) school situations, and who had encouragement from their parents or adoptive parents. It's true that Patti and Tony, who didn't have upper-middle-class parents, who had great gaps in their schooling, and who were adolescent before starting to learn their second language, were both having more difficulty with language than Lilly or Jenny. Nevertheless, the immigrants whose second language was English still had confidence in their school situations.

Iris and Carlos, Puerto Rican students; Tracy (in seventh grade), Zac, and Sonia, who spoke black English; and Tim, an American Indian, all lived with a dissonance between the view that they at first wanted to have of themselves as students and the negative view that the schools reflected to them of their performance; they had lost confidence.

On the other hand, immigrants felt that effectiveness in written expression would come in time, with hard work, and their parents encouraged them to get on with the hard work. Matt, whose parents urged him to take part in a program for "gifted" minority students, said, "You just have to get the trick"; Lilly said, "I just have to write all summer"; and Jenny said, "I just had to work much harder than the other students."

There was some evidence in my study that learning standard English was also easier for the immigrants because there existed cleaner distinctions between the standard English that teachers were endeavoring to teach and the first language that they had acquired. For students like Carlos and Iris who spoke a mixture of Spanish and nonstandard English, and for others who spoke non-standard dialects, differences were muddied. Jenny searched for differences between her first and second languages. She knew exactly why she had to deal with inserting articles and verb endings, whereas Carlos was not aware of any pattern in his continual errors in standard English until distinctions were made clear to him. He couldn't see his constant omission of plural markers on nouns or his omission of past-tense markers for what they were. He spoke English words but followed many of the syntax rules of Spanish. Though he had spent hours of classroom time doing grammar exercises, he didn't call up these grammar lessons when he corrected what he wrote. In addition, what Gardner (1986) calls the integrative motive might well have been missing for these students; the lack of respect accorded to their culture and language by society at large may well have made them unconsciously unwilling to really *want* admission into a new language group.

Hence to the most important distinction between the groups: consciousness. The group of students who came to the United States with some literacy in their first language knew that the problem with writing was really one with language, whereas participants who spoke Spanish or black English (except for Tracy after eighth grade) were confused about their lack of success. Carlos at first thought it was because he was "dumb." Zac, Sonia, Ed, and Iris had other explanations. "I'm lazy," Ed, Zac, and Sonia told me. "I don't care about writing," said Iris. All explanations showed a lack of consciousness that language was a real reason why they had not been successful students in the eyes of their schools. These students were oppressed and trapped by their unconsciousness of the fact that their language differences mirrored and exacerbated their social differences. Further, most of their parents were caught in the deep despair of the inner-city experience and were caught in similar traps. Immigrant ESL students, however, were fully aware that they were struggling with problems of language, and they had more faith in the potential good results of hard work.

Threat posed a serious problem for many participants who began their schooling without standard English as a first language, but it wasn't a problem for students who entered American schools partially literate in their own language. This is yet another validation for bilingual (and bidialectal) education in early school years until literacy in the home language is established. Bilingual education for students provides good models of the written code of both languages. It seems that establishing a positive view of oneself as a learner and a writer is far more important to future success than rapid acquisition of the new language. It's difficult to try to develop intellectually, to learn to read and write, when one has only partial control of the language that becames one's tool for learning.

Motivation for Writing

Jenny and Lilly were sent to the United States so that they might have a better life than they would have had if they'd stayed where they were born. Hence Jenny, Lilly, and the others were willing to put tremendous effort into the education they saw as valued by their families and useful to their future. What they viewed as possible became possible. Gardner studied the motives that people have for learning second languages. Two motives were particularly evident in the group of five immigrant students in this study: the integrative motive and the instrumental motive. Gardner termed the willingness of the second-language learner to become a member of the new language group as the integrative motive, and he pointed out that students who showed the integrative motive had parents who also professed an integrative orientation. Matt's and Jenny's parents (both Korean and American) knew that succeeding meant succeeding in America's educational system. Carlos and Iris did not evidence this motive as much as Jenny, Lilly, Patti, Tony, and Matt did. The bilingual educational experience may be particularly important for students like Carlos and Iris who retain a deep affinity with their first culture and first language. The desire to be a member of the new language community was so strong for Jenny that when her adoptive parents tried to ensure that she might be bilingual, she and the other Korean children resisted.

Furthermore, the immigrant students were also driven by the instrumental motive. They were taught at an early age to value higher education as a way of making a better life for themselves. Sacrifices were made for them to get an education, and those sacrifices which indicated the valuing of education were remembered. We have seen how this played out in Jenny's life, how she sought to live up to the expectations that her Korean and American parents had for her. Learning to read, write, and speak English were essential to the medical career to which she felt committed. Tony said, "In Vietnam we don't have many school; only rich go school because they don't have to work. We worry about living every day. Now in summer I get money for school next year." For Lilly, schooling in Korea was a privilege she had to earn:

> My sister have to quit school and start to work. I thought I had to
> quit school too, but I didn't. I really lucky; I stay in school. In the

morning I get up early at five o'clock and cook breakfast for my brother and clean the house, and I go to school from seven to twelve. Twelve-thirty I at home cook my brother, eat, and clean the house, everything during the time till seven. My promise to keep if the house clean, everything go well, I will be in school. Otherwise, I have to stay home. Seven to twelve, that my free time, then that's my school, rest of the day work.

It's no wonder that Lilly works hard. Regarding schooling in America, she said:

I still do pretty good. I do all kinds of report and term paper by myself. I gotta spend much time on it than other kids their writing. It's really hard for me right now. When I compare with other kids, I'm far behind. I want to make writings really good for my college, and I'm trying hard as I can in writing.

The instrumental motive for writing is a motive closely connected with the desire for self-determination and competency, the ability to have some power over their future. Nevertheless, we can see the same lack of enthusiasm for writing in Jenny and the other immigrants that we saw in the successful writers who were more interested in excelling than in what they were writing about. Perhaps their strong instrumental motive for writing counted on rewards that were too far in the future. Matt's words seem important: "I have an intention to write well. . . . Once I get over that then I don't want to see another paper in my life."

When writing seemed impossible, delaying was a useful tactic, especially when it was uncomfortable to get help. Jenny said, "I would put it off as long as I could and then I'd ask people, 'Well, how do you do this because I don't know how to do this.'" Lilly said:

I have a hard time to write it. I force myself to write it; nothing will come on my mind, for five hour. My mind kind of tired. I want to go somewhere have fun. My mind tie up. I struggle a lot. Maybe I delay that paragraph. Tomorrow I will do it. And when I look at that paragraph again, I feel I don't want to do it. Maybe I do a different paragraph and then I delay it again. I delay that same thing for week. I don't want to do it.

Matt struggled, but he still had to perform as the successful student that he had proved himself to be. He had earned the right to be in a special program, and he had to excel to stay in that program.

There is a lot of pressure on me, eight classes you know, I hate seeing C's on my papers, disgusts me. I like B− or better. The problem is that I wait to the last day; like some people start way early, and they rewrite it. I wait to the next to last day. Why? I

don't know; that's something I want to find out myself. So I have
the habit of not proofreading papers. It's like I'm in a rush to get it
over with. I have an intention to write well, and I'm not even half
way through the process. I may be in a position to write a dis-
sertation paper. Once I get over that then I don't want to see
another paper in my life.

As with the other successful students in the study, we owe it to
these writers to help them to find reasons for writing beyond the
still important instrumental reasons of grades and of success at the
next educational level. The Jennys in this world will struggle, but
they will become doctors. Matt will learn the trick. The instrumental
motive will work though it may limit other intrinsically motivated
uses for writing.

On the other hand, the parents of the low-status second-language
learners who are caught in poverty haven't been able to model the
possibilities that an education affords. And for their children who
view themselves as poor students, the struggle of learning English
in its most acceptable form may be too great. It's probable that
many of the functionally illiterate adults in our nation are not
literate because the struggle to become so was too great.

In the Classroom

Need we make a choice between a curriculum based on "acquisition"
(through extensive exposure to lánguage) and one based on "learning"
(through rule-based instruction)? We have seen that the remedial
curriculum based on rule-learning and exercises did not serve Carlos,
Iris, and nonstandard-dialect speakers, yet we are warned that if
correctness is not addressed, fossilization of incorrect structures
will occur. This seems to call for an approach that integrates both
acquisition and learning. An acquisition component seems particularly important. A curriculum should make speaking, listening,
reading, and writing geared toward what they are intended for: self-
expression through language. Whether these students are mainstreamed or are still in ESL classrooms, writing topics connected
with real interests, written for real audiences, and with real purposes
tap the strengths that students can bring to becoming competent in
a second language: their own rich experience, their desire to be
understood and accepted by those around them, and their desire to
express themselves. These are instrumental motives that are closer
to the person than the more abstract instrumental motives of success
in some future phase of one's life. Real communication for *real*
purposes is where early language acquisition starts and where it

ought to continue, in either first- or second-language acquisition.

There were only four times when I heard ESL students excited about writing. Carlos was excited in writing about the demise of his apple tree (excited about making sense of an important experience); Jenny was excited about updating the Cinderella story (a group project); Matt was pleased with his paper on the value of passion in the physical education class (a paper that drew him positive attention from his peers); and Lilly was pleased with the paper she wrote about parting from her father (making sense of experience) — at least before it was read aloud to the class. If all students (ESL and others) could focus on language as a social and meaningful activity, if they were shown possible ways to keep their writing process simple enough at any one stage so that overload would not occur, if they wrote about subjects that held their interest, to comfortable audiences, and for self-selected and real purposes, they would have inner inclinations to write, and the overwhelming struggle inherent in a complex process would be eased.

Rule-based learning should be integrated into the final phase of ESL students' writing: editing. With ideas at the center of the writing process, correctness should be an important and final step in any writing program. Though correctness of English forms and usage can be acquired, often it needs special attention from adults and peers if fossilized incorrect forms are to be avoided. Grammar and spelling logs (see Figures 2–1 and 2–2, pp. 37 and 38) give us an opportunity to help students help themselves in coming to distinguish between the correct and the incorrect. These logs might be used in combination with whole-language activities that Freeman and Freeman (1989) suggest: the daily personal journal, interactive journals, literature and content response journals, cross-curriculum assignments (they describe a class that followed a compelling court case). Further, the qualities of the project-based writing and/or the workshop setting seem important for these students. Imagine Jenny and Carlos working in collaboration with two American students to prepare a handbook for new ESL students. Imagine Toni and Patti interviewing recent immigrants and immigrants who came to the United States earlier in the 1900s to compare those two different immigrant experiences. Imagine Lilly writing about her parting from her father in a workshop setting where she could share her writing with two or three peers she had learned to trust. What we imagine, we and our students can experience.

Chapter Seven

Doug and Joseph
The Straitjacket of the Secondary Writing Curriculum

A man should learn to detect and watch that gleam of light which flashes across his mind from within, more than the lustre of the firmament of bards and sages. Yet he dismisses without notice his thought, because it is his. In every work of genius we recognize our own rejected thoughts: they come back to us with a certain alienated majesty.

—Ralph Waldo Emerson (1841)

Until now I've been focusing on what went wrong for developing writers as individuals and as groups, but in this next-to-last chapter I'd like to take a hard look at the writing curricula adopted by secondary schools and advocate changes based on what I have learned from the students I interviewed. Before we begin with Doug's view of his writing program, however, we need to examine a popular pedagogical myth that gets in the way of change.

I talked to a teacher I met in Doug's school about what Romano (1987) and Atwell (1987) and Wigginton (1985) were doing in their classes; she was instantly resistant, and she based that resistance on her belief that "Students these days are afraid of a little hard work. They are spoiled by teachers that they had before who seem to think education is entertainment." I've heard this in other contexts: "He who has not been flayed has not been educated." But the students I talked to weren't afraid of work. They worked hard at things that were important to them, even those who called themselves lazy worked hard at nonacademic things in which they felt some success. They didn't mind work, but they did mind drudgery. Drudgery occurred when they were not engaged in what they were doing, when writing was, at best, "like brushing your teeth" and, at worst, "like scrubbing the bathroom floor." When they saw purpose or felt interest, they didn't mind work.

By eleventh grade most of the students in this study were disenchanted with writing. Doug was one of the very few writers who still had an active writing life outside of school in eleventh grade, and perhaps because he still found satisfaction in that writing, he is best able to articulate what bothered him about school writing. Doug wrote poetry, as did Heidi and Joel—when the spirit moved them. Another five writers still wrote in their journals when life was intense. Otherwise, students had stopped writing unless it was demanded of them.

I've quoted Doug before. He was the young man who couldn't keep his lost wallet out of his mind while he was writing, and he was the budding young actor who used his perfectionist tendencies to benefit his stage career but groaned under them while writing something he didn't want to write. We'll join Doug's description of his writing experience midway so that I can bring in another student, Joseph, toward the end of the chapter. Doug began by talking about a sixth-grade assignment.

A Profile of Doug

In sixth grade, I remember one essay . . . well, a kind of essay. We were supposed to write an autobiography on ourselves and into the future, and that was fun. I really came to use my imagination and kind of created a whole new world for myself, and the teacher liked it and encouraged me. I mean very young teens are very egocentric. Even if it is a phase, when you're a teen *you* are everything. You're not really concerned if the president sent troops down to Nicaragua. You're more concerned about how people are gonna react to your sweater. I'm just being honest. I always thought that was kind of funny, about myself, because I'd write happily if it was about myself. I got a *B* on the autobiography. Never to this day can I get an *A* on an English writing assignment. Well, I've gotten one or two *A*'s, but even when I do, I'm still kind of shaky on what I did to get an *A*.

In seventh grade, the teacher said, "Do you know what analysis is?" I hadn't been introduced to it. And he said, "Do you know what symbolism is? Imagine you see a man driving in a big limousine with jewels on his fingers ... blah, blah, blah. What do you think [that means]?" "That he is rich." "There, see, right there you're analyzing. That's analysis. That's what you've gotta do during the book." So I understood analyzing: the English teacher tearing that book apart, trying to [create] future English majors. From then on I was pickled in analysis.

Lord of the Flies, that was my first introduction to symbolism, and I thought that was really neat, that a writer would do that. After that for like two essays I tried to use some symbolism in my writing. We weren't doing story type of writing; I finally figured you can't use symbolism in analytical writing, so I pretty much quit after that because I didn't have time to write on my own; I could be putting symbolism into my work and who would care. I used to come home and write a little bit, but I just got too busy, and I put it away and eventually stopped. I haven't been assigned to write a story in an English class in three or four years. There is no support. I've never been introduced to how to write a good descriptive story. I've just always been shoved into the mode of analyze this, analyze that, and boy that's the one thing that makes me mad about writing. Analyzing works is good, trying to see what the writer is looking at is good, but I think there's a point where you overanalyze, and it loses its beauty. You have to try to dive into the depths of everything.

Freshman year, the big thing was, "Don't pad your writing, keep your points concise, know what you're talking about, no flowery things." Generally I work until I find out what the teacher wants, and then once I get there, I just write that way. I learned to be concise, come to the point and don't waver off it at all, so then I found out the next one wanted length. Pleasing the teacher's really hard for me 'cause every teacher's so different. In tenth ... one crazy teacher. I was getting *C*'s and *D*'s on essays. "There's not enough material," she said. "It's good to be concise, but if you don't write enough, you can't show what you know." I B.S.'d my way through my papers, and she loved it. Big swing. I said, "Okay, fine." So the next essay I wrote ten pages, and I got a big *A* on that paper. Shakespeare, that's all we studied all year long. I got a good introduction to Shakespeare, but the way she taught us to write was flowery. I think she wanted us to write like Shakespeare. She just worshipped the man.

Writing this year, oh boy, I've been really upset. The first essay

I wrote, I got a 60 on, out of 100. And I thought, "Oh no, another year when I'm going to spend the whole semester trying to find out what the teacher likes, figure it out, make my parents happy." The purpose of a bad grade to me is to worry my parents. The purpose of a good grade is to please my parents. That's the only purpose grades really have in my mind. The only essays we've done this year are style analysis, which makes sense to prepare for the English A.P. exam. We have been dealing with diction, detail, point of view. The next essay I spent a lot of time on. It wasn't especially long, or too concise, or too flowery, and I got a *B+*. In this essay now, a style analysis of Steinbeck, the thing I'm worrying about is not the writing but the style analysis. That's gonna be tough because there's an absolute rock-hard format that you have to follow: the thesis, then a chunk—a statement with woven quotes and two example sentences—and you're supposed to have three or four of those chunks. There's an exact format that you have to follow, and how am I gonna work that into *Grapes of Wrath*? It's like going back to the mechanical stuff again. It's just more worrying. Style analysis is just a new thing for me, and the main reason why it's important to me is because that's how you get a good grade in class.

I wrote for myself for a long time, but I realized I'm not gonna go to college this way, so I have to please the teacher. But this year I'm still really vague on what Ms. Summers wants. With Ms. Summers, I'm just not motivated as much. The aura about her is [of] an English teacher and a very intelligent person, but it's hard to respect someone who snaps back at you when you ask for help in the A.P. class. If you don't understand, she gets really upset. I mean she knows what she wants in good writing, and I don't think it's just length or flowery language, but I am vague on what she wants. Half the people in the class didn't know what style analysis was. She is very tight about what she wants. I think a lot of times my writing is better than other times because I can say what I mean, kinda belt out what I'm trying to say rather than just kind of mushing. Ms. Summers says I write passive a lot. I still don't understand what she means. She rambles, so you keep asking [about passive], and you look dumber and dumber and turn all red. Then last essay she said, "Great, not a single bit of passive in this," and "That was a good essay," but I didn't know what I did.

Sometimes I can really get a lot of kick into my writing. I'm actually starting to get a little pride in my term paper on movies that I'm writing in history. My mom is very critical of my writing, and she read the introduction and said it was great. Mr. L., he's the best teacher I've ever had. You go in that [A.P. History] class, and you're quiet and you're in your seat, and you're interested. He asks me how my plays are going and stuff like that. I think I'm past the level of performing for him. I write the way I want to write; I always thought humor was good in essays, because it gives the person that's reading it a break. I think Mr. L. appreciates it. I always try to do that, but I don't do that with Ms. Summers — a little scared to let loose. I try pretty hard, but I don't push myself like with Mr. L. He's a pretty hard grader, but I get A's in essays. It's really important when I find something to write on that's something that I know about. I mean I did a lot of reading to make sure it's the right topic. Which area to concentrate on was basically my decision. Being vague on a subject just fuels the fires of confusion, worry, and everything like that. I watched forty movies, and I studied them. That was the thing that I really liked about this report, I analyzed each film and grouped them into cycles. I watched them all [before] I read a single book. The books already did the analysis for you. Note cards just didn't work for this report; I wrote down notes on a piece of paper. I tried to explain to Mr. L. about it, and he said, "Well if it works for you, then do it." And it worked fine, because all my organization came together very well, so I was glad that he understood that. My final copy was beautiful, and shiny, and crisp, and clean.

Analysis of literature didn't just become tougher [through the years], it got to be a real pain; we were always analyzing stuff, taking it apart till there was nothing left. Analysis for me is a heavy writing project. It wasn't that it was boring; it's just that it gets to be the same thing. Every time you read a book make sure you look for symbolism; analyze every sentence. I like to do essays because practice makes perfect, but I think it would be good if we did short essays, maybe a long one every once in a while, and like maybe one week a story, and maybe the next week creative poetry, and the next analysis and then more analysis, and then more creative. But constantly having to regurgitate it and put it into an essay form all the time, that's the writing we've done in the past three years. You have to be serious about it, but how creative can you get? With creative sorts of writing, I think it would develop your writing skills to the point where the analysis would be more effective; you could use metaphor. And it would give you a break.

I think if someone read my poetry, they'd like it, and they'd think it was interesting. That's because I'm doing it my way. I think I'm a little scared to let go and write that [my] way in an essay because I've always been beaten on the head by my English teachers. I mean not literally beaten on the head. I think I should do my writing my own way, not stand-uppish and polite, but well done and everything. Too many people live their life trying to please other people. I always thought that I could be a good play writer, but I've always kind of chucked the idea because plays have to be so long, and I don't have time. I'd write a teenage sex comedy. I've always been interested in common tragedies because I thought they were the biggest tragedies because they hit so close to home. Writing is so important because your knowledge of words and how they work is important in theater. Writing helps you understand more. If I didn't write my poetry, I'd be a really unsatisfied person. I have to do my work, and I have to do my poetry. Whatever my writing skills are, I'm in more harmony. If I just write analytically for school, I think I'd have negative feelings toward writing. I've been thinking that I should just say, "Go jump in the lake!" to my English teachers.

Problems with Writing Curricula

When I went to Doug's school, I was particularly interested because I was told that most of the teachers had participated in a Writing Project, and indeed they seemed to be teachers who taught writing "as a process" effectively. But though the students in this school did more writing than others, took time to get their ideas and plans in order before they started drafting, did multiple drafts (though many resented it), and worked with others to improve their drafts (unless pushed by procrastination to a last-minute finale), the rest of their experience was all too familiar. They had "the process" down pat, but only their history teacher, Mr. Lawrence, seemed able to get them enthusiastic about it.

Doug's disgruntlement with school writing throws light on three problems with the traditional writing curriculum that must be overcome if secondary students are to want to use writing after graduation: overemphasis on analysis of literature, emphasis on format-based instruction, and emphasis on grading. These emphases are so entrenched in secondary writing curricula that it's hard for many teachers to picture how things might be different. As misplaced as I feel these emphases are, there was an even more noticeable problem: a lack of the kind of engagement that results when students are allowed to pursue things that are important to them. Though teachers like Atwell, Romano, and Wigginton have written of ways to engage students by using workshop and project settings, it's hard for many teachers to see how important it is that they work toward that end and how to go about it in the context of their teaching situations. In order to show why we must value, yet go beyond, "writing as a process," I've used mostly students from Doug's school in this chapter, so we can see how students who are adept at "the writing process" still have problems with school writing.

Pickled in Analysis

From seventh grade on, Doug felt "pickled in analysis." Almost every successful writer in the study talked about the predominance of literary analysis in their secondary English classes. For the most successful writers and readers, analyzing literature wasn't in itself dissatisfying. We know that students come away from reading with responses to and questions from what they have read. Students reported that they liked working through the questions that literature left them with, the puzzle of it, and the thinking and insights it involved. Nevertheless, they were tired of figuring out what they thought each teacher wanted, or they missed the variety of writing they had done in prior grades, or they just wanted to read literature and respond "in peace."

Successful students often came out with a rendition of the dispirited "all we do is read it, analyze it, read it, analyze it" phrase in their second interview. Joy in reading was undercut. For the less successful students, the perpetual link of reading and writing was a double burden. Reading wasn't easy for them, and when they had to read knowing that writing about it was the inevitable next step, a nonproductive tension was superimposed on the reading. Basic writers usually haven't read broadly, and this penalizes them because they haven't internalized structures of the written code that might help them with reading and writing. They have little sense of what to expect or what must be accomplished.

There's irony here because literature was something students were generally enthusiastic about in grade school and often in junior high, and teachers usually are drawn to teaching English because they too love literature. But though the link between reading and writing is an important one (and one that is currently in vogue), this link needn't always be played out in analysis. Students can write in many ways about literature, discovering meaning in the process. Furthermore, it's important for us as teachers to realize that students learn about writing simply by reading good literature, and learn about literature as they write poetry and fiction and essays (Cleary and Lund, 1989).

Another issue is development. The thinking processes that go into many forms of literary analysis may not be fully developed until late high school years or after. Piaget (1957) establishes the lowest age when "formal operational thought" is evidenced as age eleven. Though researchers still debate both Piaget's stages and their actual ages, it's clear that abstract thought does not click on at a certain age between eleven and eighteen; in any secondary classroom different students will be at different stages of developing such thought. Some perfectly intelligent students under the age of eighteen (or over) may not be ready to do the kind of analysis of literature that's demanded of them. Donaldson (1979) talks about the "disembodied thinking" (similar to what Piaget talks of as "formal operational thought") that she sees as further developed in students who come from the middle-class homes where that kind of thinking is encouraged. She warns that our schools fail children who are not ready for disembodied thought when it's required of them and begin a pattern of failure. Not all students will catch on to analysis as quickly as middle-class, white Doug. Connecting literature with personal experience and moving naturally toward analysis as a way of understanding this experience is the kind of literary approach that some students need and that all will enjoy. The need to figure out what the teacher wants may be heightened by students' inability to do the kind of analysis being required. I don't believe that most English teachers are looking for their own ideas in student papers. We'd all be pretty bored, as well as weighed down with papers, if that was all we received. But that seems to be what Kevin and other students thought was wanted:

> I had to learn to take his key points and then make them my key points, and then summarize them and then argue them the way I would argue them. Writing is trying to make your thought process match the thought process the teacher is looking for.

It may be that because many students aren't ready to do the kind of analysis that we want from them, they solve the problem by getting clues from teachers that will allow them to get the writing done.

Certainly the link between reading and writing is important. The problem comes when the connection becomes drudgery or agony. Learning literary conventions through reading can be both an inductive and a deductive process. Students learn inductively about the craft of writing fiction just by reading, by absorbing as if by osmosis, *and* they learn deductively by consciously attending to what authors do. Teachers can let students have homework and class time to read and learn by osmosis; they can also focus them consciously on literary technique, letting them *discover* those techniques in text.

From listening to the forty students, I've concluded that it's important to vary the kinds of things we ask students to do with literature. Not every piece of literature must be formally analyzed to initiate understanding of literary forms and figures. Doug's idea of practicing the symbolism that he saw in his reading by applying it in his own writing might allow him a deep understanding of the technique, which in turn would inform later analysis. Moffett (1980) advocates a similar technique by having students read and then write from different points of view as a way of discovering craft in writing. Response journals, practicing literary conventions, discussion, conscious analysis of author's style, all will feed later analytic ability and may better fill college literature courses with enthusiastic majors, minors, and students seeking electives. Literary study needn't lead exclusively to written analysis of literature.

I'll let Peco, an aspiring young film director, be responsible for summaries in this chapter. He was a perceptive young man whose anger matched Elana's. Though he, like Chris, had been nominated by his teachers for an NCTE Achievement Award for his writing, he didn't think of that writing as being thinking.

> If they gave you the option and it wouldn't affect your grade, I wouldn't write about books anymore. I can get something out of the book by myself or in discussion. Why don't you write about something that you either haven't covered before, or something that's very personal, rather than writing about a book that first of all you didn't choose to read and [second] that you've probably analyzed already in class? Sometimes you'd like to write about things that happen to you. I went to my junior high school math teacher's memorial service. And I wanted to write about it because I had strong personal feelings, and it was an unusual time, people I hadn't seen in years, and I had gotten older since. If I had anything I'd like to write about, that'd probably be it, not books. There just never seems to be enough time.

Format: Stricture or Structure

Tom described the change in the writing he encountered upon entering high school:

> I had to get through that first struggle; it was all a very new type of writing. Pretty much fifth through eighth grade I had liked to describe things in details and determine things like stories in my mind. It was pretty fun. When we got in high school, we didn't do it anymore. It was brand new, and it got hard when we started writing essays. You had to follow a certain format, putting all ideas together, staying on the same track, and supporting your thesis. The whole idea was hard; writing is hard.

Almost every student described a sense of loss when they learned that there was one way to do things, when they learned that content was less important than form. They felt format as stricture instead of structure. In elementary school, the focus was on meaning-making and correctness. In junior high and/or early high school, format descended. Students described the jolt of learning the paragraph format, and just as their paragraphs were ordered, the clamp of the expository format was applied. Meaning took a backseat, and confidence waned. Constance Weaver describes elementary students (while referring to Graves [1976]) who are "convinced that they can't write because they can't do it 'right.'" Children learn that writing is done to "command various conventions," and there is danger that they many never "get form and meaning back together" (Weaver, 1979, p. 60). This dichotomy between form and meaning seems even more heavily established when students get into secondary school.

The secondary students in this study detected two sources of stricture: the teacher-specific formula and the more general expository formula. Kevin described the teacher-specific formula:

> In the beginning of the year I am uncomfortable 'cause I know there is a standard, and I don't know it. Towards the end of the year I know what the teachers are looking for and so when I write, I take enough of me to get it written, but I know what they are looking for, so I just sort of follow the formula. They will allow certain flexibility, so I'll flex it to whatever level they like, add enough twist to make them happy but not too much so that it annoys them. I'll try to come up with an angle, something that's close enough so it's acceptable but different [so mine won't be] the twentieth duplicate essay.

Students tend to see "what the teacher wants" as arbitrary and as a function of the submission/dominance power structure set up in the classroom. The irony is, of course, that most teachers establish these teacher-specific formulas because they believe they'll help students meet their futures.

The second source of stricture is the expository formula. The expository formula is teacher-imposed, but certain stock formulas are used nationwide. Though clear organization is important to establish in students' writing, we must work against the exclusivity of writing according to formulas. The "five-paragraph essay," the "CSC" (claim, support, conclusion), the "chunks" that Peco and Doug described, and many other formulas may be useful formats for students to analyze and even model occasionally. To use these formulas, students normally take the rules for the structure and apply them; they begin with form instead of meaning. These formulas took an extraordinary prominence in the students' minds when they talked about secondary writing. In part, formula-bound writing may explain the sense of loss, the loss of ownership, and the growing ambivalence that students feel toward writing.

Tom Newkirk's (1987) analysis of the discourse structures that surface naturally in young children's writing suggests that young children induce and acquire increasingly complex expository structures quite naturally through reading and writing. Secondary students might also "acquire" increasingly complex expository structures if they were permitted to explore them through both reading and writing. Deductive attention to expository discourse structures may further "learning" of these structures, but exclusive and arbitrary use of narrative and expressive writing in elementary years or of expository writing in secondary schools is not only unnecessary but destructive to students' sense of discovery and destructive to their writing motivation (Moffett, 1968). As Emig (1967) suggests, there are two things that we can lend to students in writing instruction: freedom and constraint. I certainly don't advocate an "anything goes" approach to the secondary writing curricula, but the excessive constraint in format that the students in this study felt may well be counterproductive. They rarely got "meaning and form back together."

We need to be realistic. Our world grades, promotes, and values writers on the basis of how well they can replicate the written structures of their profession (or what Bartholomae [1985] and others call "discourse communities"). Businessmen have to know how to write good memos; teachers have to know how to write notes home to parents; mechanics need to be able to write up work requests; literary critics need to be conscious of the school of literary criticism they come from and must write according to its conventions; and researchers have to know how to write abstracts and how to present their results with voice and format appropriate to their targeted journal. Before students leave high school, they need to become conscious that "discourse communities" exist, and they need to become familiar with (though not necessarily adept at) the structures they'll encounter after high school. However, this writing need not constitute their whole secondary writing experience. Apprenticeship or formal higher education is designed to accomplish this learning. If students want entry into a discourse community, that in itself will establish purpose. Students will want to become familiar with the discourse communities that they might want to enter in the future. Let that be conscious exploration, discovery, and experimentation, rather than what seems to be application of arbitrary formulas. Through reading, students can consciously identify characteristics of different kinds of writing that they might have to do in the future, and if the students can find real purposes for such writing, they might experiment with new structures using what Bartholomae identifies as the special vocabulary, system of presentation, interpretive scheme, and form of analysis. This will help students have conscious purpose in their writing. They will understand better what teachers like Ms. Summers know: writing in certain ways gets you ready to enter a vocation. Again, I will defer to Peco for our summary:

> I find it pretty ridiculous to use this five-paragraph thing over and over again. I find it very rigid, and if you try to vary what you're doing, you're gonna kill your grade. "This is well written, but I'm gonna give you a low grade because it's not what I asked for." I heard that in freshman year. Since freshman year, they've been teaching you format: "If you want to write a good essay, write it in this format, even though you're never going to use it again." If you look at the good authors, they don't follow the rules. "Don't address your reader"; authors address their readers. "Don't make long lists"; authors make long lists. It's very hypocritical, especially when the teachers say this is such a great novel. Why aren't they [authors] sticking to the formal styles teachers taught us? Teachers sit there and say, "Analyze the style of this novel. It fits perfectly into a six-paragraph essay." So for four years, you're gonna use a format that you're not gonna use again. That's pretty ridiculous to me.

Grades

I have to have a little confrontation with myself every time I try to slip out of facing the issue of grades. Grades are a subject that educators tend to avoid; they are as connected with the American Way as mother, apple pie, and grammar. Teachers always see grading as a stumbling block to what they wish they could do differently. But in analyzing these forty students' experience with writing, I came to this conclusion: *It isn't productive to connect writing with grades.*

As stated in three prior chapters, grades for the sake of grades mainly have a negative effect on writing. Participants in this study viewed grading (evaluation without collaboration) as a form of criticism or a form of praise, as a mirror by which to view themselves or as a means of comparing themselves favorably or unfavorably with peers. In that respect, grading had more effect on writing confidence than on the development of writing ability. If grading was perceived as continual criticism, any intrinsic motivation for writing was destroyed. In some instances, perceived praise made students more willing to go about writing, but the long-range effect of grading was to seduce students into a pattern of pleasing the teacher or, as Doug suggests, to get their parents off their backs.

There are more productive ways to enhance writing confidence.

Students, however, do need the feedback that grades have been assumed to offer. Yet, unless collaboration between student and teacher is a part of the feedback given, the process takes place entirely outside the writer. Participants valued corrections and suggestions most if they were connected with what they perceived as collaboration with a teacher who respected them. Then students viewed evaluation as information about how to tackle further complexities in the writing process. When response was used to prime intrinsic motivation (as in Ms. M.'s response to Lisa's whale topic), or when response was given in conference with the writer to point to areas of competence and to next steps (as was the case with Mr. O'Neill's conferences with Orion), evaluation fostered writing as a meaningful mode of expression that would continue after school years.

Grades are useful feedback about writing only when students interpret them as information about a new competence or a need for competence. And again there are more useful ways to indicate competence or the need for competence. Evaluation is essential; grading is at best seductive, at worst destructive. In reality, as Peco says, teachers give themselves grades:

> If I got an *A* on the paper I just said, "Big deal." I threw it away because I knew that it was only what she wanted to hear. The only reason I was getting a good grade was because she was just seeing her opinion.

If this is so (though as teachers I know we don't intend it), the good grades mean we have brought our students to think and act the way we want them to think and act. Extending Peco's line of logic, bad grades then mean we haven't succeeded; we fail. (Strategies for grading, when you have to grade, are discussed in the final chapter.)

Struggle for Voice

I made a promise to Jessica that it's time to fulfill. When Jessica marched into her first interview session, she was a young woman with a mission. Her first words:

> My teacher said you might write a book to writing teachers. Tell them I don't like to write when the teachers assign something and say, "Here, you have to do it this way, you have to have an introduction, you have to have the body, and you have to have the conclusion, and here's what you have to write about." I hate writing essays, and I don't like writing, period, for school 'cause I don't feel like I'm getting anything out of it, 'cause I have to write

it in a certain way. When I do it on my own, I can have some feelings for it—"This is my paper, and I'm writing it my way." That's the way I've always felt toward writing, you know.

Every student in this study came up with a variation on this statement which Jessica managed so forthrightly during the first few minutes of her interview sequence and which she repeated with variations until I finally promised her that I would quote her in whatever I wrote.

And, of course, in listening to these students, I have become, like Jessica, a woman with a mission. Students entreat us to let them regain control of their voices, to preserve, as Emerson said, "the gleam that flashes from within." As teachers we need to create situations that permit students to find voices in which to say things that are meaningful to them; we need to show them the power that their voices hold. Years ago Vygotsky said:

> Writing should be meaningful for children, that an intrinsic need should be aroused in them, and that writing should be incorporated into a task that is necessary and relevant for life . . . Writing should be "cultivated" rather than "imposed." (Vygotsky, 1978, p. 118)

Some elementary teachers have taken this advice to heart, but most secondary teachers have not. With form as the guiding focus of our curricula, the driving force of meaning is lost.

Throughout the previous chapters, we've seen what it was like for students to write when they couldn't focus their attention on that writing. Kathy will remind us of the struggle that ensues:

> If I'm not interested in it, I get frustrated so I wanna throw it down and burn it, and go away and go outside and not think about it any more. But I have to, and I'm forcing myself to sit there, and I get mad at myself for not being able to bring it out and I'm angry and grumpy, and I don't want people to talk to me. And I don't want interruptions 'cause anything stops me thinking about it.

In order for students to sustain the focused attention that permits growth in writing, it's important that there be links between writers and their material. There needs to be what Sondra Perl (1986) calls a "felt sense," a sense of what the writer wants to say that will act as a guide in the structuring of that writing.

> In writing, meaning cannot be discovered the way we discover an object on an archeological dig. In writing, meaning is crafted and constructed. It involves us in a process of coming-into-being. Once we have worked at shaping, through language, what is there inchoately, we can look at what we have written to see if it adequately captures what we intended. Often at this moment discovery occurs.

We see something new in our writing that comes upon us as a surprise. We see in our words a further structuring of the sense we began with and we recognize that in those words we have discovered something new about ourselves and our topic. Thus when we are successful at this process, we end up with a product that teaches us something, that clarifies what we know (or what we knew at one point only implicitly), and that lifts out or explicates or enlarges our experience. In this way writing leads to discovery. (Perl, 1986, p. 34)

I would like all secondary writers to write from a felt sense of what they want to say.

I believe that the problems with sustained attention and passive voice that the more successful students in this study were concerned about may well come about because they have no felt sense of their topic. It was a curious phenomenon that so many students struggled to deal with the passive voice. At first I explained students' use of passive voice as their attempt to sound formal. If that's the case, it's no wonder that students adopt the passive voice. It's certainly modeled in most of their textbooks, a model for voiceless writing. But use of passive voice may well be more complicated than that. Perhaps students' adoption of that voice is indicative of the passive stance they take toward their writing. I find that I slip into the passive voice when I'm not sure I believe what I know I must say to please the audience, or when I would prefer not to take responsibility for saying what I know will irritate the audience. Passive voice indicates to me that I'm disconnected from a felt sense, that I'm not sure I really want to own up to what I'm saying. Perhaps for many of the forty students, passivity was an alienated response to their topic.

If we permit choice in writing topics, we increase the chance that felt sense will drive the composing process. Further, if students are encouraged to write from their interests or passions, felt sense will bring strong guidance to that writing. Doug described his desire as a young adolescent to be able to write about himself or things connected to him. The links between self-discovery and writing are strong; they feed self-knowledge and self-actualization, things our adolescents could use more of.

It's ironic that Doug had never had a chance to bring his poetry into the school. His literary self is diminished because it goes unacknowledged: "I think if someone read my poetry, I think they'd like it, and they'd think it was interesting. That's because I'm doing it my way." There needs to be more room in our curriculum for students to do at least some things their own way. Decisions that they make about form and topic are writers' decisions. They won't begin to think of themselves as writers until they begin to exercise some control in those respects. The scope of many schools' writing curricula has narrowed to emphases on form and literary analysis, even though our professional organization, The National Council of Teachers of English, advocates "that much practice with expressive language (oral and written) is important, leading to writing with various purposes in a wide variety of forms for many audiences" (NCTE, "Guidelines for the Preparation of Teachers of the English Language Arts," 1986). I certainly don't advocate cessation of literary analysis or cessation of reasonable attention to and experimentation with form—even Doug sees the need for those—but I do think students need to establish personal links with their content in order to learn about themselves, in order to establish a voice, in order to experience power through their writing.

There's also a practical reason why we need to let students regain their voices: If students have a history with writing that they have cared about, most will care enough to give their writing the sustained and focused attention that will improve their writing skills. They'll give this time and attention not because they'll be "flayed" if they don't but because they'll want to. They will care enough to find out how they can best structure their writing so that it fulfills its purpose, and they will seek to know what conventions it should follow so that their audiences may focus on its message. The burden for effective writing is shifted to the student.

The consequences of not permitting students their voice are many. There are consequences to teachers, to students, and to our society. Perhaps the greatest consequence to us as teachers is that we'll have to grade what our students think we want to hear—dull voiceless papers. Furthermore, we won't get sincere effort from our students. Peco can show us how he ceased to take his work seriously. He will end this section before I move on to the consequences to society. Peco was a young man who, like Elana, was angry at the loss of his voice, and like Elana he sought revenge in little ways. He would end his junior high writings in dreams or root-beer fights to irritate his teacher, and in high school he became a little more sophisticated in his revenge:

> Last year I remember her being strict on these stupid essays. She was forcing a topic on us. If anybody forces a topic on me, I just can't stand writing. What she liked in the paper was just pure regurgitation from what she was saying. I think that's affected me because even if I want to get something done on time, I get writer's block until the last night. Actually there was a project this year that I was excited about. We had to do an analysis of *Billy Budd*, and the only reason why I liked doing that project was because I

was doing it with a friend, and we were taking a viewpoint that we knew that the teacher might not like: we said the plot had elements of a communist revolution. We didn't take the project too seriously, and we put pictures of Stalin and things like that all over our report.

The loss to teachers is worsened by the loss to students. I worry about the alienated students that our school systems create, both the successful ones and the unsuccessful ones.

The Social Consequences of Voicelessness

There's a logical consequence to the heavy "please-the-teacher" mentality that pervaded the successful students' experience. Some students who felt disconnected from the writing they had to do did that work with a touch of anger; a loss occurred for them when the secondary school writing straitjacket was applied. Still other students, however, scared me because they accepted "pleasing the teacher" without perceiving it as a sellout, without seeing it as a loss of personal integrity. They learned to distance themselves from their writing, to please the audience, to be untrue to themselves. Furthermore, they became good at it. Joseph had mastered the art of pleasing his high school teachers.

A Profile of Joseph

In fifth and sixth grade, I got the urge to write a story once in a while. I remember writing about my dog. I guess I don't write for fun anymore. It's just writing for like a teacher or a judge. Most of the writing I do now can go back to learning from sixth-grade composition, like topic sentences of paragraphs and things like that. I guess the past set a good foundation for my writing now, about 50 percent of it, and then I think the rest of the 50 percent came recently, organized it, perfected it, made it easier.

In seventh grade our teacher was tougher, and we did have to do reports every once in a while. Before that we were learning grammar and stuff. We had a textbook with certain stories and interpretation of the stories, and I did really poorly. I didn't know exactly what kind of answers the teachers wanted to particular questions. I didn't really know how you're supposed to go about telling somebody about a story. I started telling the story, and my teacher stopped me and said, "Just tell what mainly happened; go to the end or something." It wasn't that hard to learn once you got the hang of it. You know what the teacher wants, and that would be a good summary. I didn't like literature. I guess I haven't liked it until recently because I didn't do too well. I didn't like spelling until I started doing well in it. I guess I didn't know exactly what was a good answer and what wasn't, and how specific to get. Our teacher was pretty hard.

In eighth grade we did start learning how to write formally, more formally, with the introduction and summary and topic sentences. The first essay that we did for him [was] just a regular article about science. I wrote it, and he brought it up in front of class and said, "This is an example of a good essay." So I guess that was my first. After a while it was actually pretty nice because I liked it better when I wrote better.

We wrote reports, essays, and things like that in ninth grade — more practice and learning new ways of writing. I did have a speech class, and we'd do a lot of writing there: essay, informative, and persuasive. But the first day I can remember in that class, we all stood up and said our names and a hobby that we had, and the next day we had to write an essay on that hobby. I had a friend who had two three-wheelers. That was really fun for me; I liked what I wrote about. That's probably the first time I started speaking in front of a class. It's pretty scary the first time. I always read what I was saying, but we were supposed to ad-lib a little bit. I got A's in the class; maybe she wasn't that strict.

I really have had to worry about what I was gonna write, always worrying if the audience will like it or not. It's been hard because I didn't know what my classmates would accept. The popular ones were really relaxed; I wasn't. I had to worry what I was gonna read in front of class. I'd worry about sounding awkward. I tried to stay away from jokes, I didn't know what kind of joke would work, and I'd get embarrassed if they didn't laugh. I usually tried to stay in the middle of acceptable. I wanted to be creative, but the worst fear was getting too creative. I wasn't writing it for something that I would like. It was more something that they would like. I remember when we had to write an advertisement about a certain product. You had to get creative and that worried me. What if you tried to be funny, and it wasn't funny. I remember in the end I just took a song, and I spoke with the song in an excited way. It was an airline vacation to Europe. They kinda liked it because of the song. It was an acceptable attention getter.

In debate we have to be persuasive and we have to be understandable, make a point that the judges will accept. In an essay it's just writing about something and the teacher grades it, and you are arguing basically. That's what debate is about. We use a lot of analogies, and I've used some of them in writing in English class, for ideas and organization. It's kind of a game. It takes a while to find out how or what exactly the audience is going to believe. In English I usually stay neutral. I used to not like literature, interpreting literature because I didn't know what the teacher would want. But once you debate in speech you know what or which arguments will basically be accepted. When I start writing a speech, I feel strongly for that particular side, and so when I switch over to the opposite thinking, I start believing that side. I wouldn't say that I have any major opinions. A lot of it is presenting arguments that aren't really true. It's just whether or not the other debater can take it apart, or whether the judge will like it or not.

I don't really write for myself. I can't think of any time . . . Oh, okay, I did a voice of democracy thing once. They have a contest at each school where they gave us a topic, and they took the top three people from each school, and the first person got $100, the second got $75, and the third got $50. They'd send the speeches over to judges. And it was called The Challenge of American Citizenship. It was a really tough topic — a lot of ways you could interpret it. There was really no way you could tell what would be a good speech. I was thinking the normal ones would be voting and public service and all that. Voting is so obviously American citizenship that I decided to do something about citizenship and world peace, racism. It was the one time when I didn't do what I thought the judges would like. I did what I thought would be a good speech. I liked it, and I didn't win. People who did win did things like voting. I wish I had won the $100. I thought next time though I wouldn't be so original. I decided to do what would win. School writing is the same basically; I need to get the grade.

I guess with my English teacher it would be better to be original 'cause she'd be looking for that type of thing. When I gave the Voice of Democracy speech, they would be more likely to look at what they would want to hear, while if I was doing it for my teacher, she would take a look at it more objectively, and, "Okay, this is more original." If too many people in the class were going one way, I chose differently. I just wrote this paper on "To Build a Fire." We were supposed to pick a topic sentence from seven that she gave you, and then just write an introduction and conclusion with a couple of paragraphs to support it. The first thing I did was to look at the topics; 90 percent of the class was doing the same topics. I decided to look for other topic sentences and put them together. I've never rebelled about what the teacher wanted us to write about. If the teacher chose something to write about, she usually gives us choices on how to approach it. A lot of kids in the class get mad because the teacher says you have the wrong opinion. I guess I haven't really had any problems with that, I just try to write what the teacher wants. I have my own decision to do it whichever way I want to do it, but still I do it in the general way that she wants.

I don't know, I guess it's nice being a good student. I have friends in debate and in a class like Enriched English, A.P. History. I have other friends, I have to change my line of speaking, and I guess that's a burden. I just have to be easy to understand. I guess respect is pretty important for me. It's important to fit in, to fit into some kind of crowd. I have a best friend, but he doesn't do that well, so I guess I need a group of friends that I can identify with. When I'm in a class that is intellectually oriented, it's really fun to be around that type of environment. In debate for example, I'm getting trophies, winning. The main thing that it does is get respect. When you win, when I bring home a trophy, sometimes I just forget to show it to my parents. I guess it's just respect of fellow debaters.

When Joseph finished his last interview, I felt a sense of discomfort that went beyond being sick to my stomach; the irony in his words made me sick at heart. At that moment I would gladly have handed over $100 to him if I thought it would have given him back his own voice. He had gone beyond the endeavor of considering what would be compelling to an audience in order to convince them of *his* opinion. Joseph was an earnest young man who was just coming into his own, in his own eyes and in the eyes of his fellow students. I could see him being a future senator in our Congress. Ralph Waldo Emerson said, "Nothing is at last sacred but the integrity of your own mind. Absolve you to yourself, and you shall have the suffrage of the world . . . I am ashamed to think how easily we capitulate to badges and names, to large societies and dead institutions" ("Self-Reliance," p. 631). Joseph had capitulated, and I'm not sure that our democracy can withstand an educational system that rewards capitulation anymore. Has its demise started with the power of grades? Or does it start with the conformity that is permitted to rage rampant in the adolescent years? The forty students in the study did not sense tolerance for their differences, for their diversity and interests. They sought to discover what was "acceptable." If students aren't encouraged to develop their own opinions and to articulate them, I fear for what we call our democracy.

Jefferson envisioned a democracy that would depend upon the education of the citizenry. He wrote in his "Bill for the Diffusion of Knowledge":

The most effectual means of preventing tyranny is to illuminate, as far as practicable, the minds of the people at large, and more specially to give them knowledge of those facts, which history exhibiteth, that possessed thereby of the experience of other ages and countries, they may be able to know ambition under all its shapes, and prompt to exert their natural powers to defeat its purposes. (From "Bill for the Diffusion of Knowledge," 1779)

Jefferson would not have seen Joseph's capitulation as education. Unfortunately, he saw young women as "too wise to wrinkle their foreheads with politics," but his hope was that young men would learn to read (as we would say, to learn to read critically), to safeguard our democracy from ambition and mediocrity of mind by having opinions about what legislators were doing, and to state those opinions in word and vote. Joseph couldn't see the way his own desire for acceptability caused him to sell out. Some students like Elana ("Well if that is what they want, that is what they'll get") and Peco capitulated angrily, and even though I probably would have been delighted with Joseph as a student, I would prefer trusting our future government to Elana.

Actually, de Tocqueville in *Democracy in America* recognized in the 1830s that capitulation might be a problem for American democracy: "The multitude require no laws to coerce those who do not think like themselves: public disapprobation is enough; a sense of their loneliness and impotence overtakes them and drives them to despair" (vol 2, pp. 274–275). Loneliness, fear of not being popular, was a strong motivator in Joseph's attention to being "acceptable" instead of pleasing himself.

> It cannot be doubted that in the United States the instruction of the people powerfully contributes to the support of the democratic republic; and such must always be the case, I believe, where the instruction which enlightens the understanding is not separated from the moral education which amends the heart. But I would not exaggerate this advantage, and I am still further from thinking, as so many people do think in Europe, that men can instantaneously be made citizens by teaching them to read and write. True information is mainly derived from experience. . . . (de Tocqueville, vol. 1, p. 329)

As discussed above, students felt best when writing was connected in some way with their experience. Though until now I have had to rely on our fore*fathers*, it is a pleasure to hear what a woman has to say on the subject. Janet Emig talks about how this relates to the less successful students:

> One wonders at times if the shying away from reflexive writing is not an unconscious effort to keep the "average" and "less able" student from the kind of writing he can do best and, often far

better than the "able," since there is so marvelous a democracy in the distribution of feeling and imagination (Emig, 1971, p. 100).

Erik Erikson stated that America was generally successful in educating children "in a spirit of self-reliance and enterprise," "free of prejudice and apprehension," and, therefore, having "hope for equality." He said that our educational system "encouraged children of mixed backgrounds" until the "shock of American adolescence: the standardization of individuality, the intolerance of 'differences'" (Erikson, 1950, p. 218). I believe that secondary students whose language deviates significantly from standard English have differences that are too great for the system as it stands to tolerate. Their voices are drowned in remedial exercises, and the large majority are, for all practical purposes, disenfranchised and rarely even understand their hidden injuries of class.

Ironically, vestiges of the European system of "top down," teacher-dominated education are still alive in the United States. Reformers like Dewey advocated educational change for a more democratic America, and they certainly have had partial success in some segments of our educational system. Some elementary schools have adopted a more child-centered approach.

Most secondary schools, however, are still run according to an antiquated system that makes capitulation look attractive to the successful students. Teachers tell students what they need to know, and students prove they know it by telling the teachers what they think the teachers want them to know (also see Applebee, 1981). Then teachers tell students if their guesses were accurate by "correcting" what they have done and awarding a grade. Students begin to see their futures tied to grades; intellectual integrity falls by the wayside. Hence, students like Joseph have become masters at capitulation.

John Dewey said in his seminal book, *Democracy and Education*:

> A society based on custom will utilize individual variations only up to a limit of conformity with usage; uniformity is the chief ideal within each class. A progressive society counts individual variations as precious since it finds in them the means of its own growth. Hence a democratic society must, in consistency with its ideal, allow for intellectual freedom and the play of diverse gifts and interests in its educational measures. (Dewey, 1944, p. 305)

Writing may seem to be a small part of a student's education, but it's a very important part. It's through writing, even more than speaking, that students can discover what they know and believe. What happens when students don't write from themselves, with a sense of integrity? There's a huge price. If we're concerned with developing writing skills, it means that students learn to write for a very narrow audience (the teacher), that they have limited attention and felt sense to bring to the structuring of what they want to say, and that they learn to dislike writing. But the price is even bigger than that. They write to get the reward (and in Doug's case, to get his parents off his back). Does the reward start off as grades and acceptance, and end up as votes and money? Could the number of ethics problems in our government be lowered if our future politicians developed a sense of integrity in their adolescent years? Could adolescents work to know what they think rather than to know what others want them to think, work for personal satisfaction rather than reward, work to discover what will make their world better for themselves and others?

We need our writing curriculum to reattach students to their souls.

Chapter Eight

Kathy
Signs of Hope

As my research progressed, I found myself wanting to talk with students who were connected to their writing in ways that made it compelling for them—students who were writing to discover who they were and what their world was all about, students who were writing to act upon that world. But out of the forty, I talked with only four eleventh-graders who seemed to be doing school writing guided by what Emerson termed the "gleam from within": Kathy, Peco, Doug, and Portia. They had just finished a term paper for their social studies teacher, Mr. L., and each had found the process to be a meaningful experience. I have picked Kathy to tell you what it was like because she talked the most about her forty-two-page love affair with writing. Then again, Kathy talked the most about everything; she managed to pack more words on a sixty-minute tape than any other student. In her profile, we can see how she established a real audience and a real purpose for herself while writing about something important to her. I've focused Kathy's profile primarily on the term-paper assignment to leave room for shortened profiles of other writers and further analysis of the kind of writing programs that foster writers' inner inclination to write.

A Profile of Kathy

I used to like making stories up that I could relate to, put myself into. "This little girl, her dad bought her a horse." I liked using my imagination. And I'd show it to my dad to prompt him, but I never did get the horse. I would get into it, and I would think about it for a long time, and [then] I'd write the stories. It was just for fun, for me. [Even in] fourth grade, I enjoyed writing, especially when I illustrated it. In school I used to get really bad grades in handwriting. That sort of turned me off. Here I was writing something, and I'd get cased on for my handwriting. It wasn't the neatest, but I could read it. I do more writing now, and my handwriting now is fine, but I don't like it.

In fifth grade I had this very strict teacher. Before that I was writing some things sort of off the subject 'cause I wanted to do what my imagination wanted to do. She'd come down on me, and I would get so offended. I'd get so upset and, "Well, fine, I won't write this stuff as well." I thought writing was being truthful about what you were thinking. After that I'd always do the writing, I just wouldn't have the enthusiasm, I'd just do the bare minimum. We were supposed to described what month our birthday was in without actually telling it, and I said, "In the month I was born in, we like to give each other things in the shape of an organ with lumps of brown stuff in it." And she said, "Well, that's just not appropriate." And I can guess what she thought. That sort of irritated, offended me. I wasn't trying to be gross. And I could see why it looks gross when I wrote it. And people still guessed, "Oh yeah, it's February, boxes of candy shaped [like] hearts with chocolate in [them]." My mom said, "Well, that's not gross; were you trying to be gross?"

After those years, when we wrote, it was often on the books we'd read, and those books were chosen by the teachers. I like them now. I look [back] at *Lord of the Flies* as a great book now. I didn't enjoy it as much then because it was work. We had to read it, and we couldn't read it at our own pace. I thought it was very interesting learning all the symbolism, but I missed writing about what I want to write about. The only other kind of writing I do that has as much meaning in it is when I am writing in my journal. Writing them gets out what I couldn't get out. One whole year, I wrote in a journal every day. I just wanted my kids to see it when I was older. It started January, and it ended December 31. I will be portraying history in a way. Who's going to write in a journal and lie about it? I started doing it monthly.

Wednesday I turned in a humongous paper in history. He gave us the choice of our topic as long as it had to do with American history. I did it on the right to bear arms. I . . . I've had people killed with guns, so I really got into that. I was real happy with it, and it was still work. Sometimes it wasn't fun. I don't know if you can call fun and interesting the same thing. It was interesting enough because I was proving something. The question I was trying to answer was, "Is this, the right to bear arms, right or practical for today?" That was great for me 'cause I could analyze it, make conclusions, and I could prove it to you. I mean I am going to send it to my senator. As soon as I get it back, I'm going to smarten it up and send it to him. He's already antigun, but I'm just real happy that I could prove it. I didn't think I could do that. This paper took me beyond my wildest dreams as far as my capacity for writing. I've never done anything longer than about six pages, and that was about forty. I feel like I've done something for Stan. That was always on my mind.

Four years ago we had a personal friend called Stan. He was a good friend of my dad's. They'd worked together, and they played poker together. Stan had a good friend who got married to some guy she hadn't known very long. After like a week, she came to Stan and said, "I made a big mistake." They were talking and this guy came, and he had a shotgun or a rifle or something, and he shot Stan, and he shot her in the street, and he reloaded while he was in the street in front of everybody and shot her again. When it came to court, he [her husband] was called emotionally unstable. Well, I don't buy that. I don't think there is any excuse for that sort of thing. Stan had been a good friend to me too. I've had somebody destroyed that I loved. It just wasn't fair, and it doesn't seem fair that somebody can go out and buy a gun.

When Mr. L., my history teacher, told us that we were going to be doing this big research paper, it was like October/November. We had to figure out three topics we thought we might be interested in. I chose the guns one, horses and history, and "Was war inevitable?" I chose the war as inevitable one because I knew the teacher'd like that. I wanted to do something about the horse and its effect on history, but that didn't have a lot of meaning in proving what the horse did somehow. I knew right away that I was gonna do guns because it interested me so much. We had to go to the library and look for the information there was, and see how much there was to gather, and then we had to choose between those three after thinking about them. He said to us, "Be careful what you choose 'cause you are gonna be stuck with it for this long."

What's a gun for? It's for killing, I mean . . . obviously. Gun advocates say to me (I interviewed a couple), "It's just as fundamental as having an automobile." But automobiles are for transportation; guns are for killing. It just drives me up the wall that people support guns. All the information that I came across about "buy guns for protection" . . . they're more likely to get killed by that gun themselves. I thought, "Well, isn't that stupid. Why don't they realize this?" Stan really made a mark on me. I don't think there are many people that come across friends that have been killed. It was very important to me. It's not something that's forced upon you, you chose your own topic, and that way it meant more to you. I wouldn't hardly have done such a good job if I'd done it on anything that didn't affect me.

We were trying to answer a question. We had to do a question that's a focusing statement, what we were gonna try and prove. It was supposed to serve as a rough introduction. And that was *so* helpful, because it's hard later getting started, especially on something that's that big. I had a list of about twelve things I wanted to prove. And he just went, "You've gotta narrow this down to about three." I was pretty upset because I wanted to know all the answers to these questions. And then we had to make an outline. That was such a crucial step. That was like your framework for what you were gonna write, very important in the writing process because you didn't go off track, writing about stuff that wasn't really pertinent to your topic.

And we had to get all our bibliography cards together, that was just going and seeing how many sources we had to collect, trying to find books that would help you prove your thesis. I just went through and looked at guns, firearms, and things like why it was ever included in our constitution. I knew I had to get history of what guns were like before we even became a nation, what were the founding fathers' ideas about guns, how had Britain's laws influenced us, how guns developed over the years, and how they'd changed, and how society had changed so that now made it impractical, which I was trying to prove. And that was hard. He knew it was tough, something we were going through, and he was very encouraging. When we were getting our bibliography cards together, he showed up at the library the night before all the cards were due. It was so much fun to go down there and see everybody! We could run and ask him questions. He's a pretty tough teacher, but that was good.

When I was doing the research, that was the most interesting part, coming across stuff. I just kept going, "Wow, this proves my point. I can use this." I would find points in the reading that would focus in on parts of my paper. I changed what I thought about. I saw why people would want to have guns, but I was fixed in my mind from the start that I was gonna prove that guns were impractical. I bumped off some information. I mean I just didn't use it if I thought it sort of contradicted what I was trying to prove. So I knew in my mind what I needed to collect. But we had to get varied sources, like books, magazines, microfiche, movies, VCR tapes; and

I did three interviews. I thought that was so important to my paper. I knew two people that had handguns, one was for hunting, one for safety. And I interviewed a member of Handgun Control, and I always had my own inner interview with my friend Stan to go by, even though he was dead.

We had to turn in note cards twice. We had to turn in 15 percent of our note cards we had our information on and then 75 percent. And I thought those checkpoints were very important because when a paper's that big, when it's a sixteen-week-long project, you're tending to forget about it. When we turned in our note cards, we had to go have a little talk with him. Everybody came up with their note cards, he'd flip through them, and he'd say, "Is the process going well for you?" In class you are generally one in a million, and it's hard to say, "I'm having this individual problem," because you're afraid of taking up time. So that conference was good. He was always willing. I was going fine with the writing process, I just wanted to share with him that I thought the research was interesting. It was a good, good feeling that he was really interested.

We had done this focusing statement thing earlier, so I could look at it, and I revised it, and then I typed up my introduction. And that was great, it got me started. I knew how I was gonna get started. [I had] a mass of information. That's where the outline really helped me. We wrote on our note cards where this information would go. So you would have Roman numeral IV A and a little 1 or whatever. You just sorted the piles and you could write paragraph after paragraph. I was quite choosey, making sure that I didn't collect information that wasn't part of my outline. I rearranged my outline because I saw it didn't make sense. I could see that it needed to be switched 'cause it went better.

We had to turn in a first draft before the final draft, and it was supposed to be as close to the final as possible. Writing it the first time, that was the hardest part of the whole schmear. I had to be at home, and I had to be sitting on a hard chair. I'd be in sweats, something totally comfortable. I mean I had to put my mind on just it. My friends can work with music. I start thinking about the music, get up, start dancing around. I try to get through a major support at a time, and a transition so that I could launch into the next one. I typed double-spaced, so I could stick stuff in, and that was much easier. If I could do it over again, I'd use a word processor, but I knew people that didn't go to bed all night; they just thought, "I can just stick in all the things, hit print and I'm done." It was exciting though. It was one of those nights where you coulda called anybody at three o'clock, and they were still up. That final draft was tough. I write something then I'll review it and it looks fine to me. My mom reviews it, a fresh mind, and sees stuff that didn't make sense and was out of order. We had two students review it and that was great. Mr. L. said, "Give them the positive and give them suggestions. Don't say, 'This sucks.'" So that really encouraged me that I was doing well, but they still said, "Well, this needs a little work," and I could say to myself, "Yeah, it does." I might not have admitted it before. One of the papers I read was terrible, so I could see where I was on the right track. It was pretty long. I could see that something super long on a topic such as this might not be too good of an idea. You might wanna cut it down. I could sit back and think, "Wait a minute, does this apply to me?" The endnotes were so tedious, and then I had pictures and graphs and a cartoon and amendment typed out on separate pieces of paper. I had a great sense of accomplishment; it's like the biggest thing I've ever written. I had a real proud feeling. I mean I'll probably get a *B+* on it, but I was happy with it, and I felt good that I'd gotten it done.

The best thing he did was to give us this two-page ditto thing that said, "OK, in two weeks' time you have to turn in three topics, two weeks after that you have to have it focused," and he gave us points for everything we turned in, twenty points for this and that. That was great because I just would have died if he just said, "Sixteen weeks you gotta turn in a paper." I'm gonna keep that forever and use it in every big paper I do. Periodically he'd say, "How's the research paper coming? What's working? Share your thoughts with people." And that was good — "Don't go to this library, they don't have anything." And after the paper was turned in, he asked us to evaluate the process we'd gone through. I feel comfortable with writing as long as I stay with my deadlines and I have the information.

Congress spends more time on guns than any other crime-related factor. It's obviously something that's a big deal. I was getting all fired up in writing it 'cause I could do something about it. I would really like to see some action on the right to bear arms. So I mean it's not like I've turned this paper in and that's it. I want to use it. I got better at writing I think, and I think this year especially since we've broken out of that five-paragraph essay thing. That irritated me because people who write books don't have to do that. You don't think of history as a place to write an essay, but it's very valuable, and it helps you learn American history better. And you don't feel under the confines of an English class, using correct grammar, rigorous form, and third person, but you still do. We got out of this structure and where you better use your vocabulary and you gotta use transitions, but we used some of it anyway 'cause it made sense.

The biggest thing in the paper was for me and not for the teacher. It's such a good tool to have, to put something down permanently. Like *The Grapes of Wrath*. I mean Steinbeck went through that. He went through the hunger and stuff, and he witnessed that. I think that really made him write that book much better. There's times when writing for me can be hard, but it was work you could enjoy. I mean I can get cramps, my muscles ache, but I'm getting toward the goal. It's like runners who like the pain. That doesn't sound too good, but it's work, but you like it. I got all fired up. "Oh, look, this proves that guns aren't practical," and I didn't want to stop. Mom was calling for dinner, "Wait just a minute." 'Cause I couldn't stop. There were points I'd get that way because I had information that really proved it for me, by me analyzing it. My ability to analyze was beyond my wildest dreams. In essays on books we were restricted, but here I had a reason for proving it. I had already answered my question to myself, but I had to prove it to other people. I coulda written a book.

There have been times when writing has been grudging hard work, but there are other times when it's been really exciting, and I think the hard work is when I didn't have interest in the thing we were writing about. The gun-control paper was like the best thing I've ever written because it's something I wanted to write. Writing is so much better if you're geared up and fired about it. My mom suggested that I send it to our governor. I thought it would be interesting to get him on my side, to try and convince people, reform all these pro-gunners. Once it was almost done, and I saw how nice and neat it looked, I could see myself going down to Washington, DC, passing out my paper.

I wish I could tell you who Mr. L. is because he deserves the praise that Kathy and the others conferred upon him. But to maintain the pledged anonymity of the participants, he must remain symbolic of those sensitive and challenging writing teachers out there who manage to orchestrate their curriculums to tap the energy, commitment, and strong interests of their students. Content was obviously the focus of Kathy's carefully crafted writing; thus her words speak to teachers in all disciplines.

Kathy had not been flayed; she had not been humiliated or bored. She brought herself, her interest, and her energies to a clearly structured, rigorous writing experience that extended her abilities at research and analysis. The experience was an important one in her education. Relevance, purpose, and satisfaction made it a task for which she had both intrinsic and extrinsic motivation. She did not resent hard work.

As I finished my last round of interviews, I began to realize that Kathy's experience with her term paper, even combined with what went well at times for other writers in my study, wasn't enough to base a chapter entitled "Signs of Hope" on. Hence, after my study was complete (data collected, sorted, and analyzed), I purposively went in search of students who were writing according to gleams from within. I contacted a writing program that had earned high praise and interviewed three eleventh-grade writers: Danny, Brittany, and Anne, who will appear later on in this chapter. It was important to find writers who could join Kathy in ending this book on a positive note.

Fostering Students' Inclination to Write

One day, about the time that I was interviewing Elana, Carlos, Chris, and Tracy, I was sitting in a linguistics class called "Brain Processes and Language." The professor listed the human attributes that allow very young children to acquire speech: natural curiosity, inclination toward self-expression, imitation, and responsiveness to feedback (Frazier, 1982). It was an important moment for me because I saw at once that these same human attributes extend to the acquisition of writing. To these attributes I've added two others that motivation theorists and others proclaim as increasing intrinsic motivation: desire for self-determination and desire for feelings of competence (Ames & Ames, 1984, 1989; DeCharms, 1984; Deci, 1975; Donaldson, 1979; Stipek, 1988). Indeed upon examination, the writing that my participants had found interesting, satisfying, and even exciting capitalized on these attributes. I've found them useful in understanding why some writing assignments, teaching strategies, and curricula make students *want* to write effectively.

Self-Determination

Power—adolescents want it. Like all of us, they want to feel some control in their world. I believe that one goal of educators should be to guide students toward socially responsible self-determination. Making sense of experience, having an influence upon the world, and feeling that there is choice make writing meaningful and satisfy desires for self-determination.

As Kathy was writing about the right to bear arms, she felt self-determination in two ways: she was making sense of the feelings of confusion and despair that she was left with when a friend of her family was killed, and she was finding a way to act on her strong feelings. As she began her paper, she was still trying to examine the outrage that she felt; as she continued writing, she started to see her experience in the context of the socio/political scene in which she lived; and by the end of the paper, she had found a concrete way to use her work for what she perceived as the public good. Writing was a tool of empowerment for her. We'll look more closely at the processes that Kathy went through.

Writing for reflection and understanding. Kathy used her term paper to make sense of an event that had jolted her family. One of her ways of evaluating what she was reading for her paper was her "inner interview with Stan." The felt sense of what she wanted to say helped structure her analysis and argumentation.

If there was one way participants still used writing outside of school in eleventh grade, it was for the purpose of reflection and understanding. Most of those who were still writing in this way did so because they had prior experience with reflective writing in journals during their late elementary, junior high, and early high school years. This writing was useful for what Paulo Freire (a man who has spent his life studying the roots of illiteracy and structuring ways to limit it) terms "conscientization," coming to understandings of the things in life that keep us from acting in our own behalf (Freire, 1968, 1985). As we have seen in chapter 4, Heidi wrote to reduce an unbearable emotion: "If I write, I notice that you don't have to carry the weight inside you." Further, students used writing to reflect, or, as Heidi said, "To see whether it [what I did] was fair or not." That kind of writing enabled them to come to well-considered action. Sullivan (1989) offers a comprehensive plan to encourage such writing in her *English Journal* article, "Liberating the Urge to Write: From Classroom Journals to Lifelong Writing."

A question remains: Does writing for the purpose of under- standing something in one's world have a legitimate place in the school curriculum? I hope to convince you it does by reminding you of something Tracy said:

> There weren't many black people in my city who had made it, so when my teacher assigned me to interview the first black man to work in the school systems of this city, I got so excited. I began to understand how it might be for me as a black person — easier than it was for him, but still not all that easy. I learned a lot writing that one.

And by adding something Meg said:

Despite all my gripes I think writing gives me an opportunity to pull some thoughts and ideas together. It really does serve a much greater purpose. In this "Death and Dying" course I was working through some things that were going on in my life, and even though it wasn't real creative, it was analytical.

Tracy and Meg were learning analysis; they were integrating course content with what they knew in their lives; and they were coming to an understanding of themselves in relation to the world. They felt more in control of their world, better able to determine their own lives. Certainly these skills have a place in the school curriculum. Brittany, Danny, and Anne did this kind of writing in their writing workshop classes, where they were permitted to explore things that were on their minds in fiction, poetry, and essays. Brittany said, "Poetry helps me figure out my feelings and what to do with them." It's clear to me that *writing for personal understanding has an important place in the writing classroom.*

Self-determination and ownership of writing edge into the writing classroom when students have choice in form and content (see Hudson [1988b] for an important discussion of ownership in writing). Though students initially may be overwhelmed by having choice if they have never had it before (they will still be trying to figure out what the teacher wants until they feel the power in their own voice), it's worthwhile seeing them through this period of discomfort. Perl and Wilson offer a wonderful procedure to guide students in connecting themselves to writing topics (*Through Teachers' Eyes*, 1986, pp. 266–269). Reflective autobiographies were used by many teachers in junior high schools; and I think this kind of writing is legitimate on the high school level as well. Similarly, a focused journal, such as Vance's Basketball Journal (chapter 4), makes an excellent model for a high school project. Not only did it include personal response to reading and reflection on his circumstances, but in it he made plans, strategies for action to make his basketball career more possible. He experienced feelings of self-determination; he wrote to act upon his world. Ken Macrorie (1988) sets forth a research model in *The I-Search Paper* that begins with what students know and care about and nudges them beyond to search for answers to the real questions they have. His structure might have extended Vance's Basketball Journal into research of the most meaningful kind.

Writing to act upon the world. Students also felt self-determination when they saw *real purposes* for their writing, when they wrote knowing they would do something important with the assignment. Kathy's momentum in her work picked up when her mother suggested a practical outcome for it. "I could see myself going down to Washington, DC, passing out my paper."

John Doe was probably the most recalcitrant writer in my study, and hence, he definitely needed real purposes for his writing. "I won't write unless it will benefit me in some way, like a business letter, a résumé," he said. "That's the only time I'll write—for some reason. Other writing will get me a grade, but it don't do nothing." Practical outcomes are particularly important for unsuccessful students like John; academic success had been beyond his grasp for some time and had lost any of its motivating power. Letters to Congress and letters to mayors or to governors usually bring answers even though they have stamped signatures. There's excitement in a classroom when students share this correspondence. Proposal writing, a variation on this strategy, worked well for Matt's teacher, Ms. M., who had her students write letters to the board of education, requesting programs and equipment.

Sandy talked about letters that her English class wrote to complain to companies about defective products. They shared the packages and letters that came back in the mail from public relations people. There is a great source of consumer power in our secondary schools, and letters that get a response give students feelings of self-determination.

Amnesty International has developed letter-writing campaigns to leaders of foreign countries concerning human rights violations of individuals in those countries. Recently they have initiated The Children's Campaign and relay carefully documented case information and guidelines for letter writing to groups who are willing to write letters for individual children and adolescents around the world whose human rights are threatened or abused. Many of these children have been imprisoned because of the religious or political beliefs of their relatives (address: Children's Campaign, Amnesty International, 655 Sutter Street, Suite 406, San Francisco, CA 94102). Such social action not only gives students a better understanding of world affairs and of the relative privileges of democracy but also gives them some feeling of power in the face of an intimidating world. This kind of letter writing could certainly be used in connection with literature like *Cry, the Beloved Country* and *Diary of Anne Frank*.

Project-based writing programs give students a real sense of the power that can come from writing. Some years ago when I was teaching in Maine, our faculty went out of their way to encourage projects that gave students a sense of purpose. Students were actively engaged in projects such as writing a local cross-country ski guide with maps and text. They created a nature-trail guide and wrote speeches to give to the state legislature when the Bottle Bill was being considered. They produced school newspapers, put together dating-tip handbooks, and made up their own Mad Libs. Real audiences and purposes gave students feelings of self-determination and gave rise to integration of reading, writing, speaking, and listening. Students also were encouraged to try their hand at the cultural journalism sponsored by *Salt*, Maine's version of Wigginton's *Foxfire*. At that time I asked one of my students, Cindy, why she liked being a part of the *Salt* staff so much. She answered, "It's important. Because like this article I am doing on Sam Polk. He might not be around much longer, and he was fishing for seventy years. He knows a lot that could get lost. This way it is down for people to read now and later."

Cultural journalism creates a sense of urgency that stems from a strong sense of audience and purpose. It's no wonder that Eliot Wigginton has had such success (see *Sometimes a Shining Moment: The Foxfire Experience*). Cultural journalism unites students in the spirit of collaboration and in a sort of collective self-determination and perpetuation of culture. There's potential for this kind of writing in every community.

The teacher's role in fostering feelings of self-determination must be that of guide and resource: a guide because the teacher can provide a structure and encouragement for such endeavors, and a resource because the teacher can point students to the materials and information and provide advice when requested.

Natural Inquisitiveness

Just as children bring curiosity and a desire for self-determination to speech acquisition, adolescents, when given the chance, bring the same natural inclinations to bear on writing. Kathy wanted to understand why the "right to bear arms" was so much a part of the American way, and her curiosity led her to look for historic reasons why the United States had such a provision in the Bill of Rights; she wanted to know so she could support her stance that such a provision was out-of-date. Her curiosity, combined with the process that Mr. L. used to ease his students into the complexity of their tasks, kept Kathy at her investigations. Answering questions that are *real* and *felt* heightens the interest that the writer has in the process. When students wrote about subjects they were curious about, they felt excitement. Prior to criticism, Lisa too was excited about her coral-reef poem, Elana about writing her grandfather's biography, and Carlos about writing about city dogs.

Teacher interest in students' inquiry fueled further endeavor.

When Lisa found out that Ms. M. was interested in whales, she found courage to write about the sea again. Teachers can prolong interest in a piece by asking questions like, "What do you think you need to know more about here?" If topics must be prescribed, teachers can provide prewriting activities that will help students develop personal interests in the topic, or, better yet, if teachers allow topic selection to be open enough, students can find ways to engage in the writing. Again a caution: when students are not used to having a choice in what they write, such choice can make them fearful. They must come to trust that it's permissible to go in their own direction. Teachers can ease students into choosing their own topics by providing lists of topic possibilities and format options, and then, as a next step, by having students brainstorm their own lists. Open options might be permitted for those who trust enough to take them. Students will soon feel the compelling nature of following their own interests, of discovering their own opinions and thoughts.

Simulation of real events or problem-solving situations also foster student curiosity. They write to know. Peco said:

> We had to do a journal log through Europe. My English teacher in seventh grade was also my social studies teacher. We were representative of a country supposedly meeting at the UN. And you had two weeks before the meeting to do whatever you wanted and record it in a journal. I was the representative of Yugoslavia, and I journeyed across certain points in Yugoslavia, Romania, and then across through Italy to the meeting. It was a real search to find out what was happening in those countries in that year. Then we had a mock UN meeting where each [of the] representatives had to go up in the class and give an oral presentation on a problem in their country.

Individualization permits students to plant their souls and their curiosity firmly within their work. The excitement of discovery was what Kathy described. As she discovered arguments that furthered her thesis, even her mother's dinner call seemed unimportant. Further, she was encouraged to "come to know" in many different ways: films, interviews, observations, library research. Macrorie's *The I-Search Paper* (1988) discusses in some depth the rationale and search for alternatives to doing strictly library research.

Students can also bring their natural curiosity to bear on writing about literature. Marshall (1988) talks about discovery in writing when that writing is about literature:

> We can initiate and support their own process of discovery through writing, knowing that they may arrive at readings different from and perhaps less informed than our own. To follow the latter

course would involve relinquishing some of the authority we have traditionally held over the meaning of literary texts (p. 56).

My argument here is that writing should serve also to initiate such inquiry, that it become a means of opening and sustaining the discussions in which we engage. If the mutually supportive relationship between writing and literature is to be preserved in our teaching, we may need to give writing a larger, more flexible, and finally a more powerful role. (p. 57)

Teachers have to give up some control of topic and format if students are to follow up on their own lines of inquiry (see Hudson [1988a, 1988b] for further discussion). If students are interested in the topic, their curiosity helps them develop the felt sense that Perl (1986) suggests guides the composing process (see p. 217).

Curiosity about the self is strong in adolescent years, and writing about literature can help in self-discovery. If students seem way off base in their initial responses to literature, it's often because they are superimposing their own lives on the literature. In such cases it's useful for them to be able to rehearse and get feedback about their thoughts in small group discussions. Rosenblatt (1976) said that students often come to know themselves better by examining their idiosyncratic responses to literature. Portia said: "The more time I have in writing some things, the more I see my point, and the more clearly I can see myself." Listening to others often helps students find an interpretation that is both well grounded in the text and true to their own experience.

Finally, we've heard students talk about the effect that interest and curiosity have on concentration. These students agreed with Larson (1985): writing goes best when writers achieve command over their attention. Encouraging students to write about what interests them in literature or in their lives gives them two tools to improve their writing: a felt sense to direct their writing and command over their own attention.

Inclination Toward Self-Expression

Just as curiosity leads us to discovery, our human nature leads us to want to *express* that discovery to others. Students' use of writing for self-expression surfaced in both public and private ways.

Students talked about the importance of public and semi-public forums for written self-expression. Joel was drawn to writing songs that would be played by his friends' band and poems that he could submit to the school newspaper. Chris talked of the "500-Page Note" that he and his seventh-grade friends stole time to write during a year of learning grammar. As five-paragraph essay writing supplanted inventive writing in their curriculum, note writing (a pervasive activity in our school systems) allowed students a chance to express themselves to those who cared very much about what they had to say. It's ironic that this was done on stolen time. The success of writing workshops is in part due to this same dynamic. That peer-response situation broadens the young writer's audience beyond the teacher to chosen peers, and in the secondary years this is an important audience indeed. We must *not* allow ourselves, as teachers, to be our students' only audience.

Self-expression can also further literary or textbook study. First, students can use response journals or peer/teacher correspondence (see Atwell, 1987) to record their initial responses to literature or texts and to connect reading with their own experience. Second, they can refine those preliminary reflections and discoveries into something they want to say about a text to a peer audience. Bursts of freewriting might be a part of this stage. Finally, after studying forms of writing connected to various discourse communities, they can begin to see how their well-rehearsed ideas can fit into more formal structures for more distant audiences. Thus, self-expression can evolve, and ideas that were germinated in the first two stages of writing can not only feed the more formal writing but also lend ownership and confidence to it.

Because adolescents are peer-oriented, real adolescent audiences can be a powerful incentive for writing. Writing groups can also help develop tolerance to others' ideas and can provide feedback to help further tentative thoughts. Part of our job as teachers is to prepare citizens who aren't afraid to express carefully considered thoughts, and to express them clearly and convincingly.

Feelings of Competence

The most depressing moments in my research came after I talked to students who felt bad about themselves and used well-entrenched defenses to hide it. As a researcher, I wasn't able to do anything substantial enough to break the pattern that led to such deep feelings of incompetence. But as I talked with students, I became clearer about the kinds of things that must happen to make these students feel good about themselves again as writers. Danny was one of the writers I interviewed after my study was complete in order to finish this book on a positive note. His tale about writing in a workshop setting was very poignant to me. I want to share a small portion of it to introduce this section on feelings of competence.

Danny's Newfound Competence

Writing has been real tough. I don't like to read. It's mostly been the kids in school making fun of me. Dad told me that to get a good job it's going to have to be passing grades in school, and that means reading and writing. That helped motivate me some in writing. It still hasn't really motivated me in reading. It's getting better; kids don't always know how slow I am. When I was in school, second or third grade, I learned to write. I was learning before, but I didn't do any writing. We had a contest, write so many letters and you win. I tried really hard. I didn't win. Decided not to do much. I didn't do homework. Mom and Dad asked me if I had homework, and I said, "Nope." Went out and play. My cursive ain't the best in the world. Then we learned commas, where to put the periods and all that. I still haven't learned too good. I was in the slow class until I was in sixth grade. I stayed down in the bottom. I guess that hurt because I'd get mad. I'd always be downstairs in the little room with the other slow kids. In sports they'd call you dummy. I didn't like it. They'd all be doing their assignments, projects, and all I'd have was a little book, doing little simple stuff. They'd say, "I did that in kindergarten." I hardly did any kind of writing.

At the end of sixth grade, I took an Iowa test to find out that I would be in regular classes. I really didn't feel better about going to regular classes with other kids. Ms. J. helped me; she stuck to me and wouldn't let me slack off. I still wouldn't do my homework. I got too macho. Seventh grade, we mainly did a lot of reading, no writing. We did write little things about what we read. I read a Star Wars book, and a book on snakes, and a book on race cars. Dad had that book about stock car racing, after that I got interested in cars. Still am—A. J. Foyt, 200 miles an hour. I'm gonna get into car racing one of these days, but right now I get scared going over the speed limit.

Got to about the ninth grade, still no homework, but then in tenth I got Ms. Goodstream's class, and it sort of helped me really begin to like it. It was challenging, first time I actually got to do anything. What really helped me was that she let me write anything that we wanted to; I thought this is the first decent grade I got in a long time, "Well, I'll try writing." I did pretty good; I got a C. I have a hard time with commas. I don't know why I have such a hard time with it. She sat down and talked it over and over. It's still floating, hasn't sunk in complete yet. Mom and Dad didn't finish high school, so if I did ask for help, they wouldn't know. I'm just on my own, or I get help at school.

We had to write, so I only know about cars, so I wrote about cars, mainly about my car, what it did, how it looked. Mom said if I graduate, I could get her Monte Carlo. I still have to graduate though. I'm pretty sure I'll graduate. I work on that car. My dad helps; he works in a welding department, makes frames. I drive Dad's car, save the miles on mine. It was okay that I wrote about cars, that and my family. Only things I cared about at the time. It made me feel good; stuff we have to write about before made me get mad, don't want to write for a while.

I'm good at basketball and track. I'm getting better at writing. I've stayed after school almost every day this year, either basketball or extra time writing or track. Once Ms. Goodstream said, "You're staying after school and getting this story done." I took it over and read it at the elementary school, and I felt better because it made the kids laugh. They asked how I made the story, how long it took to write it. It made me feel great. They think you are some sort of superman, but for you it's really average. We had a writer that came in our room. She told us how much money she got paid for her two books. That helped a lot. I mean I don't think I will make a career of it, or make a lot of money. I still like it. I didn't ask her some questions I had — too nervous.

When I got to high school, I got involved in stuff. My grades actually picked up. It was challenging. The coach wanted me to run track, writing. I find myself doing more than I did in the past. My parents used to have people over, talking about what their children did and stuff, and I did nothing. I decided to do some stuff. I didn't do nothing until tenth grade. All I wanted to do was go home, watch T.V., go outside, sit in school, do nothing. The teachers are nice here. I'm not too good at getting up in front of other people. I don't like reading. I mainly read what I have to, I like to write because you are doing something. I still ain't the hottest reader. That's part of the reason I don't like to read. Other people fly through. And I still have a hard time understanding it. Sometimes I read it, and I sit down to write about it, and my mind is as blank as the piece of time. In Ms. Goodstream's class we have to read a lot. When I read car magazines at home, all my parents ever read, it is easier because I understand what is going on in there. I have reading to do tonight in current events that everyone else finished in class, about Panama. When they had an article on the trade deficit and cars, that was easy to read.

I think the teacher makes me want to write. She sort of influences me in some way. I don't know how she does it, but every time I go in that class I want to do something. When I'm in other classes, I will do it if I have to. Ms. Goodstream talks a lot about her writing, and that helps me decide what to write. Like we are supposed to write about our birth, part of an autobiography in the writing from experience section, and she talked about how she asked her Mom about her birth and that helped me know how to go about it. Instead of her just strict out telling you how to do something, she sort of puts it a way I can understand. She reads all the time, sometimes even in class. All she talks about is books. She knows where I am so she gets me at that level. She is interested in what anyone writes, she was for me. Then I'd want to do another one and do it better.

I didn't realize that I thought about my family as much as I did. I was writing about my grandfather for the autobiography. It shocks me. I've been realizing that my family, education, future job, future family (if I can have one and support them with a job) are important to me. I write about them all. I mainly like to write about that car. My grandfather had that car. He sold it to my mother. I want to really take care of that car, keep it in the family. One day, when Mom passes on, I can say that my grandpa owned that, hand it on like my mom did, and if I ever had a kid, it would be a traveling timepiece. I didn't write about that yet, but I'm thinking of it. It would make an interesting piece. When we wrote about jobs, realized that I really wanted to graduate, go to tech school. I guess I should write about jobs once a week. It's really getting bad because everything is high tech, it's all computers, and I'm not so good at geometry.

I get mad sometimes when I don't get my way. Couple of times I took it out on my mom, and my dad get mad at me for yelling at my mom. One time in class, Ms. Goodstream read an article on how you can write that stuff on paper. I tried it once and it worked pretty good, so a lot of times I put it out on paper, so I don't get so mad at my mom. I wanted to go to Kentucky one time, and Mom wouldn't let me. She found out I was ineligible for track, and I thought I should be. I started to say a lot of bad stuff. It wasn't really her fault, so I had some paper around and I started to write. I got rid of the note. I'm not allowed to use that kind of language, but I could talk to her then. A lot of times my mom will go through my gym bag to see if I got any homework. She ran across a couple of my notes, so I got rid of it. Sometimes it kills the anger. Sometimes I reread it to see if it's something to get mad over. She did this, and what led to that. A lot of times I will be in the wrong, and I will see I didn't have no reason to get mad, and other times I've looked at it and seen that I had all the reason to get mad. It helps me figure that out.

I had Ms. Goodstream last year for one term and this year. In that class we wrote just about every day. At first I didn't like it,

"Lady, you're making us write too much." We wrote stuff, and if we read it in front of the class we'd get bonus points. I began to almost like to go up in front of the class and read my stuff. When I write, I use littler words than what the books use, so that I can fly through it. I have trouble getting the bigger words out, and if I know the words in my writing, I can make them think I'm a better reader. I have to keep writing about two or three drafts on a paper to get it better, 'cause she grades heavy on that. I need all the points I can get. I want about a "C".

If I write full-time, it won't turn out right. If I think about it, it's better. Sometimes my dog is practically in my lap. Sometimes I write on the kitchen table, closer to the refrigerator. I try to start out quick, if I just do it quickly, then I feel better, knowing I only have so much left. Sometimes I put it in a folder and revise it at school. Sometimes I do half of it and finish and redraft it at school. A few years ago was hard for me because I'd fail that class because we'd have to do an assignment every day, "Read this, write about it," so I just wouldn't do it. The zeros'd add up. You get an "F," and it'd make you hate writing. When we did some in class, it gave me more time.

I visit my grandmother, see how she's doing every summer. My cousin and me, we'd be fishing, and I'd catch a couple of fish, and I write about it, how tough they was to get in, where I caught them. I think about what I'm going to say ahead of time, while fishing. [When] I'm just in the mood for writing, I write it. Hard to explain. I just do it. I have to figure out how it will be, don't want it to turn out bad or something.

The turning point in writing for me was when I got a piece published in a magazine for writing here. It wasn't good or anything. They must have been really low on poems that year. [But] it must have been decent else it wouldn't have been in there. The poem was about my car. I did it about three or four times. She kind of suggested to put more detail and dialogue into it. I looked it over, and I agreed with her. I was doing more writing and getting better grades at it, so I thought, "I must be doing something right." I thought, "I'm pretty good at this; I ought to keep it up. I have something decent to do, something I'm good at." And I been doing it ever since.

Is there anything that is more essential to human happiness than the way people feel about themselves? Do school systems have the right to make a large portion of the population lose feelings of self-respect? The feelings of competence that Danny is beginning to have in writing will be important to the way he feels about himself for years to come, probably much more important to him than the skill he gains in writing. Teachers need to build into the writing curriculum the potential for success for *all* students. The three strategies that follow can help teachers to build feelings of competence in their students.

Accomplishable tasks and expectations of success. First, students must have tasks set before them that they can, with effort, accomplish, and they must sense that those around them trust that they can, with effort, complete the tasks successfully. Danny finally discovered that he could write when he was allowed to write about something that interested him, his car, and when he received an indication from his teacher that he was succeeding in doing it. Students take it to heart when you show them where they're doing a good job and let them know you expect that they'll complete it. Sometimes the hardest part of our job is to help students find a topic that's both simple and interesting and then to find a kernel of something good in their initial writing that they can build on. The reward is statements like Danny's: "Well, I'll try writing," which is no minor statement since he had given up on writing for years.

Even successful students, who are used to getting praise, thrive on feelings of competence, and they don't get those feelings unless they perceive a writing task as a challenge and stretch to meet it. If they perceive themselves to be good writers and then have to write something that doesn't stretch their abilities, then the task becomes a chore. If the task seems overwhelming or illogical, struggle ensues. This is an important reason for individualization in the writing classroom. Optimal difficulty (or "productive tension" as some educators call it) will increase feelings of accomplishment and competence and pride (Goodlad, 1975). Sometimes students need to be "nudged" (to adopt a word that Atwell [1987] uses), nudged to take on projects that will extend their abilities. I like the word "nudge" very much; it describes the attention I need to get me working on something that is a little bit threatening, and it's only when the new or unfamiliar is conquered that growth can keep occurring. Students who prefer safe success need a nudge now and again if they are to move on to the more distant audiences and complex organizations that are indicative of complex analysis.

Unloading the process. Feelings of competence also increase when students work out ways to prevent cognitive overload from occurring. Teachers build success into writing by helping students explore strategies that will help them maintain enough room in their conscious attention while drafting. Modeling and encouraging freewriting (Elbow, 1973, 1981; Macrorie, 1988) and clustering and brainstorming (Zemelman and Daniels, 1988) help students limit what they have to concentrate on during their drafting. Teachers can also encourage students to write drafts without worrying about the concerns of past English teachers and then to revise drafts with a designated audience in mind. Students who had help in developing these strategies were more likely to perceive a complex assignment as a challenge.

A good many students in my study hadn't internalized the importance of unloading the writing process, and for them feelings of incompetence (the emotional results of frustration and fear of failure) disrupted the thought processes necessary to complete the writing task. It's important, however, not to assume that each student will come to the same set of strategies or to assume that it's best for students to use the same process for everything they write. Though a description of a "writing process" is even included in the ever-present *Warriner's*, its authors and some teachers seem to misunderstand this process. I was distressed to have a teacher in Joseph's school tell me: "My students have just learned the writing process; they read the chapter and just took a test on it." I think Brittany, who was interviewed after my study was completed, can tell us more about working out a "process" than *Warriner's* can.

Brittany's Process

I always have to let an idea simmer in the back of my mind for a while until it comes. When I first write it, I have so many ideas going on at once. I have to go fast to get it out. Ms. Court in eighth grade said don't stop, just keep going. Mr. R. was that way too. If you don't write it fast, you wouldn't get it down. If I stop it will break my concentration, and I won't get down everything. After I have to read it through and read it through again, so I have in my mind what I have said. I have little notes in my mind, like I have to change this, and that is awful. Sometimes I make little marks while I'm writing fast, but usually I find what's wrong when I read through the first time. After the fast time, I go paragraph to paragraph, and keep going into details. What action verb can I put in there? I read it and picture it sometimes. If I picture it, I can think of better words. Then I have a rough draft.

When we have rough drafts due, I am never happy with it. When I go back, I just laugh at it. We'd do about a rough draft in a week. It could be a mess, and she'd give us pointers if we'd ask for them. She'd do what would be helpful: "What kind of response do you want on this?" Then we'd do it over, and then we'd have the final draft due. And while we were working on our pieces, we could work with other people. We'd get into a group of three and that would be the group for the rest of the semester. You would do your own stories, but they would give you tips. This smaller group was O.K., especially when you were first working on a piece. The three people would get to know you, more open, and after a while you won't hurt their feelings. They weren't my close friends, but I got to know them better. If they were my friends, I wouldn't have taken any chances. At first they would just say it was good, and then I would say, "I need some ideas on this." And then they'd say, "Let me hear this part again; maybe you could tighten this." And, "Well, what was your title?" If my stories are bad I want to know, so I can get it better in the future. By the end of the semester, I could tell whose story was whose if it was read; that's how well we knew each other's writing.

Revision is like eliminating a paragraph or a page. Tightening is my problem, and like parallelism and structure. It's probably the most important thing I learned. In past years I learned about revising, but this year I learned about tightening. Tightening is with the very littlest details. Editing is like spelling words. We've got a writing book, paperback, *Writing Your Way*. We'd read a chapter probably every other week, and then write our own piece. We'd write something every two weeks. Write, revise, tighten, edit. Ms. N. said you have to tighten it, it is a sin to her. Get rid of unnecessary words. Read it as a whole, read it by the paragraph, go shorter and shorter until you end up with the sentence. And if you got a "was" try to substitute it with an action verb. That helped out a lot. This year it was all up to us, we knew what to do, but our sophomore year, we would have one day for revising and one day for the little conferences with the teacher or other people, and it helped a lot. Editing is things like spelling and commas. We'd always have to edit in red pen.

I need about a week and a half or two for a deadline, so that I can pace myself out. I can write it in one or two days, but some days I'm stuck for a whole day, and if it's due, I'm in trouble. After we had our final draft due, we'd get in a circle, and we would share. If somebody didn't have a title, they would say, "I need a title," and others would give you some ideas. If I worked hard on a story, it makes me feel special if they clap. Then, when it is all done, I will probably want to change it tomorrow.

Recognition for competence. When students get the message through peer or teacher feedback and/or through "publication" that they have been effective in making meaning, they feel competent; this in turn builds their willingness to continue writing. Danny's self-confidence and motivation increased when his poem was published in the school literary magazine. He said, "I must be doing something right. . . . I ought to keep it up. I have something decent to do, something I'm good at."

Students know that they've been able to express themselves clearly when they are heard and understood. If teachers and fellow students are interested in a piece of writing, the author *knows* that his or her task has been at least partially successful. Large, *trusted* peer audiences worked well to give most students feelings of competence. Some of the students talked about the excitement of writing pieces that were posted or read aloud and discussed in class. Elana described her excitement in writing up and illustrating an invention for her science class. "I made something that you put on the steering wheel of your car, and it analyzed your breath, and if you were over the limit the car wouldn't start. The teacher put it on the bulletin board and that felt good."

Many students talked about getting things published in a variety of ways in elementary school, and a few students were "published" in secondary school. Nancie Atwell (1987) has a wonderful list of "ways to go public" in the appendix of her book, *In the Middle*. But, as we've seen, some students like Lilly have no intention of going public with what they write, and others are fearful of large public exposure of their writing. They do better to share their writing in small peer-response groups or with chosen writing partners. Students said things like: "They actually took my advice." "He liked my topic and approach but had lots of other ideas that helped my draft." Very sensitive writers can start off working with one other person and then, when feelings of trust and competence increase, they can be "nudged" into working with groups of three or four. If grades must be connected to the writing process, teacher and peer assessment of accomplishment that accompanies grades will permit those grades to be perceived more as evidence of competence than of a teacher's method of control. Nothing much can mitigate the message of a poor grade.

Imitation

It's important for developing writers to see their teachers as interested and engaged in reading and writing. Motivation for activities can be internalized when young people see certain skills valued by models in their social environments. This is especially important for the students who don't see their parents reading and writing for pleasure or for their work.

When I first started teaching, my mentor Mary Wilson told me that she tried to read everything that her students were reading during their Friday "Free Reading." I was astounded to hear her say it, but with a year of reading behind me, I found that I could manage, and I enjoyed the discussions I could have with my students about what they brought on Friday to read. But for ten years it didn't occur to me to write with my students. I had to read about that to get interested enough to start doing it. It was especially interesting to me to hear students like Danny talk about teachers' reading and writing. He seemed almost surprised that Ms. Goodstream spent some of her time like that.

If we see literacy as important, it's especially important for us to be more public about our reading and writing. In addition, teachers might consider having students interview a variety of community people to explore how they use reading and writing to their benefit. If each sophomore interviewed two community members who had jobs that they might be interested in having, they would have both a role model and an introduction to discourse communities. Furthermore, if teachers write with their students and permit students to respond to that writing, it helps provide a sense of community that will lessen the feeling of threat that students can feel in letting others respond to their work. They become better able to see the task of writing as a challenge (Cleary, 1986). Students can also benefit from imitating what they read. They can try variations on the styles and structures found in literature. This heightens their consciousness of what authors do well and allows them to begin to see writing as an art that they might have some control over.

Responsiveness to Teacher Feedback

Teachers can construct situations that permit students to bring self-determination, natural curiosity, inclination toward self-expression, feelings of competence, and imitation to writing, but they can also affect student motivation by the feedback they give. Unless they have been "flayed," human beings are responsive to feedback. Mr. R.'s response to the writing Anne did in a workshop setting made her want to do it and to do it well.

Anne Talks About Teacher Response

As a writer, I guess I'd put myself in the middle. There are a lot of people in my class that are really good. There are some things that I write that I get real satisfied from, but I revise it, rework it. Some people it comes off the top of their head. I'm willing to work at it more. Some teachers used to place too many limits, to write a certain way. Not what we wrote about, but the way we would write it. They would say why don't you focus on this instead, so you have to go by the way someone else wants you to write and worry, "Well, is this the way she would want me to say it?"

Mr. R. lets everyone have their own voice, that's what he calls it, and not as many guidelines. Say you already had your paper written out, he might say, "I agree this would make it stronger, this might help it, but you do what you want with it." And he would kind of go, "And how do you feel about it?" when we would get stuck. Other teachers would go, "Why don't you put this instead?" but he would let us come up with it on our own. He had us write about things that we knew about, that helped a lot. Because when we would get stuck, he would say, "Okay, put yourself in that position today, how would you react to it?" You would have a discussion about it and that helped. We would have to do a poetry, a drama, and an essay. Those were the only kind of limits he would set. He would help us come up with an idea, the brainstorming. I think the class was more relaxed, more of a comfortable setting. He would joke around and stuff. It was strange in a way, like we would have a couple of weeks to get it done on our own, and he would come around, but he wouldn't push us. But I think because he trusted us with that, everybody did it. Even if you weren't real poetic, or if you couldn't get everything to go together, you could do it in your own way, and it satisfied you. The atmosphere made you want to write.

Mr. R. would give us a certain amount of weeks, and as long as we are working on something every day was all that he was concerned about. We had deadlines to a certain extent, but we could work on things longer. This year we have to start on something, and two or three days later we have to turn it in. I do better if I do something and then put it aside, and then I go back to it, instead of do something, turn it in, do something else, turn that in. In Mr. R.'s class I don't know anybody that didn't work. Everyone in my class did really well. It takes some a longer time than others to do it or to get ideas, and when you have to turn it in right away, you rush through it and don't think about it and work hard.

To learn to write better, it doesn't matter how much I write; it matters if I work to satisfy. It is easier to sit down and write a whole lot than it is to work on it. It doesn't take much skill to sit down and write three or four pages. The more you work on it the more you can put yourself into it, and the more you want it to get better. You don't want to work for two weeks and have it mean nothing. When you revise it, you take out what's not important and put in what's important, and I think you learn more about the kinds of things you want from your writing.

At the beginning of the year I wrote about a ski trip that I had taken. I had it all written up and ready to turn it in. It ended up that the deadline was turned back. I got stuck when I was working on something else, so I went back to the ski trip and started to revise it. And it turned out completely different from what I started out with, but at the end of it I felt good about it. A lot of times I wasn't satisfied with it when I put it away. I thought I was stuck and that I couldn't do anymore. And then you start to come up with new ideas, and you get more excited when you're more into it. I don't worry so much about what somebody else would think about it. But at the end, I try to think if I was somebody else reading it, would I understand it, get the same feeling. I guess it's in my mind when I work on it, but most of the time I don't think about it, unless I'm revising it. With the teacher sometimes, if you know they want certain things, you try to go with that, but with Mr. R. it was pretty much your own. In Mr. R.'s class we'd have one or two people in the class read it. I'd usually pick someone that I feel comfortable with, a real good friend and share it. Then I could tell if they understood it, if there was things to add or take away. Then I would rewrite it and hand it in to Mr. R., and he would read it.

I got an *A* and I got it published, but it's the satisfaction that I want from it. I found out that if I'm good at it I will try hard at it. If people tell you you have to write this way or this way, and that's not the way you really write, then that takes a lot of the fun out of it. He never said, "I don't like this, I don't like that"; he let you do it on your own. He wanted to see if you work hard on it and whether you were satisfied with it.

In Mr. R.'s class, in the beginning I was just writing for me, and in the end I wanted to be just as good as the best writers. Sometimes you will write a paper, and you think, "Yeah, this is pretty good," and then you'll see someone else's and see what they did with it, and you think, "I could do what they did with it and make it a lot stronger." I guess that isn't really competition, except within yourself—you're strengthening yourself to get better and better every time. I don't stop until I know that it can't get no better. I think you find out new things that you didn't realize are in you until you put it on paper. I did a paper this year about a teenage girl that was dying. I think I was dealing with the fear of dying and of someone else dying. I found out some things I hadn't known in writing that paper. Writing is parting with things that upset you and finding part of yourself, finding what is important and all your emotions and fears. Even if it's made up, all those things are there.

Mr. R. didn't praise Anne or Brittany, nor did he criticize them. Instead, he encouraged them to write until they were satisfied with the meaning they wanted to make and until they had strengthened themselves and their writing in the process. Part of what he did was to give them indications that they were competent enough to tackle the task they had set for themselves. Teachers can find ways of responding to written work that will capitalize on students' responsiveness to feedback and minimize the teacher's impact on the students' intrinsic motivation to write. And it's important for students to learn to write for many different kinds of audiences; the teacher needn't always be the critical audience. Teachers need not be ogres to challenge students.

The conference format is an important forum for teacher response, just as peer writing groups are an important forum for peer response. Atwell (1987) used goal setting as part of her conferencing procedure. If students reach goals that they set in collaboration with the teacher, they see that as an indication of a newfound competence. Conferences are especially valuable for the student who has not been successful in writing. It's a time when teachers can give these students explicit statements about the causes of their lack of success in writing. Students can begin to see their failures as connected with their home dialect or with lack of practice, as opposed to seeing those failures linked to their self-worth or intelligence. If class size is small enough, time can be allotted to confer about grammar and spelling logs in which students are coming to their own realizations about correctness. This connects to conscientization. If they become conscious of what keeps them from success, then they have the power to work on that. Furthermore, they'll begin to see high teacher expectations as evidence that the teacher actually thinks they can meet those expectations. Written dialogue between student and teacher can also add to this conscientization process. Process journals, as described in Perl and Wilson (1986), can be a vehicle for teachers to help students become more conscious of the dynamics that affect their writing.

As we can see from what Jessica said, teacher recognition of student effort is very important:

> In my sophomore year I had that difficult teacher who would take time and help me, and he would always go over what I did wrong and help me out, and he just knew that I worked my buns off. I was reading more, writing more and better. I might not have the

ability as yet to write a good paper, but I felt like I had gotten better. My highest grade in there was a *C+*, but I still remained a *C* for the semester. I was shocked that I did that good. I'm glad some teachers realize that a student is trying even though their grades aren't good. I was struggling so much, but I was doing so good because he saw improvement in me.

Grading when you have to grade. Actual evaluation is a primary and powerful way that teachers interact with students' writing, but if grading is part of that evaluation, it's very important that it be done very carefully. Grades were useful feedback about writing only when students interpreted them as information about progress made in acquiring new and needed skills. Anne said, "The grade made me feel good, because once you work really hard on something, it makes you feel really good for it to be recognized." Acknowledging growth should be the goal of grading if it needs to be done.

Unless collaboration between student and teacher is a part of the grading process, students are much less likely to see grades as indicators of growth. If grades must be given, and if they're contingent on criteria that have been *mutually established* by teachers and students, this provides self-determined reasons for a student to work at a challenge. If we're to limit the effect of grading on writing confidence, then students need to see just what the grading measures and how their effort affects that measure. Some time ago, Coopersmith (1967) studied the *Antecedents of Self-Esteem*. Among other things, he found that situations that built self-esteem in children included clear structure combined with respect and latitude for freedom within that structure. In writing curricula and in individual writing tasks, students need to know what the structure is, and they need to feel secure about where they have freedom to connect themselves to the assignment.

Further, criteria should be set for the term and/or for each individual writing project. What are the possible criteria? We can grade on correctness of written language, on features of format, on depth of thinking, on ideas, on progress in developing specific skills, on the number of pages, on the number of drafts, on how hard students work, and by comparison of products with other peers' products. Romano (1987), Atwell (1987), and Murray (1985) make the best of traditional situations by picking carefully among these qualitative and quantitative criteria. The grading strategies they present are important reading, but I would like to suggest alternatives.

In some schools teachers have been able to convince administrators that writing courses be pass/fail. If this can't be done, teachers can get some of the same results by contract grading, a class contract or individual contracts based on a class contract. Criteria for passing or contract grading might be based on both quantity (number of drafts in the writing folder, number of finished products) and quality (correctness of final drafts, attainment of collaboratively set goals, "the gleam that comes from within," student satisfaction in the end product, effort evident in the student's work, evaluation of student-selected samples of their work). As long as the criteria are set at the beginning of the term, and as long as conferencing occurs along the way, this procedure works.

Having collaboratively set class goals and individual goals for the term is a very important part of this process. The teacher can set up a structure: "It's important that we write more than we did last term, so we'll spend more time in class writing, and I have set the number of final drafts that must be in at four, instead of two. . . ." Then the teacher can let students think about what makes for good writing until a sort of contract emerges: "Let's list some other criteria that we know make for good writing that we should concentrate on this term, and then as individuals we'll add individual goals to this contract in conference." The teacher can decide what structure is important, as long as there's some latitude for the students as a group and the students as individuals to make choices that affect their writing. If class size permits, the student and teacher can confer on grading so that each student will be able to have success during the term and will be able to grow and benefit from feelings of competence. When the contract is handed back at the end of the term, students will have clear indicators of the accomplishments their efforts have brought or of those skills that they still have to work on. Grades then become indicators of growth in writing skills that have come from student effort.

Teacher response to student writing is perhaps the trickiest task of the English teacher. Teachers need careful understanding of what enhances motivation for writing and delicate skill in implementing that understanding.

Writing Programs That Foster Gleams from Within

Writing curricula that provide clear guidelines for writing and latitude within that structure for personal choices allow students to act from a sense of autonomy and pride. Workshop and project-based writing curricula seem to provide these elements.

The writing program is Brittany's, Danny's, and Anne's school was established by committed and enthusiastic teachers. They began thinking of changing the way they were teaching when a group of them attended a writing project, and they were supported in their endeavors by the principal they had at that time. Their conviction that they were doing the right thing increased in response to the progress and enthusiasm they saw in their students. They established writing workshops in their classes that followed along the lines that Romano, Atwell, and Murray advocate.

Though many years of research indicate the changes that this English department made, many teachers fear administrators will disapprove of their efforts to change. Administrators may be more willing than we suspect to establish such programs. Two junior high teachers have told me recently that simply getting their principals to do a quick reading of Atwell's *In the Middle* gave them instant support in making changes.

Within or without a workshop setting, individuals can do research that is exciting for them. Kathy's gun-control paper has the trappings of a traditional research paper, though Mr. L. opened up the process enough so that Kathy could squeeze into the heart of it. Vance was also doing a sort of research in his Basketball Journal, though he started with his own questions, musings, and needs instead of an ordered thesis and outline. Macrorie says in the preface of *The I-Search Paper*: "For many decades high schools and colleges have fostered the 'research paper,' which has become an exercise in badly done bibliography, often an introduction to the art of plagiarism, and a triumph of meaninglessness — for both writer and reader." In the book he stretches the concept of research so wide open that even the most recalcitrant students in my study, George, Orion, and John, would have entered the process of "I-Search" and found it exciting.

Project approaches to the teaching of writing (see Rodrigues, 1985, and Wigginton, 1985) work in similar ways to actively engage students in making sense of their world. Such approaches are ordinarily premised upon some sort of publication, and students are aware that they are doing important writing for important purposes. Whereas individuals are likely to feel pride and satisfaction in workshop settings, whole groups or whole classes feel that pride and satisfaction from the collaboration that is necessary in project approaches. Grants from local historical societies or regional granting organizations might offset the extra expenses that such programs incur.

Even if administrators or school boards won't support what they see as dramatic departures from traditional programs, teachers can fall more in line with what research indicates as sound practice. Within the most traditional schools, teachers can develop means of drawing on the "gleams from within" their students. Last week I was sitting in a quite traditional classroom, and the teacher was surprised when her students became enthusiastic about a Robert Browning poem. She immediately broadened the tight structure of the writing assignment that was due the next day so that they could use the poem. After class she said to me, "When the sparks fly like that, you can't pass the moment up." And that was a beginning. Sparks, glimmers, gleams — we need to loosen up so students can draw on them. Although there are very exciting alternatives to the traditional writing classroom, much of what I have suggested here can be implemented without changing fully to the workshop or project setting.

Simply put, students like to do what they feel they do well and thrive on having choices in the directions that they might take in writing. Because secondary writing teachers are continually burdened with recalcitrant students (who have come to the defensive stances of "I don't care," "I hate writing," "I'm not a very good writer") or with jaded writers (who see writing as just "hard work" and work to "please the teacher"), it's sometimes difficult to believe that students want to be competent and self-determined. And, of course, it's our long-term goal as teachers to foster these very qualities.

The writing experiences of all the students who have shared their voices in this book show us ways to reconnect students' souls to their writing, to foster their inclination to write after they leave our schools, and to show them how they can use writing to enhance their control over their circumstances.

Bibliography

Agar, Michael H. *The Professional Stranger: An Informal Introduction to Ethnography.* New York: Academic Press, 1980.

Apple, Michael W. *Education and Power.* Boston: Routledge and Kegan Paul, 1982.

————. *Teachers and Texts: A Political Economy of Class and Gender Relations in Education.* New York: Routledge, 1988.

Ames, R., and C. Ames, eds. *Research on Motivation in Education: Vol. 1. Student Motivation.* Orlando, FL: Academic Press, 1984.

Ames, C., and R. Ames, eds. *Research on Motivation in Education: Vol. 3. Goals and Cognitions.* New York: Academic Press, 1989.

Applebee, Arthur N. *Writing in the Secondary School: English and the Content Areas.* NCTE Research Report No. 21. Urbana, IL: NCTE, 1981.

————. *Contexts for Learning to Write: Studies of Secondary School Instruction.* Norwood, NJ: Ablex, 1984.

Atlas, Marshall A. "Addressing an Audience: A Study of Expert–Novice Differences in Writing." Carnegie-Mellon University, Document Design Project Technical Report 3, 1979.

Atwell, Nancie. *In the Middle: Writing, Reading, and Learning with Adolescents.* Portsmouth, NH: Boynton/Cook Publishers, 1987.

Barnes, Douglas, James Britton, and Harold Rosen. *Language, The Learner and the School.* Penguin, 1971.

Bartholomae, David. "Inventing the University." In *When a Writer Can't Write.* Ed. Mike Rose. New York: The Guilford Press, 1985.

Becker, Howard S., and Blanche Geer. "Participant Observation and Interviewing: A Comparison." In *Issues in Participant Observation.* Eds. George J. McGall and J. L. Simmons. Reading, MA: Addison Wesley, 1969.

Berkenkotter, Carol. "Understanding A Writer's Awareness of Audience." *College Composition and Communication* 82 (1981): 388–399.

Britton, James, Tony Burgess, Nancy Martin, Alex McLeod, and Harold Rosen. *The Development of Writing Abilities (11–18).* London: Macmillan, 1975.

Bloom, Lynn Z. "Anxious Writers in Context." In *When a Writer Can't Write.* Ed. Mike Rose. New York: The Guilford Press, 1985.

Bogdan, Robert C., and Sari Knopp Biklen. *Qualitative Research for Education: An Introduction to Theory and Methods.* Boston: Allyn and Bacon, 1982.

Brooks, Charlotte K., ed. *Tapping Potential.* Urbana, IL: NCTE, 1985.

Bruner, Jerome, J. Goodnow, and G. Austin. *A Study of Thinking.* New York: Wiley, 1956.

Clark, Margaret S. "A Role for Arousal in the Link between Feeling States, Judgments, and Behaviour." In *Affect and Cognition.* Eds. Margaret Clark and Susan Fiske. Hillsdale, NJ: Erlbaum Associates, 1982.

Clay, Marie M. *Reading, the Patterning of Complex Behavior.* Auckland, New Zealand: Heinemann, 1972.

Cleary, Linda Miller. "A Profile of Carlos: Strengths of the Non-standard Dialect Writer." *English Journal* 77.1 (1988): 59–64.

―――. "The Fragile Inclination to Write: Praise and Criticism in the Classroom." *English Journal* 79.2 (1990): 22–28.

―――. "The Unsuccessful Writer: Treating the Malady Instead of the Symptoms." *Minnesota English Journal* 16, (1986) 2, 17–25.

―――. "Affect and Cognition in the Writing Processes of Eleventh Graders: A Study of Concentration and Motivation." *Written Communication.* 8.4 (1991 in press).

Cleary, Linda Miller and Nancy Lund. "Debunking Some Myths about Traditional Grammar." *Minnesota English Journal* 19.2 (1989): 1–8.

Collins, Allan, and Dedre Gentner. "A Framework for a Cognitive Theory of Writing." In *Cognitive Processes in Writing.* Eds. Lee Gregg and Erwin Steinberg. Hillsdale, NJ: Erlbaum Associates, 1982.

Collins, James L. "Dialect Variation and Writing: One Problem at a Time." *English Journal* 69 (1979): 48–51.

Cole, Michael. "How Education Affects the Mind." *Human Mind* 5 (1968): 50–58.

Cole, Michael, and Sylvia Scribner. "Literacy Without Schooling: Testing for Intellectual Effects." *Harvard Educational Review* 48 (1978): 448–461.

Connell, R. W., D. J. Ashenden, S. Kessler, G. W. Dowsett. *Making the Difference: Schools, Family, and Social Division.* Boston: George Allen and Unwin, 1982.

Cooper, Charles, and Lee Odell. *Research on Composing: Points of Departure.* Urbana, IL: NCTE, 1978.

Coopersmith, Stanley. *The Antecedents of Self-Esteem.* San Francisco: W. H. Freeman and Co., 1967.

Daly, John A., and Michael D. Miller. "The Empirical Development of an Instrument of Writing Apprehension." *Research in the Teaching of English.* 9 (1975): 242–249.

Daly, John A. "Writing Apprehension and Writing Competency." *Journal of

Educational Research 72 (1978): 10—14.

―――. "Writing Apprehension." In *When a Writer Can't Write.* Ed. Mike Rose. New York: The Guilford Press, 1985.

DeCharms, Richard. "Motivation Enhancement." In *Student Motivation* Vol. 1. of *Research on Motivation in Education.* Eds. Carole Ames and Richard E. Ames. New York: Academic Press, 1984.

Deci, E. L. *Intrinsic Motivation.* New York: Plenum, 1975.

DeTocqueville, Alexis. *Democracy in America.* 2 vols. (The Henry Reeve Text as revised by Francis Bowen, now further corrected and edited with a historical essay, editorial notes, and bibliographies by Phillips Bradley.) New York: Vintage Books, 1945.

Dewey, John. *Democracy and Education.* New York: The Free Press, 1944.

Dillon, David, and Dennis Searle. "The Role of Language in One First Grade Classroom." *Research in the Teaching of English* 15 (1981): 311—328.

Donaldson, Margaret. *Children's Minds.* New York: Norton, 1979.

Elbow, Peter. *Writing with Power.* New York: Oxford University Press, 1981.

―――. *Writing without Teachers.* New York: Oxford University Press, 1973.

Emerson, Ralph Waldo. "Self-Reliance." In *The American Tradition in Literature,* Eds. Sculley Bradley, Richmond Croom Beatty, E. Hudson Long, and George Perkins. New York: Random House, 1981 pp. 627—648.

Emig, Janet. *The Composing Processes of Twelfth Graders.* Urbana, IL: NCTE, 1971.

―――. "On Teaching Composition: Some Hypotheses as Definitions." *Research in the Teaching of English* 1 (1967): 127—135.

Ericsson, K. Anders, and Herbert A. Simon. "Verban Reports as Data." *Psychological Review* 87 (1980): 215—251.

Erikson, Erik. *Identity, Youth, and Crisis.* New York: Norton, 1968.

―――. "Growth and Crises of the Healthy Personality." Paper written for Josiah Macy, Jr. Foundation for the Fact-Finding Committee of the Mid-Century White House Conference, Supplement II to the Transactions of the Fourth Conference on Infancy and Childhood, 1950.

Fiske, Susan T. "Schema-triggered Affect: Applications to Social Perception." In *Affect and Cognition.* Eds. Margaret S. Clark and Susan T. Fiske. Hillsdale, NJ: Erlbaum Associates, 1982.

Flower, Linda S. "Writer Based Prose." In *The Writing Teacher's Sourcebook.* Eds. Gary Tate and Edward P. J. Corbett. New York: Oxford University Press, 1981.

Flower, Linda S., and Hayes, J. R. "Images, Plans, and Prose: The Representation of Meaning in Writing." *Written Communication* 1 (1984):

120–160.

Frazier, Lynn. Lecture in course, "Language and Brain Processes," University of Massachusetts, Amherst, Fall 1982.

Freeman, Yvonne S., and David E. Freeman. "Whole Language Approaches to Writing with Secondary Students of English as a Second Language." In *Richness in Writing: Empowering ESL Students.* Eds. Donna M. Johnson and Duane H. Roen. New York: Longman, 1989.

Freud, Sigmund. *Inhibitions, Symptoms, and Anxiety.* New York: Norton, 1959.

Freire, Paulo. *Pedagogy of the Oppressed.* New York: The Seabury Press, 1968.

———. *The Politics of Education.* South Hadley, MA: Bergin and Garvey Publishers, Inc., 1985.

———. "Culture, Power, and Politics." Lecture given at St. Scholastica College, Duluth, MN, January 7, 1990.

Frye, Marilyn. *The Politics of Reality: Essays in Feminist Theory.* Trumansburg, NY: Crossing Press, 1983.

Glaser, Barney, and Anslem Strauss. *Grounded Theory: Strategies for Quantitative Research.* Chicago: Aldine Publishing Co., 1967.

Gardner, R. C. *Social Psychological Aspects of Second Language Learning.* London: Edward Arnold, 1986.

Goodlad, John I. *The Dynamics of Educational Change: Toward Responsive Schools.* New York: McGraw Hill, 1975.

Graves, Donald H. "Let's Get Rid of the Welfare Mess in the Teaching of Writing." *Language Arts* 53 (1976): 645–51.

———. *Writing: Teachers and Children at Work.* Portsmouth, NH: Heinemann Educational Books, 1983.

Harris, Muriel. "Diagnosing Writing-Process Problems: A Pedagogical Application of Speaking-Aloud Protocol Analysis." In *When Writers Can't Write.* Ed. Mike Rose. New York: The Guilford Press, 1985.

Hairston, Maxine. "Winds of Change: Thomas Kuhn and the Revolution in the Teaching of Writing." *College Composition and Communication* 33.1 (1982): 76–88.

Hart, Leslie. "Programs, Patterns and Downshifting in Learning to Read." *The Reading Teacher* 10 (1983): 5–11.

Hayes, John F. *Cognitive Psychology: Thinking and Creating.* Homewood, IL: Dorsey, 1978.

Hayes, John F., and Linda S. Flower. "The Dynamic of Composing: Making Plans and Juggling Constraints." In *Cognitive Processes in Writing.* Eds. Lee W. Gregg and Erwin R. Steinberg. Hillsdale, NJ: Erlbaum Associates, 1980.

———. "Identifying the Organization of Writing Processes." In *Cognitive Processes in Writing.* Eds. Lee W. Gregg and Erwin R. Steinberg.

Hillsdale, NJ: Erlbaum Associates, 1980.

Heath, Shirley Brice. "Toward an Ethnohistory of Writing in American Education." In *Writing: The Nature, Development, and Teaching of Written Communication*, Vol. 2. Eds. Carl Frederickson and Joseph Dominic. Hillsdale, NJ: Erlbaum Associates, 1981.

———. *Ways with Words: Language, Life and Work in Communities and Classrooms.* New York: Cambridge University Press, 1983.

Higgs, Theodore V., and Ray Clifford. "The Push Toward Communication." In *Curriculum, Competence, and the Foreign Language Teacher.* Ed. Theodore V. Higgs. Skokie, IL: National Textbook Company, 1982.

Hodges, Richard. *Improving Spelling and Vocabulary in the Secondary School.* Urbana, IL: NCTE, 1982.

Hudson, Sally A. "Beyond Process: Writing and Teaching as Thinking in the 1990's." *The Iowa English Bulletin* 36 (1988): 23–33.

———. "Children's Perceptions of Classroom Writing: Ownership Within a Continuum of Control." In *The Social Construction of Written Communication.* Eds. Bennett A. Raforth and Donald L. Rubin. Norwood, NJ: Ablex, 1988.

Issen, Alice M., Barbara Means, Robert Patric, and Gary Nowicki. "Some Factors Influencing Decision-Making Strategy and Risk Taking." In *Affect and Cognition.* Eds. Margaret S. Clark and Susan T. Fiske. Hillsdale, NJ: Erlbaum Associates, 1982.

Jefferson, Thomas. *Bill for the Diffusion of Knowledge.* State of Virginia, 1779.

Johnson, Donna M., and Duane H. Roen, eds. *Richness in Writing: Empowering ESL Students.* New York: Longman, 1989.

Johnson, John M. *Doing Field Research.* New York: Free Press, 1975.

Jones, Stan. "Problems with Monitor Use in Second Language Composing." In *When a Writer Can't Write.* Ed. Mike Rose. New York: The Guilford Press, 1985.

Kagan, Spencer. "Cooperative Learning and Sociocultural Factors in Schooling." In *Beyond Language: Social and Cultural Factors in Schooling Language Minority Students.* California State Department of Education. Los Angeles: California State University Evaluation, Dissemination, and Assessment Center (1986): 231–298.

Krashen, Stephen D. *Principles and Practice in Second Language Acquisition.* Oxford: Pergamon Press, 1982.

———. *The Input Hypothesis: Issues and Implications.* New York: Longman, 1985.

Labov, William. "Academic Ignorance and Black Intelligence." *Atlantic Monthly.* June 1972.

Labov, William. "Logic of Non-Standard English." *Language in the Inner City: Studies in Black English Vernacular.* Philadelphia: University of Pennsylvania Press, 1972.

Lambert, Wallace E., R. C. Gardner, H. C. Bank, and K. Tunstall. "Attitudinal and Cognitive Aspects of Intensive Study of a Second Language." *Journal of Abnormal and Social Psychology* 66.4 (1963): 358–368.

Larson, Reed. "Emotional Scenarios in the Writing Process: An Examination of Young Writers' Affective Experience." In *When a Writer Can't Write.* Ed. Mike Rose. New York: The Guilford Press, 1985.

Lofland, John. *Analyzing Social Settings: A Guide to Qualitative Observation and Analysis.* Belmont, CA: Wadsworth, 1971.

Macrorie, Ken. *The I-Search Paper.* Portsmouth, NH: Boynton/Cook, 1988.

Maehr, Martin. "Meaning and Motivation: Toward a Personal Investment." In *Research on Motivation in Education: Vol. 1. Student Motivation.* Eds. Carole Ames and Richard E. Ames. New York: Academic Press, 1984.

Manheim, Karl. *Ideology and Utopia.* New York: Free Press, 1975.

Marshall, James D. "Classroom Discourse and Literary Response." In *Literature in the Classroom.* Ed. Ben F. Nelms. Urbana, IL: NCTE, 1988.

Maslow, Abraham H. *Farther Reaches of Human Nature.* New York: Viking Press, 1972.

———. *Toward a Psychology of Being.* New York: Van Nostrand Reinhold, 1962.

Mayher, John. *Uncommon Sense.* Portsmouth, NH: Boynton/Cook, 1989.

McClelland, David, John W. Alkinson, and Russell A. Clark. *The Achievement Motive.* New York: Appleton-Century Crofts Ltd., 1953.

McDermott, Ray P. "Social Relations as Contexts for Learning in School." *Harvard Educational Review* 47 (1977): 498–513.

———. "Achieving School Failure: An Anthropological Approach to Illiteracy and Social Stratifications." In *Theoretical Models and Process of Reading.* Eds. Harry Songer and Robert Ruddell. Newark, DE: International Reading Association, 1976.

McNeil, Linda M. "Contradictions of Control, Part I, II, and III." *Phi Delta Kappan.* January–March 1988.

Mellon, John. "Language Competence." In *The Nature of Measurement of Competency in English.* Ed. Charles Cooper. Urbana, IL: NCTE, 1980.

Mishler, Elliot. "Meaning in Context: Is There Any Other Kind?" *Harvard Educational Review* 49 (1979): 1–19.

Moffett, James. *Active Voice.* Portsmouth, NH: Boynton/Cook, 1980.

———. *Teaching the Universe of Discourse.* Boston: Houghton Mifflin Co., 1968. Available from Boynton/Cook, Portsmouth, NH.

Monahon, Brian D. "Revision Strategies of Basic and Competent Writers as They Write for Different Audiences." *Research in Teaching of English* 18 (1984), 288–304.

Moskowitz, Breyne Arlene. "The Acquisition of Language." *Scientific American* 239 (1978), 92–108.

Murray, Donald M. "The Essential Delay: When Writer's Block Isn't." In *When a Writer Can't Write*. Ed. Mike Rose. New York: The Guilford Press, 1985.

———. *Learning by Teaching*. Portsmouth, NH: Boynton/Cook, 1982.

———. *A Writer Teaches Writing*. Boston: Houghton Mifflin, 1986.

National Council of Teachers of English. "Guidelines for the Preparation of Teachers of English Language Arts." Urbana, IL: NCTE, 1986.

Newell, Allen, and Herbert A. Simon. *Human Problem Solving*. Englewood Cliffs, NJ: Prentice-Hall, 1972.

Newkirk, Tom. "Is the Bay Area Model the Answer?" *English Education* 15 (1983): 161–166.

———. "The Non-narrative Writing of Young Children." *Research in the Teaching of English* 21.2 (1987): 121–144.

Patton, Michael Quinn. *Qualitative Evaluation Methods*. Beverly Hills, CA: Sage Publications, 1980.

Pearson, P. David, and Dale D. Johnson. *Teaching Comprehending Reading*. New York: Holt, Rinehart, and Winston, 1978.

Perkins, D. N. *The Mind's Best Work*. Cambridge, MA: Harvard University Press, 1981.

Perl, Sondra. "The Composing Processes of Unskilled Writers." *Research in the Teaching of English* 13 (1979): 317–336.

———. "A Look at Basic Writers in the Process of Composing." In *Basic Writing: Essays for Teachers, Researchers, Administrators*. Eds. Laurance N. Kasden and Daniel R. Hoeber. Urbana, IL: NCTE, 1980.

———. "Understanding Composing." In *To Compose*. Ed. Tom Newkirk. Portsmouth, NH: Heinemann Educational Books, 1986.

Perl, Sondra, and Nancy Wilson. *Through Teacher's Eyes*. Portsmouth, NH: Heinemann Educational Books, 1986.

Piaget, Jean. *The Language and Thought of the Child*. New York: New American Library, 1974.

———. *Origins of Intelligence in Children*. New York: International University Press, 1952.

Postman, Neil, and Charles Weingartner. *Linguistics: A Revolution in Teaching*. New York: Dell Publishing Co., 1966.

Reed, Michael, John K. Burton, and Patricia P. Kelly. "The Effects of Audience Awareness on Drafting." *Research in the Teaching of English* 19 (1985): 283–297.

Rich, Adrienne. *On Lies, Secrets, and Silence*. New York: Norton, 1979.

Richards, Jack C. "A Non-Contrastive Approach to Error Analysis." *English Language Teaching* 25 (1971): 204–219.

Rist, Ray. "Student Social Class and Teacher Expectation: The Self-Fulfilling Prophecy in Ghetto Education." *Harvard Educational Review* 30 (1970): 411–451.

206 Bibliography

Rodrigues, Ramond J. "The Moving Away from Writing Process Worship." *English Journal* 74.5 (1985): 24–27.

Rodriguez, Richard. *The Hunger of Memory: The Education of Richard Rodriguez.* New York: Bantam Books, 1982.

Roen, Duane H., and R. J., Willey. "The Effects of Audience Awareness on Drafting." *Research in the Teaching of English* 22 (1985): 75–88.

Rogers, Carl. *Freedom to Learn.* Columbus, OH: Charles E. Merrill Publishing Co., 1969.

———. *On Becoming a Person.* Boston: Houghton Mifflin, 1961.

Romano, Tom. *Clearing the Way: Working with Teenage Writers.* Portsmouth, NH: Heinemann Educational Books, 1987.

Rose, Mike. "Complexity, Rigor, Evolving Method, and the Puzzle of Writer's Block: Thoughts on Composing-Process Research." In *When a Writer Can't Write.* Ed. Mike Rose. New York: Guilford Press, 1985.

———. *Lives on the Boundary.* New York: Penguin Books, 1989.

Sapir, Edward. *Culture, Language and Personality.* Berkeley, CA: University of California Press, 1949.

Scardamalia, Marlene. "How Children Cope with the Cognitive Demands of Writing." In *Writing: The Nature, Development and Teaching of Written Communication*, Eds. Carl H. Fredericksen, M. Whiteman, and Joseph F. Dominic. Hillsdale. NJ: Erlbaum Associates, 1981.

Schuman, David. *Policy Analysis, Education, and Everyday Life: An Evaluation of Higher Education.* Lexington, MA; Heath, 1982.

Schutz, Alfred. *The Phenomenology of the Social World.* Evanston, IL: Northwestern University Press, 1967.

Shor, Ira. *Critical Teaching in Everyday Life.* Boston: South End Press, 1980.

Shor, Ira, ed. *Freire for the Classroom: A Sourcebook for Liberatory Teaching.* Portsmouth NH: Boynton/Cook, 1987.

Scribner, Sylvia, and Michael Cole. "Literacy Without Schooling." *Harvard Educational Review* 48 (1979): 448–461.

Seidman, Earl. *Interviewing as a Qualitative Research: A Guide for Researchers in Education and the Social Sciences.* New York: Teachers College Press, 1991.

———. Untitled paper presented at seminar, "Language and the Teaching of Writing." University of Massachusetts, October 1982.

Seidman, Earl, Patrick Sullivan, and Mary Schatzkamer. "On In-Depth Phenomenological Interviewing." In National Institute Education Report on the Work of Community College Faculty. Grant Number NIE-6-81-0056, September 1983, School of Education, University of Massachusetts, Amherst.

Selfe, Cynthia L. "An Apprehensive Writer Composes." In *When a Writer Can't Write.* Ed. Mike Rose. New York: The Guilford Press, 1985.

Sennett, Richard, and Jonathan Cobb. *The Hidden Injuries of Class.* New York: Vintage Books, 1973.

Simon, Herbert A. "Comments." In *Affect and Cognition.* Eds. Margaret S. Clark and Susan T. Fiske. Hillsdale, NJ: Erlbaum Associates, 1982.

Shaughnessy, Mina P. *Errors and Expectations.* New York: Oxford University Press, 1977.

Smith, Eliot R., and Frederick D. Miller. "Limits on the Perception of Cognitive Process: A Reply to Nisbet and Wilson." *Psychological Review* 85 (1978): 355–362.

Smith, Frank. *Writing and the Writer.* New York: Holt, Rinehart and Winston, 1982.

Solsken, Judith W. "Authors of Their Own Learning." *Language Arts* 62 (1985): 491–499.

Spradley, James P. *Participant Observation.* New York: Holt, Rinehart and Winston, 1980.

Stallard, Charles. "An Analysis of the Writing Behavior of Good Student Writers." *Research in the Teaching of English* 8 (1974): 206–218.

Stillman, Peter. *Writing Your Way.* Portsmouth, NH: Boynton/Cook, 1984.

Stipek, Deborah J. *Motivation to Learn: From Theory to Practice.* Englewood Cliffs, NJ: Prentice-Hall, 1988.

Sullivan, Anne McCrary. "Liberating the Urge to Write: From Classroom Journals to Lifelong Writing." *English Journal* 78.7 (1989): 55–61.

Udall, Morris K. "The Right to Write." Originally printed in a Congressional newsletter, January 20, 1967.

Van de Weghe, Richard. "Grammar and Spelling Logs." In *Non-Native and Non-Standard Dialect Students.* Ed. Candy Carter. Urbana, IL: NCTE, 1983.

Vygotsky, Lev S. *Mind and Society.* Cambridge, MA: Harvard University Press, 1978.

———. *Thought and Language.* Cambridge, MA: M.I.T. Press, 1962.

Weaver, Constance. *Grammar for Teachers: Perspectives and Definitions.* Urbana, IL: NCTE, 1979.

Weiner, Bernard. "The Emotional Consequences of Causal Attributions." In *Affect and Cognition.* Eds. Margaret S. Clark and Susan T. Fiske. Hillsdale, NJ: Erlbaum Associates, 1982.

———. "Principles for a Theory of Student Motivation and Their Application within an Attributional Framework." In *Research on Motivation in Education: Vol. 1. Student Motivation.* Eds. Carole Ames and Russell E. Ames. New York: Academic Press, 1984.

Wells, Gordon. *The Meaning Makers: Children Learning Language and Using Language to Learn.* Portsmouth, NH: Heinemann Educational Books, 1986.

White, Peter. "Limitations on Verbal Reports of Internal Events: A Refutation of Nisbett and Wilson and of Bem." *Psychological Review* 17 (1980): 105–112.

Wigginton, Eliot. *Sometimes a Shining Moment: The Foxfire Experiment.* New York: Doubleday, 1985.

Wilson, Stephen. "The Uses of Ethnographic Techniques in Educational Research." *Review of Educational Research* 47 (1977): 245–265.

Zamel, Vivian. "Writing: The Process of Discovering Meaning." *TESOL Quarterly* 16 (1982): 165–187.

Zemelman, Steven, and Harvey Daniels. *A Community of Writers.* Portsmouth, NH: Heinemann Educational Books, 1988.

Index